HA

Reuter Reporter
among the Communists
1958–59

For our daughters-in-law,
Angie and Janis

Reuter Reporter among the Communists 1958–59

Peter B. Johnson

TAGMAN

www.tagman-press.com
London, Sydney, Los Angeles

First published in Great Britain 2000 by The Tagman Press,
2 Elmdon Court, St Leonards Road, Norwich NR1 4JP

ISBN 0-9530921-7-8
A CIP catalogue record for this book is available from the British Library

Edited by Bridget Bagshaw
Designed by Dick Malt

A *Tagman Crown Laurel* book
Printed and bound in United Kingdom by
MPG Books Limited, Bodmin, Cornwall

Also by Peter B. Johnson:
Reuter Reporter in Divided Germany 1955–58
(Adler Publications, 1998)
£6.95 including postage & packing from the author at:
47 Braeside, Beckenham, Kent BR3 1ST

Contents

Acknowledgements

I am indebted above all to David Childs, Professor of Politics at Nottingham University, who edited my first volume, *Reuter Reporter in Divided Germany 1955–58*, and encouraged me to write this one. My thanks go also to former Reuter colleagues Michael Nelson, Terence Davidson and Nick Carter, who read the manuscript and made valuable suggestions.

The author and publishers are grateful to the following for permission to reproduce photographs: ADN/Zentralbild; Associated Press; German Federal Press Office; Inter Nationes, Bonn. Every effort has been made to trace the holders of other copyright material.

Preface

Like my previous volume, *Reuter Reporter in Divided Germany 1955–58*, this book owes its existence firstly to a forgotten experienced someone who, in about 1946, told me that would-be journalists ought to keep diaries – mine is now more than 53 years old. This volume, like its forerunner, concentrates mainly on Germany which, by what I think is chance, has played a major part in my life.

I was already fairly fluent in German when, as a 21-year-old Royal Naval Voluntary Reserve sub-lieutenant, I was posted to Royal Naval Headquarters, Germany in the summer of 1946. At first the headquarters were in the former building of the well-known Melitta coffee company in Minden, Westphalia, but were moved a few months later to refurbished barracks in still largely devastated Hamburg. There I got to know an intelligent and beautiful East Prussian refugee, Elfi Kowitz, 22, who was one of the headquarters' interpreters. As I related in the first volume, she was at first reluctant to go out with the former enemy, but an old Anglophile aunt told her the British were human too, so she relented. We became engaged about eight days after we had first gone out together.

Our marriage in my hometown, Bradford, Yorkshire, in May 1947, was one of the first Anglo-German marriages after the Second World War. Our elder son, Robin, who became a German teacher in Yorkshire, was born in 1948. We had to wait until 1953 for the arrival of our younger son, Christopher, who became an electrical engineer and went to work in West Germany.

A few months before our marriage I had started my journalistic apprenticeship on such colourfully named weeklies and dailies as the *Whitley Bay Weekly Guardian* in Northumberland, the *Cleckheaton Guardian* and its companion, the *Heckmondwike Herald*, the *Halifax Courier* and the *Bradford Telegraph & Argus*, all in my native Yorkshire. Then, in 1954, Reuters took me on as a sub-editor, quite a lowly post, in its Fleet Street headquarters and, a year later, I was happy to be sent off to the Cold War – to the Bonn office. Reuters did not actually expect me to fight in the Cold War, but to write about it as fairly as I could.

I found myself first in a West Germany on the verge of rearmament, emerging from occupation rule under the impressive conservative leadership of Konrad Adenauer. Berlin was already divided between the two blocs, even though the Berlin Wall had not yet been built. I managed to interview refugees streaming out of Hungary during the abortive revolt of 1956. The first book ends by detailing my first visit to the interior of Communist East Germany in late 1958.

That first volume produced some encouraging echoes from various readers around the world. I was particularly moved by an unsolicited comment from Baron Rudy von Wechmar, who was a colleague (or enemy!) in Bonn during the fifties, when he worked for the American agency, United Press, before entering the diplomatic service. He rose to be, among other things, West German ambassador to the United Nations and the reunited Germany's ambassador in London. From his retirement in Munich, he wrote in part:

Peter Johnson's . . . account of how he saw both sides of Germany during the crucial years 1955–58 is fascinating . . . His report is a masterful blend of very personal impressions plus a good description of the political landscape in those years and the problems the Germans and their allied occupiers were facing at that time.

This second volume – I hope, at 74, that it will not be the last – takes up the story in late 1958 when I was one of several Reuter correspondents based in Bonn. Routine events were soon over-shadowed by Khrushchev's 'Berlin Ultimatum' of 10 November 1958, which threatened to cause a major East–West crisis, including a repetition of the Berlin blockade of 1948–9. I first experienced the Soviet leader in the flesh when he visited Leipzig and East Berlin in March 1959, and I was both impressed and charmed by him.

The main part of the book deals with my posting by Reuters to be the first Western non-Communist correspondent stationed in the so-called German Democratic Republic, which was not genuinely German but essentially a Russian puppet, and was certainly not a democratic republic. During my five months on that assignment, from May to October 1959, I gained a closer insight into the real nature of the German Communist regime.

My unique position, allowing me to travel freely throughout East Germany, except in its closely guarded frontier areas, helped me to obtain some scoops, including a widely-publicized interview with Dr Klaus Fuchs, the German Communist spy who had been imprisoned in Britain for betraying Western nuclear secrets to the Soviet Union and, on his release, flew to East Germany. I also followed Khrushchev round Poland – he had a plane and I a Volkswagen Beetle – and reported on a visit to Warsaw by the US Vice-President, Richard Nixon.

Working for Reuters in the fifties was more than just a job. It was like being a member of a large family, scattered worldwide, or – as my onetime boss in Germany, Gerry Long, once put it – belonging to something like a religious order.

Reuters was founded in London in 1851 by a German Jew, originally called Israel Beer Josaphat, who converted to Christianity and took the name Paul Julius Reuter. He became known as Julius Reuter, later Baron de Reuter after he had been given a barony in 1871 by the Duke of Saxe-Coburg-Gotha. Reuter retired as managing director of the agency in 1878 and was succeeded by his son, Herbert. Baron de Reuter died in 1899. Herbert committed suicide in 1915, ending the family connection with the agency.

In 1941 the Press Association, representing UK provincial newspapers, which had been the majority shareholder in Reuters Limited – a private company – since 1925, became an equal partner in the company with the Newspaper Proprietors' Association, representing British national newspapers. In 1947 the main news agency of Australia and that of New Zealand were taken into the partnership. In 1948 the main Indian agency, the Press Trust of India, was also brought into the group but this agency withdrew in 1953.

From the start, news provided to bankers and stockbrokers produced most of Reuters revenue. That subsidized – and strengthened – the news service to the media. Initially the shareholdings of the news agencies and newspapers were not seen as financial investments, but as a way of ensuring a good news service as economically as possible.

However, by the early eighties, thanks to the success of the agency's electronic systems distributing news to business, it became evident that Reuters could become a big money-spinner. Some of the newspapers who held Reuter shares had financial problems and realized that they could obtain large sums if the firm were floated as a public company, enabling them to sell their increasingly valuable shares, or part of them. There was considerable opposition to the proposed change. But, after prolonged debate between shareholding companies and within Reuters management, the agency was floated in April 1984.

A main concern of the owners, management and staff was to maintain the principles of the 1941 Reuter Trust guaranteeing the agency's independence. This was achieved; in fact the trust arrangements were strengthened. The flotation, simultaneously in London and New York, provided the funds to enable Reuters rapidly to expand its business and its media services worldwide and also to make numerous acquisitions, particularly of firms in the computerized information sector.

Since the flotation, Reuters growth has been enormous. At the end of 1984 the firm had 3,865 employees; at the end of 1998 it had 16,938 – including 2,072 journalists – drawn from more than

50 nationalities. By then there were 218 Reuter offices in 96 countries. In 1984 Reuters revenue was £313 million and its profit before tax £74 million; in 1998 its revenue was £3,000 million and its profit before tax £580 million. Of course, I preferred the old Reuters, even if it was hard to get a wage increase!

Peter B. Johnson
London, July 2000

Map of Germany in 1959

Interzonal autobahns

Denmark

Rostock
Schwerin

Hamburg

EAST GERMANY

Bremen

Netherlands

Poland

WEST GERMANY

Helmstedt   BERLIN
Hanover   Magdeburg   Potsdam   Frankfurt
                                   an der Oder

Essen
Düsseldorf
Cologne

Belgium

Bonn

Halle   Leipzig

Bacharach
Frankfurt
am Main

Czechoslovakia

Luxemburg

France

Stuttgart

Munich

Switzerland   Austria

1 Chasing Elvis

16 September 1958 : After a visit to Communist East Germany, I was back in the capitalist West with a vengeance today. Was sent to Frankfurt/Main to report the signing of an agreement between the Deutsche Bank, one of the main German banks split up by the Western allies after 1945, which has since reconstituted itself, and the Anglo-American Corporation of Johannesburg, holding company of a vast mining concern. Under the agreement, the Deutsche Bank is floating a loan of 50 million marks on the German capital market on behalf of Anglo-American, which needs the currency to buy a diamond mine. This marks Germany's return to the world capital market as a lender for the first time since 1914.

After the signing, Harry Oppenheimer, son of a German-Jewish emigrant who became diamond king Sir Ernest Oppenheimer, addressed a press conference along with Hermann Abs, who signed for the bank. Oppenheimer, the chairman of Anglo-American, is small, sallow and moustached. He obviously equivocated when questioned about an alleged ban by the London Diamond Syndicate, which his firm controls, on sales to German diamond-cutters. The alleged ban was reportedly imposed because of price-cutting by the Germans and because of Sir Ernest's dislike of the Nazis. The ban is now apparently to be lifted, as a *quid pro quo* for the German money.

Abs, who negotiated the London Debts Agreement of 1953, consolidating Germany's pre-war debts, is a large broad-faced

1

man with a small moustache and rather pleasant face. His manners are gentle but authoritative and I found him an appealing personality. *[He had held a senior post in the Deutsche Bank in the Nazi era, when the bank helped to finance wartime projects, including the construction of the Auschwitz mass-murder concentration camp in occupied Poland. However, after the war, Abs was credited with having moderated the harsh expropriation of several German-Jewish firms during the Nazi era. He died on 2 February 1994.]*

Oppenheimer told me over a cocktail afterwards that his father had been only 16 when he left Germany to go into the London diamond trade. The Deutsche Bank loan is part of the efforts to reduce West Germany's balance of payments surplus and has been welcomed in London.

17 September 1958 : Driving back home to Bonn, picked up a one-legged 42-year-old rosy-cheeked and somewhat whimsical-looking man in a German army forage cap and an old suit, who told me he'd lost his leg in the *Wehrmacht* in Italy. He started by cursing people for not picking him up earlier – he'd been waiting several hours. He said people were inhuman these days.

He was an orphan who believed his father had been a court painter somewhere, and he himself had the obsession that he must become a painter, poet or musician. Up to now he'd earned money – apart from an 80-marks-a-month (about £7) pension for the loss of his leg – by playing his mouth-organ and selling postcards in holiday resorts, bringing him another 200 marks (about £17) in some months. He showed me some of his drawings, which were poor, and said he'd refused to take jobs as a porter or suchlike, or in factories.

'I don't want to be a slave,' he said. 'I want to be free. I've got talent and when one has talent one must do what one has the talent for.'

I suggested he should get a half-time job and then develop his talents by schooling, and when I dropped him near Bonn he thanked me for the advice. He hobbled off on his crutches, rucksack on his back, into a wood.

[I recalled later that when Hitler was a young man in Vienna he also thought he had talent, and sold not very good paintings. If he had been accepted into the Vienna art college which rejected him, that might have spared Europe much tragedy.]

My old woman has become 34 in my absence and says it's depressing to think you're going on for 35! Told her not to be so daft.

18 September 1958 : Reported on the trial of 39-year-old Robert Schneider who, like Hitler, is an Austrian who served as a junior NCO in the army. Unlike Hitler he did not go into politics, but amazingly became the chief psychologist in the West German Defence Ministry, allegedly by forging documents purporting to show all kinds of qualifications. Schneider had served as a doctor's assistant in the Austrian army, but evidently without obtaining proper medical qualifications. He had been jailed for fraud in Austria in 1951.

To get his job in the West German Defence Ministry, Schneider provided documents stating that he had worked as a psychologist in London, Paris and elsewhere. The court was told his method was to forge a document, get some notary to make a copy of it, with the official stamps, then to destroy his 'original'. At the Defence Ministry, where he worked for about six months in 1956, he brought out a handbook on the psychological screening of soldiers – based on other people's work, but put into understandable language – which was used for the screening of some 80,000 of the 100,000 soldiers currently in the forces. He was unmasked when, like Hitler, he applied to become a German citizen and a local official detected some irregularity.

The presiding judge, Schroeder, is obviously convinced of Schneider's guilt on the main charges of using false titles – Schneider admitted some minor charges – and is making ironic bitter remarks to the accused like, as one German journalist put it to me, the presiding judge of a Nazi 'People's Court'. *[My diary does not give the result of this trial.]*

20 September 1958 : Had my last outdoor swim of the year at Bad Godesberg, just as the baths were closing for the winter. It was as warm as in midsummer in Britain, but people here are comparatively soft, so baths are closing now.

24 September 1958 : While I was away in East Germany recently, Elfi behaved as a well-trained Reuter wife by immediately phoning the office when she heard on a local German radio that there had been a major accident on the steep rack railway which runs from the nearby Rhineside resort of Königswinter up a hill to the Drachenfels ruin, a favourite tourist spot. About 17 people were killed and about 90 injured in the accident, when a train left the rails. It was the first accident on that line in 75 years. Thanks to Elfi, Reuters beat other foreign agencies on this story.

25 September 1958 : Read an East German article about the foundation of a cooperative (collective) farm, which sounded very reasonable. Unfortunately, in practice it often happens that the collectives are founded by applying so much pressure that the farmers have not got their hearts in it. The idea, I think, is a good one – better, anyway, than the semi-feudal Junker system.

27 September 1958 : With our elder son Robin, 10, visited the Brussels World Fair. In the large Soviet pavilion, a vast statue of Lenin dominates. In front of him are models of the sputniks. I was particularly touched by the leather harnesses for the sputnik dogs and the little padded metal chamber, like the one in which Laika, the dog that died in Sputnik 2, was placed. Two of the latest Soviet cars – very hard to tell from American ones – gleam on their stand. No prices stated! Various slogans and excerpts from the constitution. (The Americans do that kind of thing more cleverly – for instance, by showing some voting machines.)

There was a large crowd around one painting, showing a Russian mother looking defiantly at a German officer in the Second World War, as her son was carried off to be shot for being a partisan. Indicative of the mood behind the exhibits – 'We're not as backward as you thought' – was that the Russians had put on show some ordinary joints of meat, in several refrigerators.

My Belgian landlady said she was sorry to say she was nowadays getting some arrogant Germans who behaved like those of 1940. They had not been like that shortly after the war, she said. What particularly annoyed her was the type of German who considered that, as the Germans worked harder than, say, the French, they were therefore the better people. She said the French were willing to work hard too – for instance, in cooking and in designing and making clothes.

29 September 1958 : Walter Ulbricht, the East German Communist leader, has told officials that only persuasion is permissible to get people to join cooperatives. What was the use of having a craftsman join a cooperative if he did not want to, he asked. He would not produce more or better goods. I could have told Ulbricht that a long time ago, and that was the drift of many remarks I made to Communist officials on my recent visit to East Germany. I am finding it difficult to write a background piece about East Germany, because it is so hard to be fair in describing the situation there.

30 September 1958 : The five-year-old daughter of one of my British colleagues, David Rees, who has not been long in Germany, calls the German language 'rubbish'. After being in a German school for a few days she told her Mum, 'Our teacher told us a story all in rubbish this afternoon.' But she is already starting to put German words into her English sentences – she asked her Mum if yesterday was 'washing *Tag*'.

1 October 1958 : To Friedberg, small town near Frankfurt/Main, to report on the arrival of the United States' best-known soldier, Private Elvis Presley, 23, star of rock-and-roll music, which he performs with much hip-waggling while playing a guitar. 'Just a sex symbol,' said one of my colleagues. Elvis was a country lad, a truck driver I believe, when he sprang to fame a few years ago.

5

One of his records sold six million copies; he's made several films and is worth several hundred thousand dollars. But now, since he was drafted some months ago, he's a private with army pay of about 100 dollars a month. Teenage girls swoon at the sight and sound of him. There were a few hundred waiting at Friedberg's old railway station tonight, in sweaters and jeans, but the army disappointed them by having Elvis, and 200 other men, arrive at an army siding some distance away. Several teenagers, including three I took in my car, managed to get to the siding where Elvis, in trim grey-green uniform and peaked cap, emerged from a railway carriage in the glare of floodlights, behind a fat military policeman.

I was surprised to see that, though he looks common in photos, he is really a pleasant-looking lad, a little Italianate, with shapely hands. He waved rather effeminately, and a sapphire ring worth 1,500 dollars flashed on the little finger of his left hand. He picked up his kitbag, like the other men arriving, and walked along the platform through a milling crowd of pressmen, with the fat MP by his side. As he was getting into a bus, photographers called to him, so he grabbed three of the girl teenagers, put his arm round a couple of them, smiled nicely and posed for pictures. That was all we had of him tonight.

2 October 1958 : Elvis – reveille for him at 05.30 – was paraded at a press conference at 09.00, answering questions for an hour or so, until too many journalists started asking for autographs. He answered simply, in a friendly way, without side. He said he had not got into trouble in the army, didn't play crap (dice) because he did not want his teenagers to stop admiring him.

4 October 1958 : Although the press has been kept out of Presley's barracks since yesterday, a sharp Italian photographer, Manlio Lucentini, talked his way in and I was able to accompany him. At Presley's barrack block we were told he was out, but Lucentini spotted him hiding behind a bed. He stood up rather shamefacedly, but let the Italian take some pictures.

Later Presley went to a hotel in Bad Homburg, some 12 miles from his base, where his father and grandfather were staying. Presley at first refused to pose for pictures with a guitar, which Lucentini – of course – had borrowed from a waiter. But Elvis later relented, when assured it was not against the code of military discipline. Lucentini and another Italian had me laughing my head off with their antics in adjusting Presley for shots, shoving his arm a little one way, gabbling at him in Italian and saying, 'See me!' when they meant, 'Look at me!' I admired the way Elvis, who was dog-tired by now, stood up to it all. He'll be a good advert for the United States, that lad.

Lucentini told me he is shortly to be tried for sacrilege. He and a colleague found out the whereabouts of Mussolini's grave, beneath an altar, and dug it up.

Our younger son, Chris, who is now five and a half, addresses our Indian neighbour, Mr Naga, a low-level diplomat, as 'Herr Indian'. Naga told me he would rather live in India than in Europe. Main reason: servants are cheaper in India. His wife is having to manage with less help than she, a Brahmin – i.e. a high-class person – has been accustomed to in India. I have suggested to my non-Brahmin wife that she has a charlady in once a week, but she prefers that we use the money for other things.

6 October 1958 : With our sons to Bad Godesberg's autumn fair, where Robin took part unsuccessfully in a draw for some pots of flowers, something I've never seen at a fair in England. There are more flower shops in Germany than in Britain too, I'm sure. For a while we listened to a very poor Punch and Judy man, made a bit more interesting by the fact that it was all in German, with an accent I took to be Rhineland mixed with Berlin. Punch is called 'Kasperle' here and Chris says the word with such tenderness when he talks about Punch and Judy shows.

7 October 1958 : We four helped for a couple of hours in the harvesting at the vineyard of our friend, Franz Müller, in Niederdollendorf, one of the most northerly vineyards in

Germany, on the eastern bank of the Rhine near Bonn. The Müller family run a wine restaurant and hotel called 'Bredershof', lovingly described in Brian Connell's 1957 book, *Watcher on the Rhine*. In the vineyard we learned that the bangs, like rifle shots, going off every minute or so, were produced by a carbide device to frighten birds. It works with starlings, but blackbirds, apparently brainier, see through it. A green-uniformed employee of the local parish patrols along the vineyard paths to prevent stealing by humans.

There were about 20 people harvesting, including several fulltime workers. One of those told me he liked working in the vineyards, even though the wage was only 150 marks (about £13) a month. We cut off the grapes with clippers or scissors and put them into a *Schlotte*, a flattish bucket with parallel sides, which normally stays upright on the vineyard slopes. From the *Schlotten* we poured the grapes into bigger containers, shaped like upturned bells, which men carried around until they were full. These were then emptied into what looked like a giant coffee-grinder, about a yard wide, operated by turning a wheel like those on old wringing machines. This pulped the grapes as they dropped into one of two large barrels on a horse-drawn cart.

The cart went at intervals to the Bredershof buildings in the village, where the grapes were put in a wine press to squeeze out the must and leave most of the pulp in the press. We were told to throw away bunches that had dried up into mouldy brown raisins, but to keep wet mouldy ones, which were said to be good for the bouquet. We all munched grapes as we worked. Never have tasted grapes lovelier – must have been the sunny day, the smell of the vines and actually being in a vineyard. Herr Müller insisted that we took home a large pile of grapes. After today I think I have come to the conclusion that wine, of itself, is not evil, but only its misuse.

8 October 1958 : Because British banks have recently gone into the hire-purchase business, London asked us for an article on the situation here. Today I interviewed an executive of the Bonn

Kaufhof, which belongs to a big department-store chain doing much hire-purchase business, in conjunction with a specialist bank. He told me the hire-purchase banks were frightened that the normal German banks would copy the British banks, which would force the hire-purchase lenders to reduce interest rates.

Hire-purchase agreements state that the interest is 8–10 per cent on the sum borrowed, but this is in fact 22–25 per cent in normal interest terms. The trick is that borrowers pay the 8–10 per cent on the total sum borrowed during the whole of the repayment period. The normal banks charge only 10 per cent genuine interest for a loan and only 7 per cent for an overdraft. But the mainly poorer people who go in for hire-purchase don't generally have bank accounts. There are good things about hire-purchase, but it would be better if it were state-run at reasonable interest rates. Until about two years ago most hire-purchase in West Germany was for clothing. Since then the tendency has been to increase the amount of durable goods bought in this way and durables now account for more than half of the total – this another sign of economic recovery.

Realized I'd spent too long at the Kaufhof, so ran through the streets to jump into my car and pick up my colleague, Terry Davidson, at the office. We tore out to Cologne–Bonn airport and, as Terry dashed out on to the tarmac, I rang up the control tower to find that Harold Macmillan, the British Prime Minister, had just touched down. Phew! Macmillan made quite a long airport speech, emphasizing British–German cooperation. We didn't know just what questions had prompted him to accept Adenauer's invitation, or maybe to ask for it. As well as his talks with the Chancellor, Macmillan also called on the Federal President, Theodor Heuss, who is to pay his first official visit to Britain in a fortnight.

9 October 1958 : The Macmillan visit, which seemed to produce little of importance, was in any case overshadowed by the death early today of Pope Pius XII. As the news came through last night that the Pope was dying, Adenauer's driver, a military police

9

sergeant-major in plain clothes, told me the Chancellor was very cut up, as Pius was an old friend dating from his days as Papal Nuncio in Germany before the Nazi era, when Adenauer was Mayor of Cologne.

[Pius XII, Eugenio Pacelli, who became Pope in 1939, was a conservative. His critics argued that he could have used his influence in partly Catholic Germany to prevent the Nazis' mass murders of the Jews, while others contended that any such attempt would have been futile and might have worsened the situation of the Church. In 1950 he had pronounced the dogma of the bodily assumption of the Virgin Mary into heaven. Protestants particularly criticized his restatement in 1951 of the doctrine that the life of a baby must not be sacrificed to save a woman in labour.]

Our guest this evening was my main Bonn Communist contact, Boris Yurinov, pale-faced 35-ish correspondent of the Soviet news agency, TASS. *[For a time Yurinov had a TASS colleague called Yuri Borisov. I never knew whether those names were genuine.]* I had Yurinov stumped once or twice, when I spoke of the need to expose wrongs in the state, such as the mass pre-war purges in Russia. When I asked whether there was any guarantee that such things could not happen again, he did not answer. I said I had hopes that the Communists might one day become more democratic, while the rest of the world became more socialist. Yurinov is yearning for his little son, whom he has not seen for three months and whom his wife will soon bring back from Moscow.

11 October 1958 : To a cocktail party held for Walton Cole, Reuters imposing fat bespectacled blond editor, a Scot. Cole greeted me cordially as 'Peter' – it was 'Mr Johnson' or 'Johnson' last time he was here. He indicated I was to get a rise, which I had been pressing for. Cole is a bit too smooth for my liking, but I think he is able and I know he is a hard worker. We had a good laugh to hear that heavyweight Cole had broken a spring in our colleague Fred Ungeheuer's Mercedes sports car, when Fred gave him a lift to his hotel. Fred is wondering whether he dare put in an expense account for such an item.

10

When Robin was sick in the lavatory, Chris sympathized with the lavatory for having to be at the receiving end. To be fair, he also sympathized with Robin.

12 October 1958 : Cole and our Bonn boss, Gerry Long, chief correspondent in Germany, told me that, because costs are rising faster than revenues, one of our two remaining men in Berlin is being withdrawn. *[Cole, who became general manager in 1959, died in 1963. Long succeeded him as general manager.]*

2 Camp guards on trial

13 October 1958 : To the trial of Gustav Sorge and Wilhelm Schubert, two former SS guards in concentration camps, who were charged with complicity in the murder of about 11,000 men during the Second World War. They had been sentenced by the Russians to forced labour for life in 1946, but were released to West Germany in 1956, on condition that the West Germans prosecuted them too. Both men looked pretty nasty.

Schubert, who appeared still to be a Nazi, showed hatred for the Russians in his evidence today, and no sign of repentance for the thousands of Russians he helped to kill in cold blood. And Sorge said that, after ten years in Russian hands, he had chosen to come to West Germany, even though he knew he would face a new trial, which is virtually certain to end in another life sentence. Schubert looks just like a stage Nazi in the way he bares his teeth when speaking each word, standing stiffly to attention and snapping out his replies with lots of *Jawohls.* Sorge, who was nick-named 'Iron Gustav' even before the Nazis took power, for his toughness in street fighting, is much more down to earth, speaking simply and almost modestly.

Lunch separated this war crimes trial from a press conference at which we were told the *Bundeswehr* would start training in West Germany on United States ground-to-ground Honest John missiles – this while efforts are still being made to deal with the leftovers of the last war in Germany. The Defence Ministry spokesman said West Germany would dispense with nuclear weapons if disarmament talks were successful. But whoever thinks they will be?

14 October 1958 : The concentration camp trial continued. Sorge began telling about the general set-up at two concentration camps where he was a guard after the Nazis came to power in 1933: Esterwegen, in northwest Germany close to the Dutch border; and Sachsenhausen, near Oranienburg, north of Berlin. This trial underlines the need, in any society, for a humane legal system and prison administration. Prisoners at the camps were whipped, hung by their bound wrists from poles, beaten and kicked. And the two camps were not planned as mass-murder camps; those were deliberately sited in occupied Poland. *[That made it easier to keep secret the mass murders, mainly of Jews and gypsies.]*

Sorge said he had not felt that his actions were wrong, as they had been ordered by his highest superior, Hermann Göring, then Prime Minister of Prussia. But the former guard said that on one occasion, when he had suspected that a prisoner had been shot dead unnecessarily, he had asked an old friend, an SS officer, how far they ought to go. The officer had told them that if actions were ordered they were correct. This trial also underlines the need for independent media, which can show up such things.

Chris was awake late and asked Elfi if there were such things as ghosts. He'd seen something of the sort on TV. Elfi told him they didn't really exist, they were just jokes. That cheered him up a lot. Later he said he had been woken up by an *Engel* (angel) and he asked what angels ate. We told him, in his language, they were abstemious.

15 October 1958 : Chatting with a Social Democratic journalist, Hardy Eckert, we agreed that his party, the main opposition party, is in a difficult position. For one thing they lack the type of leader who would appeal to Germans. Further, they are frightened to be socialist, for fear they will be accused of being communist. The result is that they are so wishy-washy that many potential supporters regard them as not much better than Chancellor Konrad Adenauer's Christian Democrats, and are not inspired to work for them.

13

I did a report on the decision by Krupps of Essen, which made arms for the Kaiser and Hitler, to go into the joint production of civilian and military helicopters with the American helicopter firm, Sikorsky. The head of Krupps, Alfried Krupp, was tried for war crimes by the Western allies at Nuremberg, instead of his ailing father, and sentenced in 1948 to 12 years' imprisonment. In the wake of the improved relations between the Western allies and democratic West Germany, Krupp was released in 1951. When he took over control of the firm again in 1953, Krupp said he had no interest in making arms. I mentioned this to the firm's spokesman, Burandt, today and he said the firm did not regard aircraft as arms any more than lorries for the *Bundeswehr*, which Krupp also makes. He said the firm was keeping to its decision not to make arms any more.

16 October 1958 : At the concentration camp trial, Sorge said that one punishment at Sachsenhausen had been to make men run 40 to 50 km (25–30 miles) a day, to test experimental shoe soles. This had quickly reduced the men to wrecks. New prisoners had been beaten and punched 'to put fear into them straight away'. One sign of humanity in the evidence so far was that two SS guards had been brave enough to be kind to prisoners. As a result they were given 25 lashes each and imprisoned in the camp themselves for a year, then put into a *Wehrmacht* penal battalion.

Sitting in the courtroom making notes reminds me of when I used to do criminal court reporting for the *Telegraph & Argus*, the paper in my hometown, Bradford. But what a different kind of trial this is! It would not fit in decent peaceful old England, even after the recent Notting Hill race riots. *[Today it is my view that if a dictatorship had been imposed on Britain, local men like Schubert and Sorge would have been found to man British concentration camps.]*

At teatime Chris again brought up the subject of ghosts, and once again we laughed it off. He seemed satisfied. But Robin nearly spoilt things by saying, 'What about the Holy Ghost?'

18 October 1958 : London tipped us off that the American agency, Associated Press, was carrying a story about a Soviet-made Tupolev jet airliner crashing between Peking and Moscow, with four West German diplomats, including the Moscow ambassador, among the dead. London asked us to try to get a matcher.

I managed this quickly by ringing up the Foreign Office spokesman at home. He told me they had received a telegram from their Moscow embassy stating that four people with German names had been killed, but that it was extremely unlikely they were diplomats and they were certainly not diplomats from Moscow. He could not give me the names, so I rang the Foreign Office, was put through to a teleprinter room and persuaded a clerk to give me the names. Not wanting to get him into trouble, suggested he seek permission from the spokesman at home to give me the names, which he successfully did. The West German news agency DPA, which buys a service from us, used our version of the story! *[This was a good example of the relative openness of West German official bodies towards the media, compared to their counterparts in Britain.]*

19 October 1958 : A very good sermon by a young pastor at our local Lutheran church today. When he said that one's property should not set the limit to one's Christian feeling for others, I felt that in that respect very few of us were Christians. I thought of the German family who were still having to live in a partly converted air raid shelter in Bonn a year or two ago.

Elfi, not for the first time, whacked me at Scrabble tonight after I had built up what I thought was a commanding lead. The more often we play, the cleverer I think she is! However, I maintain it's just because she uses so much verbiage whereas I, professionally, have to restrict it. *[We often played in German and English.]*

20 October 1958 : At last I bought a dinner jacket and trousers – needed for an important coming function. Could not really afford it at the moment, but when will I be able to? I chose one made of a light West German synthetic fibre, Trevira, for

15

179 marks (around £15), about as cheap as one can get here. The average gross monthly wage in West Germany at present is 512 marks (£45). *[I still wear that suit.]*

In Cologne, visited an exhibition of paintings by Russian-born Vassily Kandinsky (1866–1944), who worked mainly in Germany and is rated as one of the founders of abstract art. The exhibition ranged from representational works done around the turn of the century to modern stuff that he started doing, I think, around 1910. Although I get nothing from some abstract painting, I enjoyed all of this. His abstract stuff is pleasant to look at, bright patterns suggesting all kinds or no kinds of things, or sombre works conveying moods. His paintings appealed to me more than many of Picasso's, even though his work does not have Picasso's breadth. *[I can still remember vaguely and with pleasure the look of some of those abstract works.]*

As part of my efforts to learn Russian, in the hope of being posted to Moscow, have completed the 65 lessons of a Russian course I started in January 1957. Have also done a Russian course as an extra-mural student at Bonn University *[the first – and last – university I attended]*.

22 October 1958 : Wrote a story about a man who was accused – and acquitted – of fraud. He had been the top leader of a religious sect preaching the world's approaching end and obtaining donations to build a kind of Noah's Ark on a German mountain near the Swiss border. A place in the 'ark' was to be offered to the Pope, in spite of the fact that one of the sect's leaders was an excommunicated Capuchin monk.

I thought the affair had a typically modern West German touch in that, when police started investigations, the former monk and a lay sister fled the country in a three-litre Mercedes. The court found that the leader of the sect, who said he still believed in its teachings, had acted in good faith, and stated that the persons who had fled were probably the guilty parties. *[My diary does not give the names of the accused.]*

23 October 1958 : I told TASS correspondent, Boris Yurinov, about Elfi's distant relative, Hans Ratzenberger who, after fleeing from his East Prussian homeland at the end of the Second World War, was given farmland in Communist East Germany, following the expropriation of large estates there. Hans, who was an efficient farmer, fled again, to West Germany, in about 1955 because he did not want to be forced into a collective farm.

Yurinov agreed with me that collectives could be badly run if people took the view that they were no longer working for their own benefit. But, he argued, they could be well run if the members felt that the collectives were a better system than individual farmers' just serving their own interests. I agreed with that, but said I thought it wrong to force people into collectives by the threat of arrest and other pressures, which Hans has told me was the case in East Germany when he fled from there. Hans has meanwhile become a winegrower near Bacharach, on the Rhine, aided by cheap credits given to refugees.

24 October 1958 : Attended a dinner in Baden-Baden of the West German Chemical Industries Association, appropriately wearing my synthetic dinner jacket bought specially for this occasion. Main speaker was the British Paymaster-General, the Conservative politician Reginald Maudling. Maudling had flown from Paris, where negotiations are taking place under his chairmanship, in a committee of the Organisation for European Economic Cooperation (OEEC), on the foundation of a 17-nation free-trade area linking the six Common Market countries with 11 others, including Britain. The gist of Maudling's speech was that if the free-trade area did not come about, that would mean not only economic but political division in Europe.

From what Maudling told me unpublishably afterwards, one stumbling block in the negotiations is the French desire, reluctantly backed by the other five of the six, that voting in the governing bodies of the free-trade area should be unanimous. That means that France would have a veto, enabling her to continue protectionist measures while paying lip service to free trade. An even bigger problem, Maudling said, was how to prevent free trade within the 17-nation area of those goods from outside the area which were subject to differing import tariffs by the 11 non-members of the Common Market.

I nearly had a scoop this evening when the public relations man of a chemical firm told me that Maudling – probably unknown to him – had been flown from Paris in the private plane of the convicted war criminal, Alfried Krupp. I obtained confirmation of this from Professor Hans Haberland, the chairman of the Chemical Industries Association and managing director of the Bayer concern.

Haberland was unable to tell me how it had come about that Krupp's plane was used, so I asked one of the Association secretaries, who realized immediately what a bombshell the story might cause in Britain, especially after the cool reception of President Heuss by some British papers when he visited Britain last week. The secretary begged me not to use the story, saying he would be sacked, and Professor Haberland joined in this plea. The secretary said that Krupp did not know that his plane had been used by Maudling; the Association had hired it from the Krupp concern after failing to get one from commercial airlines.

I told them I would not be doing my duty as a journalist if I suppressed the story, but promised to put their representations to Gerry Long. I phoned Gerry and he decided, rightly I think, that to publish such a story would make it seem that Reuters was trying to discredit Maudling and that we should therefore leave it alone. I must confess, though, that I was just a weeny bit sorry that it did not get into print – though I don't want to harm efforts towards European cooperation.

25 October 1958 : Driving back to Bonn on the autobahn, learned, line-by-line, some Russian verse which I had clipped to my dashboard. Came across an interesting word: *nyeboskryeb* – skyscraper. *Nyebo* means 'sky', and might be cognate with German *Nebel* ('fog'), whereas I think that *skryeb* is just a Russian version of English 'scrape'.

27 October 1958 : John Bush, our new news editor – deputy to the chief correspondent, Gerry Long – pointed out to me that I had not issued a story on 25 October about demonstrators throwing stink bombs at one of Defence Minister Franz-Josef Strauss's meetings in the Hesse state election campaign. *[The source of that story was almost certainly the West German news agency DPA, with which we had a contract. We had the right to translate that agency's stories and put them into Reuter style.]* I had decided that sort of thing had happened so often that it was no longer news. But John had resuscitated the story, issued it yesterday and it was used by one or more of our clients.

I also had a note from Gerry today pointing out I had not inserted some comparative figures necessary to make a recent economic story more comprehensible. *[As well as that kind of editorial supervision in Bonn, our stories were edited in London too.]*

To mark the twelfth anniversary of our engagement, we saw the film version of a delicious German political satire, *Der Maulkorb* (*The Muzzle*), based on a famous book by Heinrich Spoerl (1887–1955). Set in the era of, I think, Kaiser Wilhelm II, it's a story of a public prosecutor who, while on his way home drunk, fixes his dog's muzzle over the mouth of a statue of the Kaiser, who was intending to introduce a law muzzling criticism of royal personalities. The next morning the prosecutor, a loyal monarchist, is told about the case, remembers nothing and tries to find the culprit. Eventually he realizes that he was responsible, but is saved from disgrace by a couple of jolly louts, one of whom accuses the other, who admits the crimes, so that the first can collect a big reward. The accused gets off lightly after telling the court he was drunk and thought the statue was 'a kind of Goethe' and not a Kaiser at all.

28 October 1958 : An official of the opposition Social Democrats told me the government was intending to start a second television programme, probably organized at the federal or national level, which would allow the federal government to control its political colour. The items in the present national television programme are provided by the various broadcasting corporations of the states, which are of differing political complexion.

29 October 1958 : Today I presented at my German bank a cheque drawn on my London bank and was immediately able to obtain some of the money. Shows how small Europe is becoming, or how trustful my bank is!

31 October 1958 : Wrote about a speech by Gerhard Schröder, the Christian Democratic Federal Interior Minister *[and namesake of the Social Democratic Chancellor who took office in 1998]*. Schröder called for legislation to give the federal government the right to use emergency powers under certain circumstances and for increased powers for the security organs. There are suspicions, not only from Social Democrats, that Schröder wants to use such emergency powers as he chooses – maybe against Social Democrats some day. He has already shown a tendency to resort to state power rather than argument in ideological matters, something which the Communists are rightly criticized for.

3 Secrets of a family vineyard

1 November 1958 : We are staying for a weekend with Elfi's wine-growing East Prussian relatives, the Ratzenbergers, in the quaint village of Steeg, just outside the Rhineside town of Bacharach, south of Koblenz. Today we helped, a little, to harvest some of the remaining grapes on one of the 14 little vineyards owned by the Ratzenbergers – only 2½ acres in all. These little vineyards, which used to be owned by various people, resulted from the old system of splitting inheritances among heirs, which is no longer practised, as it became uneconomic. The steep hillsides glowed golden with the autumnal vines. The air was nectar.

Elfi and Hans' 52-year-old wife, Hedwig, in old clothes, headscarves and boots, set off first to walk up a muddy track to the vineyard. Hans, two metal teeth shining in the sun, two of his three sons, Robin, Chris and I, all piled onto a tractor or the cart it pulled up the steep winding track to a vineyard about ¾ mile away. As we cut off bunches of grapes, working our way – and slithering – up the soggy steep slopes, we could see the thousand-year-old keep of a castle.

Back at the house, the grapes, in the vat that had been on the cart, were electrically milled to pulp them, then put into an electrically operated pressing vat, developing very high pressure. As the must – grape juice – oozed from holes in the bottom of the pressing vat, it was pumped into normal vats and will stay there until January or February, fermenting. The fermentation makes a popping bubbling sound, as though the vats are talking to one another. It produces carbon dioxide, which can be dangerous

21

if the cellar is the lowest room in the house, which it usually is.

In January or February the wine is poured, except for sediment, into other vats. It stays there for about a year and is then bottled. In most years in this area it is necessary to add a permitted amount of sugar, so that the wine is not too sour. This is done within a day or so of the pressing, the sugar normally being added in hot water. Tests of the relative amounts of sugar and acid in the must are made to show how much sugar to add to the wine. This year, an October with little sunshine meant that the wine will not be of the best quality, but the harvest was a large one. In one vineyard alone, Hans produced 600 litres of must; two years ago he had exactly ten grapes in that vineyard. Frost took the rest.

2 November 1958 : As refugees, the Ratzenbergers were given a calf by an American Christian sect, with the proviso that, if it calved some day, they should give that calf to another refugee family. Their calf is now a cow, but I think it's not old enough to calve yet. It recently recovered from an operation to remove a nail it had swallowed. Today, as she was milking the cow, Hedwig let me try my hand at one teat. To my amazement, milk actually squirted out when I went through the motions. I'd never thought it would be so easy, but maybe it was because Hedwig had got things going.

Hanfried, 19, one of the Ratzenbergers' sons – they also have a daughter, Hannelore – took Robin to see about two of the four hours of *Gone With the Wind*, in spite of the fact that this Hollywood epic is *verboten* for Robin's age-group. He seemed to have quite enjoyed it.

The staple diet of the Ratzenbergers is brown bread baked by a local baker from their own rye, milk from the cow, and the products of the regular slaughtering of one pig after another. Our evening meal was composed of these elements, plus a few gherkins, probably home grown too, sliced tomatoes and some bought cheese.

Hans told me how he and his family come to be in the Rhineland. After fleeing from their East Prussian homeland in late 1944 or early 1945, as the Soviet army swept in, they came first to Western Germany. But in 1947 they went to Eastern Germany, not yet a separate state, but under Soviet occupation. Hans knew he could get land cheaply from one of the great estates being broken up in the Communist land reform. West Germany, he said, was near starving at that time. Hans was given 25 acres, for which he had to pay only 100 marks (about £9) annually.

It was not until some years later that the Communist authorities started applying pressure on private farmers to join cooperative (collective) farms. Hans agreed with me that working in a collective could be better than working as a farm labourer for a big landowner, but not if the collective had been founded compulsorily. He said that most of those who joined the early collectives were people who had fallen behind in compulsory deliveries to the state. Collective members do not have to make such large deliveries, and get more and cheaper credits. Hans said he fled when warned he was about to be arrested for opposing collectives – he'd been offered the chairmanship of one, but had turned the offer down, as he wanted to work for himself and his family.

At present he has a job in a factory as well as working on the farm in his spare time, with his wife and one of his sons, 14-year-old Jochen, employed full time there. *[Jochen later studied wine-growing at an agricultural college and took over the business when Hans retired. The vineyard was extended and became one of the best in all Germany, with its wine being bought for federal government functions.]*

3 November 1958 : As we left for home, the Ratzenbergers presented us with several hundred apples, four bottles of grape juice and a big basket of grapes. I also bought four bottles of wine and insisted on paying something for the other things, in spite of protest.

4 November 1958 : Was told today that Reuters general manager, Sir Christopher Chancellor, had approved a rise in my salary – something I've been seeking for quite some time. The increase, bringing my salary to £1,125 per year, amounts to about £2 8s [£2.40] a week, the largest salary increase I've ever had, except when I joined Reuters. My total emoluments are now £1,550 per annum (including foreign allowance and car allowance), which seems a phenomenal sum compared with the £275 I got when I started in journalism in 1947. Shall use much of the extra money to clear off income tax arrears and my car loan. My rise is, in one sense, the more pleasing, as it seems I was the only staffer to get one as a result of Cole's visit, and Reuters is in the midst of an economy drive.

6 November 1958 : Started my fourth term as an extra-mural student at Bonn University – again in the advanced Russian section. Our lecturer, Dr Kandler, an ethnic German born in one of the Baltic states when it was part of Tsarist Russia, commented after today's class that I had been working hard in the holidays.

Listened to a long-playing record of songs from *My Fair Lady*, the Broadway show based on Shaw's *Pygmalion*. Fred Ungeheuer, Harvard-educated German colleague, had lent it to us. It's delicious, especially one song entitled 'Why don't the English learn to speak', making fun of regional British accents.

One day late, because I was busy yesterday, we held a British Guy Fawkes' Night on spare land near the Söhners' flat, joined by them and their children. The Söhner clan and some of their German neighbours were delighted with this bit of British folklore. Later we ate Gunpowder Plot parkin, as we used to do in Yorkshire, baked by Elfi.

7 November 1958 : Saw Chancellor Konrad Adenauer – unchanged at 82 – meet John G. Diefenbaker, the burly friendly-looking Canadian Prime Minister, at Cologne–Bonn airport. Diefenbaker has an appealing grin and a comic high-pitched laugh. He seemed genuinely pleased to be in West Germany and the Germans seemed genuinely pleased to welcome him. About 600,000 people of German descent now live in Canada, and the two countries have important trade relations.

10 November 1958 : Our news editor, John Bush, is annoying some of us by not reducing the undue number of stories he thinks worth writing. He worked from 09.00 to 23.00 today. At one stage he asked me if I thought he had handled one story in the most interesting way. It was an old story, so I told him, in a friendly but blunt fashion, that it could not be interesting in any form. He's such a nice fellow that he did not react angrily even at that.

11 November 1958 : To a press conference at which the Interior Minister, Gerhard Schröder, a man suspected of authoritarian leanings by the Social Democratic opposition, gave some details of the emergency powers law which is shortly to be introduced into the *Bundestag*, the Federal Lower House, the most important parliamentary chamber. The government argues that the law is necessary to supersede the powers that the three Western allies, the former occupation powers, have retained to take action in an emergency until the *Bundestag* has passed a law on the subject.

I found Schröder quite appealing today. His argument was that the *Bundestag* could not pass the law without the cooperation of the opposition, as a two-thirds majority is required by the constitution and the opposition controls more than one third. Thus it was up to the opposition to ensure, in considering the law, that any fear they had about the misuse of the proposed powers was removed by the inclusion of safeguards. Sounds reasonable enough to me.

On a duty drive to Hamburg, made a brief stop in Bottrop, in the industrial Ruhr area, to visit my widowed mother-in-law, Helene Kowitz. It's now 12 years since we first met when, as a junior naval officer, I was allowed to visit her and her husband, Ludwig, in an internment camp in Denmark, where they were held after fleeing by ship from East Prussia. They were kept in the Danish camp until 1947, because of the housing shortage in devastated Germany, and were allowed to return to Germany only when relatives in Bottrop offered them a room. Later they obtained a flat.

My mother-in-law, whom I call '*Mutti*', is a sterling type. She is also a devout fundamentalist Lutheran, so I, the doubter, try not to discuss religion with her.

Have nearly finished learning another poem by a Russian poet, about how he spent his birthday in Peking and, in spite of his advanced years, was cheered by the sight of the youth there who, in his view, represented the successful fight against egotism and so on. Just depends on how you see things. I am at least glad that Soviet poets usually write in the manner of Socialist Realism – it's easier to translate than abstract stuff.

12 November 1958 : Driving on to Hamburg, was thankful for the autobahn, as the remaining 200 miles of my journey from Bottrop were in fog, with visibility in parts down to about 50 yards. At least on the autobahn you do know that – as a rule – there's no one coming the other way on your side of the road.

I'd come to Hamburg to report on a meeting of officials of the International Transport Workers' Federation, held to prepare a boycott, from 1 to 4 December, of 'cheap flag' ships, which now account for about 13 per cent of the world merchant fleet in tonnage, a figure which is growing at about 2 per cent a year. Such ships, registered in countries like Panama, Liberia, Honduras and Costa Rica are subject to little taxation and few regulations. Most of them are owned by Greek companies, with a lot of American capital behind them. The planned boycott, which can affect only ships that are in port, is not intended to end the use of 'cheap flags', but to press the ship-owners to sign agreements with the unions. So far only about a sixth of 'cheap flag' ships are subject to such agreements.

15 November 1958 : Drove from Hamburg to Berlin. You cannot drive directly between these two cities unless you are a German or specially favoured by the East German Communist regime. Foreigners must, as a rule, drive southwards from Hamburg for about 100 miles before turning eastwards to cross into East Germany on the autobahn just east of the small town of Helmstedt.

26

On my way I picked up an unusual hitchhiker, who turned out to be Dr Schulz, a medical specialist in x-ray diagnostics and next-door neighbour of West Berlin's Social Democratic Mayor, Willy Brandt. Dr Schulz told me he had recently opened a practice in Brunswick, close to the East German border, and was going home for the weekend. He had not wanted to wait another six hours for the bus, which travels down the interzonal autobahn from the West.

We talked much about politics and religion, he being a staunch Catholic who kept quoting from books by Graham Greene, which I had never read. He believed in God, he said, because he felt God's presence in his affairs. Though apparently not a Social Democrat, he spoke very highly of Brandt.

As we went through the frontier formalities at Helmstedt, I chatted with an East German official about his country's single-list parliamentary 'elections' tomorrow – the reason I'm going to Berlin. I suggested that the elections were not democratic, as the result, at least so far as the majorities are concerned, is known in advance.

He gave me the usual answer that, anyway, all the parties are agreed in principle about moving towards socialism and that the people did not want other parties like the 'fascist' parties in West Germany, or words to that effect.

16 November 1958 : Shortly after 08.00, I was waved on by a West Berlin policeman, as I drove onto the ruined Potsdamer Platz into East Berlin, not far from the rubble of Hitler's Chancellery. On the Western side of the square stands a high metal framework holding a device consisting of many flashing electric bulbs, which form the letters of news messages that can be read at a distance at night by people in East Berlin.

On East Berlin's historic Unter den Linden, which starts at the Brandenburg Gate, I saw lots of election banners, posters and flags, calling on everyone to go to vote for peace and socialism and against Adenauer and 'atomic death'. In the Russian-style show street, the Stalinallee, not far from a giant statue of the former

Soviet dictator, I found a polling station in a department store specializing in children's wares.

The scene seemed much like polling day in Britain during a general election – until you looked more closely. Voters showed their identity cards to election officials, members of the Socialist Unity (that is, Communist) Party and satellite parties, which all favour the basic Communist aims, while purporting to represent groups such as Christians, farmers, ex-Nazis, Liberals and so on. After the voters' names had been checked on the electoral roll, they were handed a blue ballot and an envelope, though not all took the envelope. On the ballot were about 15 names – candidates of different parties, with a majority ensured for the Communists. To vote in favour of this list, the citizens simply had to fold up the paper, putting it in the envelope if they wished, and push it through the slit in a cardboard ballot box.

In charge was an elderly man named Gustav who told me he had taken part in the abortive Communist revolution of 1918 when he was in the navy. He said anyone had the right to go into a booth at the end of the room and vote secretly in there. To register opposition, one could strike out one or more names. About 100 people came in while I was there and I saw no one enter the booth. Gustav told me that voters had been able to turn down candidates earlier, after they had been chosen by the Communist-dominated National Front, grouping all the parties. He said that, in East Berlin, two candidates had been replaced in this way, but he agreed that this would not alter the automatic Communist majority.

From what Gustav and two other men told me, the theory is that it is impossible for parties in a Communist state to oppose the great goals of peace and socialism. So, you see, there's no need for party bickering and the kind of election where you can choose between one party and another. In other words, this election is just a big demonstration of alleged unanimity, and those who vote against are either old people who don't understand, or other misguided types, or implacable fascists. A man I quizzed outside the polling station conceded that one fine day the satellite parties would be completely swallowed up by the Communists.

A few streets away I saw a group of sweet-faced boys and girls, aged about nine, led by a plump woman, singing songs outside a polling station, exhorting people to vote. An elderly woman standing nearby told me she thought that was excellent. She agreed with me that the children did not understand what they were doing, but thought they were getting the 'right ideas' at an early age instead of being taught, as she had been, almost to worship the Kaiser. There were posters on some blocks of flats, saying their occupants were all going to vote at the same time – for the list, of course.

At another polling station, in an old pub still in private hands, unlike many which have been nationalized, one of the officials was a 40-ish man who had been in a prisoner-of-war camp in Britain after the Second World War. He recalled a farm labourer near Malmesbury, Wiltshire, swearing at the 'bloody Tories' and saying that elections didn't do him much good. I retorted that the 1945 election, which had brought Labour in, had moved Britain some way towards a democratic socialism, so it was untrue to say in Britain that the ballot box got you nowhere.

When I asked three officials at this polling station if people who used the polling booth – a few were doing so here – were victimized, they laughed, and I'm quite prepared to believe that they are not. One of the officials told me about a man at his workplace who, at a pre-election meeting, attacked the Communist single-list system. He was countered with arguments, my informant said, and nothing else. This official said other people used dirty words about the Communist system; today, he argued, the Communists could afford to be tolerant. All three agreed with me that ten years ago people could have been locked up for showing much independence in discussions.

Was a lunch guest in the West Berlin flat of our Berlin correspondent, 40-ish German, Alfred Klühs, who spent much of the Nazi era in Britain, as his father, a leading Social Democrat, was a political refugee. Also present were his charming doctor wife, Gaby, and their two daughters, aged about nine and seven. The girls are not allowed to go to Sunday school or religious lessons at school, because Alfred and Gaby are agnostics and, they say, want their children to use their own brains when they grow up, to decide then what to believe in. Alfred and Gaby spend much of their time in voluntary work for a traditional workers' welfare organization, the Workers' Samaritan League.

4 Tension over Berlin

17 November 1958 : According to the official result of the East German election, 0.13 per cent voted against the list and a further 0.13 per cent spoiled their papers. At the last election, in 1954, these two totals were added, to produce 0.54 per cent. West Berlin radio had recommended voters not to endanger themselves by registering opposition votes. Everyone realizes that is pointless at present.

Drove in a hurry to Berlin's south-western tip to see three American army vehicles – two open trucks and a jeep – leave to cross East Germany westwards on the autobahn, which they are allowed to do according to four-power agreements. Two days ago three closed American trucks were stopped by Soviet soldiers and eventually sent back because the Americans refused to allow the Soviets to look inside the trucks. The American view is that this is not allowed. British officials told us unofficially that the British have the sense to leave open the back flaps of their trucks to save trouble. Today the open trucks were allowed through, indicating that the Russians are not trying gradually to impose a new blockade like that started in 1948.

Tension over Berlin began on 10 November, when the Soviet Communist Party leader, Nikita Khrushchev, made a disturbing Cold War speech, claiming that the 1944 four-power London Agreements on the occupation of Germany were no longer valid. *[Khrushchev, in what the West called his 'Berlin ultimatum', said that West Berlin must be transformed into an 'independent political unit – a free city' in which no outside state, including the two German* states, must be allowed to interfere. The Soviet Union fixed a six-month deadline for the Western allies to agree to its terms and threatened that, if no agreement were reached, it would conclude a separate treaty with East Germany, under which it would hand over its occupation powers to the German Communist state.

On 10 January 1959 the Soviet Union called on the Western allies to conclude separate peace treaties with the two German states. This was an obvious attempt to achieve Western diplomatic recognition of Communist East Germany, which the Western allies and West Germany opposed on the ground that the East German state had no democratic legitimacy. The three Western powers rejected the Soviet demands and reaffirmed their guarantees for West Berlin: the continued presence of the Western garrisons, the maintenance of the access routes and of the viability of West Berlin.

Before the six-month deadline expired, Khrushchev gradually toned down his ultimatum. In the summer of 1959 there were talks in Geneva at foreign minister level between the four powers, with the participation of the two Germanys, but no compromise was reached. After that the Soviet Union repeatedly renewed its demands, but took no far-reaching action until it authorized the building of the Berlin Wall around West Berlin, which was started on 13 August 1961. This virtually ended the massive flow of refugees from East Germany.

The building of the Berlin Wall was a breach of the four-power status of all Berlin. However the Soviet Union tacitly accepted the right of the three Western allies to continue stationing their forces in West Berlin, to have free access to West Berlin from West Germany, and for members of the Western allied forces to have free access to East Berlin on the basis of the old four-power agreements. Similarly, Soviet soldiers had free access to West Berlin. Although the three Western allies protested at the building of the Berlin Wall, they accepted the new situation, partly because their rights in and regarding West Berlin had not been curtailed and evidently because they feared that action to tear down the Wall could result in war.

After the building of the Berlin Wall, the main thrust of the Soviet Union and its East German satellite regarding Berlin was intended to restrict, as far as possible, West Berlin's links with West Germany. The *three Western allies had vetoed an article in the constitution of West Germany, adopted in 1949, under which West Berlin would have become a* Land *(state) of West Germany. Instead it remained under Western allied occupation while, with Western allied approval or toleration, becoming* de facto *in most respects part of West Germany. A number of West German governmental agencies were sited in West Berlin.*

From 1961 to 1969, when successive West German governments were led by conservative Christian Democratic chancellors, there was repeated tension when Soviet and East German authorities sought to prevent such manifestations of West Germany's links with West Berlin as the holding in West Berlin of a Bundestag *sitting and the election there of a new West German Federal President. The Communist reaction took the form of the 'buzzing' of Western allied planes in the air corridors linking West Germany with West Berlin, and the temporary halting of traffic on the surface access routes to West Berlin.*

Much of the heat went out of the Berlin question after 18 months of negotiations between the three Western allies and the Soviet Union which resulted in the quadripartite Berlin Agreement of September 1971. The two sides negotiated, while consulting closely with their respective German ally. One reason why this agreement became possible was the détente *policy of the new West German coalition, headed by the Social Democrat, Willy Brandt, which took office in September 1969. The Berlin Agreement was politically linked to* détente *agreements made by the Brandt government with the Soviet Union and Poland in 1970.*

The Berlin Agreement was a compromise under which both sides, in spite of their differences, renounced the use of force to change the existing situation and agreed on a number of practical improvements. The Western allies made the concession that in future there would be no West German presidential elections or plenary meetings of the Bundestag *or* Bundesrat *(the second parliamentary chamber, representing the states), held in West Berlin. The Soviet Union, for its part, agreed that West Germany should be allowed to represent West Berlin internationally, under certain provisos.]*

18 November 1958 : Our main opposition, the American agency Associated Press (AP), beat Alfred and me today by quickly putting out an opening statement issued at a crowded press conference in the Soviet embassy in East Berlin.

We had expected there might be some important announcement on Berlin, linked to the Khrushchev ultimatum. Instead an embassy spokesman condemned American attempts to recruit anti-Soviet spies and said this was a danger to humanity. Then a former Soviet army officer and a circus performer, who had both defected to the West and then gone back to the East, described how Americans in West Germany had tried to persuade them to become spies.

There was no reference to Berlin's status until nearly the end of the two-hour press conference, when the army officer said activities of Russian *émigré* organizations in West Berlin breached the 1945 four-power Potsdam Agreement. One of the AP correspondents must have gone back to West Berlin to transmit part of the opening statement – about an hour ahead of Alfred, who had left halfway through the press conference. *[Telephone connections between East and West Berlin had been cut off by East Germany some years earlier.]*

I stayed until the end. We were criticized both by London and our local bosses. It was not that the story itself was a big one, but Gerry told me on the phone that, after the Khrushchev ultimatum, almost any story from Berlin is big news at the moment. All good experience anyway.

Two days ago I had a chat with George Turner, the 50-ish British spokesman in Berlin, who does not seem to take the situation very seriously. He asked me what I thought about the chances of East Germany's being recognized by the West. I told him that during a recent trip to East Germany I had said I would not bet on its not happening within five years. *[It did not come about until the seventies, after West Germany had recognized East Germany through a 'Basic Treaty' between the two German states, which took effect in 1973.]*

19 November 1958 : On East German television 64-year-old Vincenz Müller, former East German Deputy Defence Minister and onetime *Wehrmacht* general, revealed more details of an intriguing incident in the Cold War: his talks in East Berlin two years ago with Fritz Schäffer, then the West German Finance Minister, now the Justice Minister.

If Schäffer did in fact negotiate with Müller, this would have contravened the basic West German refusal to recognize the East German regime. Schäffer has in fact denied negotiating with Müller, saying he met him only because Müller had arranged a meeting for him with the Soviet ambassador. I'm inclined to believe Müller's version, which is that Schäffer knew very well he was talking to an East German government representative.

According to Müller, Schäffer had suggested creating a kind of confederation of the two German states, rather on the lines of the cooperation between the Benelux countries. Schäffer has been criticized for his action by some, praised by others. I think proper negotiations between the two Germanys will come one day and that they will be better than not talking at all, while arming.

At least some contacts still go on between the two Germanys. I took part in one today, by phoning, while in East Berlin, the Communist Deputy Minister of Education, Wilhelm Girnus, to ask him whether his mother was still alive. I did this on behalf of an East Prussian woman friend in whose house Girnus's mother had stayed as an evacuee during the Second World War. Girnus told me politely that his mother, now over 80, was alive and kicking. When I asked if our friend could write to his mother, he said she could.

20 November 1958 : To a defiant press conference given by Mayor Willy Brandt, in West Berlin's Schöneberg city hall, the headquarters of the West Berlin city government since the Communists split the Berlin administration by force in 1948. They took over Berlin's original city hall in East Berlin, called the 'red' city hall because it's made of red brick. Schöneberg city hall has a tower containing the Freedom Bell given to Berlin by the

United States after the 1948–9 Berlin Blockade. Brandt, a 44-year-old former journalist, spoke about the new threat to Berlin caused by the Khrushchev ultimatum. His theme was: 'We shall not give in. The allies are backing us.'

Spent the evening with a Belgian Communist journalist, Martin Thijs, based in East Berlin. Our discussion ranged over the theme of why Communists are deceitful in propaganda and try to force people to do things they do not want. One of the answers was that people were forced because they do not yet understand what is good for them. Was amused to learn that Thijs' wife is a Social Democrat and that they go at each other hammer and tongs in their East Berlin flat. She is not sold on East Germany at all.

22 November 1958 : The West German Foreign Minister, Heinrich von Brentano, flew in from Bonn to see Brandt. Brentano indicated, in a not directly quotable talk with foreign journalists, that there probably would not be opposition by the West if the Soviet Union made the East Germans their 'agents' in regard to their Berlin control powers, providing that the Russians did not purport to hand over their powers, which the West maintains they cannot do without four-power agreement. Alfred Klühs and I sent a message to Bonn office complaining that London had written into our story a line saying Berlin was 'gripped with fears of a blockade' which is just not true. London issued a correction.

After I'd been working for about 12 hours, one of my Bonn colleagues came on the phone asking for coverage of an editorial in the Socialist Unity Party (SED) organ, *Neues Deutschland*. Being tired and considering the editorial not very newsworthy, I asked my Bonn colleague to do the story from a shorter news agency version of the editorial which was available in the Bonn office. Then I went home to sleep, feeling, on the one hand, somewhat ashamed that I hadn't done that story myself and, on the other, justified in not having done it. We could work 24 hours a day if we wrote about everything.

23 November 1958 : To Berlin's old city airport, Tempelhof, in a built-up area of West Berlin, to report on the arrival of young-looking US Democratic Senator, Hubert Humphrey, a possible presidential candidate in 1960. Humphrey greeted Willy Brandt as 'a wonderful freedom fighter' and underlined American determination to maintain the four-power agreements on Berlin.

At a press conference later today, Humphrey said that the 1948–9 Berlin Airlift could be repeated. Actually, that is somewhat melodramatic so far as the Berlin population is concerned, for the Soviet moves do not, at present anyway, threaten Berlin's civilian supply routes, but could leave the Western allies with the choice of negotiating with the East Germans, as the Russians' successors, or flying in their own supplies instead of using the autobahn.

Apparently what Brentano conveyed to us last night, about possible Western acceptance of the Russians using the East Germans as their 'agents' regarding access to Berlin, was not the West German view at all, but just Brentano making things, as usual, unclear. It seems that the West Germans are entirely against anything tending to give any kind of recognition to East Germany in such matters. Their Foreign Office even protested to Gerry about our report. After reading my transcript, Gerry said we had better not refer again to what Brentano had said, because he seemed to have confused matters.

Lunched in West Berlin with recently widowed 45-ish Felicitas (Fee) Sauheitl, a distant relative of Elfi's. Her husband, Adolf, was an Austrian-born Communist official in the East German Trade Ministry, whom I liked because of his readiness to engage in frank and sometimes heated political discussion; he seemed to me to be one of the old idealistic Communists. *[I had driven Fee to West Berlin from her flat in East Berlin. There was still much free movement between the two halves of the city, and tens of thousands of East Berliners had jobs in West Berlin.]*

Fee, an attractive blue-eyed blonde, told me the revealing story of an elderly bourgeois couple who live in the same three-storey block of flats as herself. The couple had told her that they had almost hated Adolf and her as Communist 'bosses' when they moved in some years ago. But when Adolf had once apologized to the wife for being, as he said, too bitter in a political discussion, they had come to like him. They felt that a man who apologized when, from a power point of view, he had no need to, was genuine in his beliefs. Later they became friendly with Adolf and Fee, but made it clear they could not accept Communist views themselves.

Fee said that after losing Adolf she had no one, except for a couple now in an East German trade mission in Vietnam, with whom she could talk absolutely freely. She said it was not that she was in fear of being locked up if she spoke freely, but other people might misunderstand her critical attitude on some matters of detail in the political sphere. Although Fee is not a member of the SED, she is basically in favour of the regime, but says she is not as naïve as some party members, who lap up everything.

[It was not until after the unification of Germany in 1990 that I learned from my file in the former headquarters of the East German State Security Service, the Stasi, that Fee – who by then was dead – had been one of the informers who had reported to the Stasi about Elfi and me. I do not hold it against her; she evidently thought it was her duty and it seems she did not tell any lies.]

24 November 1958 : I keep quizzing the press section of the Soviet embassy in East Berlin about the expected Soviet Note on the Berlin question. Find I can chatter away quite nicely in Russian now, once I get going. And if I get stuck I just shove in a German word.

The friendly *Daily Mail* man, Robin Smyth, gave me a copy of the text of an interview he had secured with East Germany's top leader, SED chief Walter Ulbricht, to be published in tomorrow's *Daily Mail*. In it Ulbricht put the Berlin situation like this: 'If I want to go to London I need permission from the British government. And if the gentlemen want to go to Berlin they need permission from us.' (Meaning, of course, that this will be the East German attitude when Khrushchev hands over powers to the East Germans, or purports to do so.)

Earlier today I had popped in to see Ernst Hansch, editor of the Communist tabloid evening paper, *BZ am Abend*, in his East Berlin office. We had a good chat, he making it clear that in the long run the Communists were after the whole of Berlin, but saying there was no question of war. He seems to think the allies will not try to force their way down the autobahn, if the Russians hand over their powers to the East Germans and the allies refuse to recognize that. Told Hansch that, although I'm almost a pacifist, I feel strongly about defending West Berlin's status, though not, of course, with atom bombs.

[Hansch, born in Hamburg in 1914, was a printer by trade who became a Communist in his youth. In 1934 he fled from Nazi Germany to the Netherlands, where he was active in the anti-Nazi resistance. In 1940 after German forces had occupied the Netherlands, he was arrested, interrogated and apparently tortured by the Gestapo. In 1942 he was sentenced to six years' hard labour but, after serving only a small part of his sentence, he was put into the notorious army Punishment Battalion 999.

While serving in Greece, he crossed over to join Greek Communist partisans. After the war he became an agricultural journalist in East Germany, and was appointed editor of BZ am Abend *in 1953. In time I came to regard Hansch as a friend. He had suffered for his convictions and was also ready to concede some of the weaknesses of the regime in discussion. His time in the Netherlands, where he married a Dutch woman, had evidently taught him some of the strengths of Western democracies. It was revealed, after the collapse of the Communist regime, that Hansch had been used as a contact man between the East German leadership and the onetime Communist, Herbert Wehner, a highly influential (and controversial) West German Social Democrat, who led the party's* Bundestag *group from 1969 to 1983, when the SPD was the main ruling party.]*

26 November 1958 : East German radio announced that the Soviet Foreign Minister, Andrei Gromyko, had visited Berlin during the past few days and had talks with Ulbricht and the East German Prime Minister, Otto Grotewohl. The most the Soviet embassy would say was that Gromyko was no longer in Berlin. More interesting, though, was a statement by the US Secretary of State, John Foster Dulles, to the effect that the Western allies might recognize East Germans as 'agents' of the Soviet Union in respect of the Soviet Union's Berlin powers. This is just what Brentano appeared to hint at last week and just what caused the protest from the West German Foreign Office when we reported that. It opens a way for a compromise.

5 Soviet 'free city' proposals

27 November 1958 : The expected Soviet Note to East Germany
has been handed over and was published today by the East
German news agency, ADN. Moscow proposes that there should
be no change for six months and that during that period there
should be negotiations on transforming West Berlin into a demil-
itarized free city. Brandt reacted by calling the Soviet proposals
unacceptable and saying that there could not be negotiations on
Berlin alone, but there must be negotiations on German unity.

I think there's nothing wrong with the theoretical idea of a free
city, but that's not what the Communists really mean. They'll
swallow it up as soon as they get the chance. And if the allies go,
the chance will have come nearer. Brandt is right in arguing that
a solution is to be found only through negotiations on German
unity, but there seems no hope of such negotiations at present,
with neither side ready to compromise.

28 November 1958 : Reaction to the Soviet Note: Elfi's 60-ish
West Berlin aunt, Trudchen Gutzeit (with a twinkle in her eye, as
ever), 'You won't let the Communists come until we're dead, will
you?' Then, more seriously, 'We shall stay, whatever happens.'

A woman visiting from East Germany, 'The Communists are
jubilant. They think they have Berlin in their grasp.'

At two press conferences – US Senator Bourke Hickenlooper
gave one, four US Congressmen gave the other – US determination not to yield over Berlin was underlined. At a third press conference Brandt said the West should make counter-proposals.

Many people think young Brandt would make a good West German chancellor. *[That came about in 1969.]*

29 November 1958 : Bought Russian records and books cheaply at a Russian shop in East Berlin. The East mark prices for such items are similar to West mark prices or rather less. But West Berlin *bureaux de change* give about four East marks for one West mark. However, foreigners without visas cannot make general purchases with East marks, except for things like books and records.

I keep thinking I'd like to leave journalism and go home to work full-time for the Labour Party, of which I've been a member for about ten years. I'd like to do something to improve the world instead of just writing about what the world is like. *[The old joke ran: 'Why don't you leave Reuters and go into journalism?' That was evidently a sarcastic reference to the pressures and grind of news agency work compared to that of a newspaper correspondent.]*

This evening I saw American hotel magnate Conrad Hilton and about 60 invited celebrities arrive on the first-ever direct New York–Berlin flight, a charter affair, for tomorrow's opening of a Hilton hotel in West Berlin. This is regarded as a symbol of American faith in Berlin. When the Hollywood actor, Leo Carillo, one of my boyhood favourites, got off the plane wearing a cowboy outfit, he threw up his hands, grinned and shouted, *'Deutschland über alles.'* Those who heard it laughed. That's a bit out of date.

In East Berlin, called on Fee Sauheitl, who gave me a pair of her late husband Adolf's gloves as a memento of him. So now I wear a Communist's gloves and a coat which belonged to my deceased German father-in-law, who was very right-wing. I drove Fee to a nearby part of West Berlin so I could buy us a hot sausage and some apple juice each; as a Westerner one cannot buy food and most other things in East Berlin without a visa. Back in East Berlin, we saw a Czech colour film based on Jaroslav Hasek's famous book, *The Good Soldier Schweik.* I told Fee I thought there were probably people in the audience who felt the same about their government as Schweik did in the First World War – namely, ironic contempt, well masked.

30 November 1958 : In a radio address, Willy Brandt said that to make West Berlin into a 'free city', as Moscow has proposed, would mean turning it into a temporary concentration camp surrounded by East Germany, which would later swallow it up. I tend to agree.

A West Berlin journalist, Steinberg, working for Associated Press told me he felt, as a Berliner, that if the Western allies backed down over Berlin, they would be lost everywhere. The Middle Eastern countries would, he thought, all go over to communism if they saw that the West was weak.

Later today Drechsler, editor of the independent right-wing West Berlin paper, *Der Abend*, told me privately that he thought that the policy of Adenauer and the Western allies in rearming West Germany had come to a dead end so far as hopes for German unification were concerned. He agreed with me that what's needed now is some grand compromise.

1 December 1958 : Wading through newspapers, mainly Communist, this morning – one drawback to the Berlin job. East German newspapers are among the dullest in the world, stamped with totalitarianism and not even very dynamic totalitarianism at that. The abuse they use is enough to damn them for me, even if some of it is half-true.

Our 25-ish colleague, slim Lorelies Oehlschläger, who reminds me of a pretty squirrel, gave a party for several journalists in her new flat, which is more like a corridor. We were served grapefruit juice with vodka. Ah, modern youth! Later we were turned out of an East Berlin dance hall because Lorelies was wearing trousers.

3 December 1958 : Attended a meeting of the East German mock parliament, the *Volkskammer*, in which the voting is, I believe, always unanimous. And the parties which are not Communist – that is, the automatic minority – do what the Communists tell them, and grin while doing so. A former Social Democrat, 79-year-old Otto Buchwitz, who opened the session, repeated the prevailing East German propaganda theme by saying there was no need for any opposition there because, after all, no one wanted to go back to capitalism.

Tonight I took out to dinner Martin Thijs, the Belgian Communist journalist, and his Social Democratic wife. Thijs surprisingly agreed with my view that there was no reason why a religious person should not be able to support communism and no reason why the Communists should damn religion outright. *[Today I consider there are strong reasons why a religious person should not support communism, above all communism's suppression of human rights.]*

4 December 1958 : Differences between the British Conservative government and the Labour opposition on how to react to the Soviet threats to West Berlin emerged at a luncheon I attended today, given by the West Berlin city government for a visiting delegation of British MPs. In the absence of the Conservative leader of the delegation, its deputy leader, Labour's Ernest Davies, a former Foreign Under-Secretary, suggested that there should be discussion on military disengagement, as a way to counter the Soviet proposals on Berlin and work towards German unity. Several Conservative MPs told reporters afterwards that they did not agree with the speech and were going to notify West Berlin leaders of their dissent.

I listened to Adenauer making a speech in the working-class suburb of Wedding this evening, and found it awful. He sticks absolutely to his outworn policy of strength, instead of showing some readiness to negotiate on the German problem.

5 December 1958 : Watched Adenauer walk around the Borsig engineering works in West Berlin, before making a speech to several thousand workers, as part of the West Berlin election campaign. As Adenauer walked by, most of the workers took off their caps or protective helmets and smiled. There were hardly any Communists among them. One man told me he would rather kill eight Russians with his bare hands than come under Communist domination. The men I spoke to seemed reasonably satisfied with their standard of living – about 500 marks (about £43) a month for an unskilled crane-driver. Adenauer promised that West Germany would do all possible in face of the crisis to support West Berlin's economy.

Tonight Adenauer made his major West Berlin election speech to about 12,000 people in the vast Deutschlandhalle. Although expressing himself somewhat better than in his disjointed speech yesterday, he again made it clear that he wanted no negotiations on a German peace treaty or on reunification, but only on Berlin, on the ground that this question must be cleared up before proceeding to others.

It looks as though Adenauer always finds some reason not to negotiate on reunification while continuing to rearm; not because he wants to attack anybody, but because he wants to make West Germany more of a force in Western councils.

6 December 1958 : At an eve-of-poll press conference, Brandt appealed for an anti-Communist vote to show what West Berlin thought about the Soviet proposals for the city. *[In West Germany, the Communist Party (KPD) was banned by the Federal Constitutional Court in 1956 as subversive, but in West Berlin, the three Western allies, who exercise supreme power, allowed the Communists, in the shape of the West Berlin section of the East German Socialist Unity Party (SED), to be politically active. This was part of the Western allies' policy of maintaining, as far as possible, the principles of the four-power administration of Berlin, which provided for both non-Communist and Communist parties.]*

At a West Berlin reception camp for East German refugees, I spoke to an elderly man, who said his reason for leaving East Germany was because he wanted to go to live with relatives in the Ruhr. Why shouldn't he do so? How stupid and inhuman the Communists are, not letting people move where they want.

Our friend Fritz Söhner, a horticultural expert born in East Germany, who works in the West German Agriculture Ministry in Bonn, brought his old mother into our office to meet me. As Fritz is not allowed to visit East Germany, because he left without

45

permission, and his mother, who lives near Leipzig, is forbidden by the East German regime to visit him in Bonn, West Berlin is the only place they can meet. It is a sad comment on the state of divided Germany that I, as a Western correspondent issued with a pass, was – unlike Fritz – able to visit Fritz's mother in her home a few months ago.

7 December 1958 : In a small polling station in the pleasant southwestern suburb of Schlachtensee, crowded with photographers and reporters, I watched Mayor Brandt and his Norwegian wife, Rut, cast their votes in the West Berlin election. In the polling station I came across the doctor neighbour of Brandt's to whom I had given a lift last month. Over coffee in their nearby house, the doctor, a Catholic I think, surprised me by saying he had had some sleepless nights searching for a convincing answer to a question I had asked, 'Why do you believe in God?'

We went on to discuss birth control, which his originally Protestant wife appeared to favour, rather than producing families which could not be looked after properly. However, her husband took the view that God would provide what was necessary. I left this pleasant couple to watch Ernst Lemmer, West German Minister for All-German Affairs, a Christian Democrat, Brandt's main opponent in the election, cast his vote in a school.

Later I drove to the Heidelbergerstrasse, a street of nineteenth-century flats. It is like many others in Berlin, except that one side of the street is in West Berlin and the other in the East. No barrier in the street, but Western and Eastern police posts in nearby streets. Three weeks ago, according to the official figures, East Berliners voted 99.77 per cent in favour of the Communist-dominated single list. Today the Western side of the street will vote almost as strongly against the Communists.

People in a pub on the Western side commented, for instance, 'Anyone who votes Communist is either a madman or a criminal.' Then I visited a man who, I was told, was about the only Communist living on the Western side: a middle-aged lathe operator. He claimed that this party had been hindered in various ways in West Berlin and, were it not hindered, would win 20 per cent of the votes, compared to the 2 per cent which is expected. However, he conceded that he could vote Communist without being marked as a black sheep, whereas in East Berlin there was pressure on voters to 'cast their votes openly', thus showing up as probable dissidents any who went into the booths to vote secretly.

8 December 1958 : A victory for the Social Democrats, who took nearly 53 per cent of the vote, to the Christian Democrats' 37 per cent. Other parties failed to win seats, as they did not reach the necessary minimum of 5 per cent of the total vote. The Communists – that is, the Socialist Unity Party or SED – received but 1.9 per cent. This result may put Brandt on the road to becoming Federal Chairman of the Social Democrats one day. At present, though, the main significance of the result is the strong rejection of Communist wishes on Berlin.

9 December 1958 : On my drive back to Bonn, overnighted in Vlotho, Westphalia, as the guest of a friend, medical doctor Heinz Werner. He told me about moves to simplify West Germany's class-ridden and highly bureaucratic health service, with its many health insurance societies, each offering a different level of benefits. He appeared to favour some aspects of our National Health Service in Britain, which has only two classes – those who use only the National Health Service and a few per cent who pay additionally for private treatment.

10 December 1958 : Back home. Chris, radiant, said again and again, 'Daddy, I do like you. It was nice of you to come back from Berlin.' [*At times our sons were upset because I frequently went away on assignments. Later we often recalled Chris saying, 'Daddy, please don't go to München (Munich)' – one of the places furthest away from Bonn.*]

12 December 1958 : Willy Brandt, who had talks with Adenauer in Bonn today, told me tonight that, while maintaining his view that the Berlin question should be used to negotiate on Germany as a whole, he had agreed with the Chancellor that the first step was to say a clear 'No' to the Soviet proposals on Berlin, because they are based on the Soviet Union's unilateral denunciation of Berlin's four-power status. When I put some other question on policy, he said, 'I'm only a little *Bürgermeister*.' To which I added, 'Of a big city'. This pleased him and he grinned. Brandt is more than a little *Bürgermeister* and he knows it.

15 December 1958 : Am preparing an article on air raid precautions. The wheel has turned full circle. In 1945 and for years afterwards, the allies had air raid shelters blown up in Germany. Now it is illegal to convert an air raid shelter into anything which could no longer be used as a shelter. And soon all new buildings in places with over 10,000 inhabitants will have to have air raid shelters built in. I think it would be better if Adenauer were more flexible!

20 December 1958 : At Ostend, on our way to England on holiday, our car (without us) was hoisted in a sling onto the deck of a packet-boat. Chris was concerned for his two teddy bears, but we told him they probably enjoyed it. At Dover it took about 90 minutes to unload the boat, as it was carrying far more cars than usual – about 20 instead of the normal four. We had to stand shivering on the dockside, as the cars were unloaded one by one.

New Year's Day 1959 : Today's the day for resolutions. I intend this year to make efforts to get a job more devoted to improving the world than that of an agency journalist. (Not forgetting, however, that Reuters does help to improve the world somewhat by giving balanced accounts of what all sides are saying and doing.) At the same time I intend to learn more Russian and to get to know more about Russians. *[Reuters gave me a temporary assignment to Moscow in 1961, and from 1962 to 1964 I was the agency's chief correspondent in the Soviet Union.]*

3 January 1959 : I sent a report last night about a local German radio technician, Peter Lengrüsser, who had picked up signals from a Soviet moon rocket launched yesterday. The rocket is due to pass by the moon tomorrow and become a new planet of the sun. Lengrüsser played for me on his tape-recorder some of the 'beep-beeps' he had picked up. It now looks as though we shall see men on the moon within a few years. *[That happened on 20 July 1969, but it was Americans, not Russians, who took the first steps on the moon's surface.]*

6 The 'only hope' for Germany?

5 January 1959 : Attended the Chancellery to see many well-wishers arriving to congratulate Adenauer on his 83rd birthday. I have reported these birthday celebrations in several previous years. Today, it seemed, Adenauer had not quite as much bounce as he used to have, though this might be because he has had two colds in the past month. The affair lasted about four hours, shorter than usual, and journalists were excluded after two. The reason apparently was that Adenauer was annoyed because some intimate political talks he had last year during the same event were overheard – and printed – by journalists. Noticeable among the congratulatory short speeches by government ministers and others was their adulatory tone, depicting the Chancellor as being the only man who could have done what he had done and the only hope for Germany's future. In my view he is neither.

Our chief correspondent, Gerry Long, told me off for using quotation marks around phrases instead of whole sentences. (He meant, for instance, that we shouldn't write that a politician said the economic situation was 'improving month by month', but should leave out the quotation marks.) I consider that quotation marks lend more sparkle to even a few words said by someone, but Gerry won't have this. *[Although I found Long at times unnecessarily abrasive, we hit it off quite well, perhaps because we were both Yorkshiremen. An outstanding manager rather than a gifted journalist, Long was chief executive of Reuters from 1963 to 1981. Under his direction Reuters was modernized and its profits were greatly increased. Long died on 8 November 1998.]*

8 January 1959 : Finished a feature about the hazards of driving on Germany's autobahns. This was directed mainly at British readers, in view of the completion of the first stretch of British motorway recently in west Lancashire.

9 January 1959 : In Wiesbaden, capital of the state of Hesse, for a conference of European federalists, including several British MPs, among them a former Prime Minister, Lord Attlee. The conference ended with proposals for the coordination of the foreign policy of the Common Market countries and a call for the election of a European Parliament, which would be a watchdog over the supra-national organizations already established. I believe that one day, Britain will be brought into the movement towards European political unity by the force of circumstances, just as Rhode Island, which originally stood aloof, later joined the United States.

12 January 1959 : My second time ever on skis, near the Rhineside town of Bacharach, on a fairly gentle slope. I fell about four times and appear to have sprained a thumb.

13 January 1959 : Gathered some saddening inside information about conditions in East Germany from two refugees, Herr Panser and Herr Gerhardt, who recently arrived in Bonn. Panser told me that he and a colleague founded a private radio factory in Halle, Saxony-Anhalt, in about 1946. It remained a private concern until early 1953, when he and his partner were warned they were about to be arrested – in those days a frequent method for preparing the nationalization of a firm under some pretext. Both families fled to West Germany by way of West Berlin. After the abortive anti-Communist revolt in East Germany on 17 June 1953, the SED changed its tactics, put a brake on nationalization and promised their property back to those who returned. Panser went back. At that time Gerhardt was the firm's technical director.

For over a year the firm flourished, expanding from about 100 to 450 employees and becoming the largest private radio concern in East Germany. The state bank had a nominee director, an ethnic German from Romania who had been close to the Russians. In 1957 he denounced Panser and Gerhardt to the authorities because they had illegally bought some measuring gear from West Germany to keep pace with technical developments – they had previously been refused permission to buy the gear. The two men were each sentenced to about 22 months' imprisonment. After their release in the summer of 1958, they fled to the West with their families. Their firm had been taken over by a state-owned radio factory in Halle. The Communists could claim they had scored another 'victory'.

14 January 1959 : Called at the Bonn office of the Soviet news agency, TASS, for a discussion with the chief correspondent, Panshin, a smoothie whom, however, I quite like. I suggested that a possible basis for the reunification of Germany would be the neutralization of Germany, recognition of present eastern frontier of East Germany as final, reunification through free all-German elections and big German deliveries of reparations to the Soviet Union – like Austria's oil deliveries to the Soviet Union which, along with Austria's neutrality, were part of the price paid for the withdrawal of Soviet troops from Austria in 1955.

Panshin came out with the old argument that East Germany is a sovereign state. I sought to disprove that by saying that it would not last long if Soviet troops left. He neatly checked that one, by saying the Soviets had offered to go, but Adenauer would not agree to a withdrawal of both NATO and Warsaw Pact forces, which is true. *[Several of my suggestions became reality when Germany was reunified in 1990 – but it was not neutralized.]*

Called on Panshin's deputy, Boris Yurinov, at his flat. His pretty wife, Inna, refused to emerge from their kitchen as, Yurinov confessed later, she had curlers on. How bourgeois!

16 January 1959 : Interviewed Bernhard Lepkes, a 45-ish ex-policeman who sells all kinds of consumer durables at 25 per cent below list price. He has had a hard fight since he started doing this (legal) trade in 1953. Fellow shopkeepers tried to do him down, so they could hold on to their large profit margins – often about 100 per cent gross profit or 12 per cent net, compared with the 3 or 4 per cent net that Lepkes is satisfied with.

Lepkes told me that thanks to 'influence' and snobbery, ministry officials and others high on the social scale can get 30 per cent (illegal) discounts on goods in normal shops, while a journalist can usually get 20 per cent and an ordinary citizen nothing. Lepkes said he sold at the same price to everyone, which is legal. He paid his employees at least the union rate. Other local traders tried to combat him by dropping their prices for a short period to less than his, but he refused to follow suit. They soon gave up.

18 January 1959 : Read a long article in the news magazine, *Der Spiegel*, on the latest researches into the historical Jesus. Many experts, it stated, claimed that quite a lot of Jesus' supposed statements are apocryphal. However, whether Jesus really said what he is supposed to have said, or whether he existed at all, is perhaps secondary to the inestimable benefit that his teachings have brought to humanity.

An example of how literal religious people can be was a story Reuters carried today from Israel about a conference of Jews held to decide how the Sabbath was to be observed on the moon, where each day lasts as long as several earthly days. I think they decided to act according to world time and give a dispensation to anyone living on the moon to cut out a prayer or ceremony connected with the rising of the new moon!

23 January 1959 : Chris, who is nearly six, is now quite useful in helping to wash the car. I gave him the wheels to do today and he was reasonably thorough, as befits his part East Prussian ancestry.

Elfi and I tonight saw *Die Wunderkinder*, one of the best German films I've seen, a biting cavalcade tracing the lives of some average Germans from 1913 to the present day. The line that produced the biggest laughs was a scene in which a Nazi tells a lavatory attendant on New Year's Eve 1932 – a few weeks before

Hitler took power – that things will soon get better. The attendant replies in Bavarian dialect, 'People will always pee.'

24 January 1959 : Interviewed white-haired rosy-cheeked Princess Oskar, the 70-year-old daughter-in-law of Kaiser Wilhelm II. Her real name is Cecilie, but Prussian princes' wives are described by the first name of their husbands when they are widowed. Her husband, the last survivor of the Kaiser's six sons, died last year. I interviewed Princess Oskar in connection with a family reunion to be held on 27 January in Berlin, marking the 100th anniversary of the Kaiser's birthday.

She lives in a seven-room house in Bonn full of royal mementoes: jars with Kaiser Wilhelm's portrait on them, toy soldiers in Prussian uniforms, furniture like that seen in palaces. The princess is friendly and not at all snobbish in manner. When I asked her housekeeper if the princess would receive me, I referred to her as 'Her Highness', but when I spoke to her, I just addressed her as '*Sie*' (you). Officially royal and noble titles were abolished in Germany in 1918, but many royals and members of former noble families continued to use their titles, which were then regarded as part of their names.

Quite a number of members of Germany's former ruling family, the house of Hohenzollern, live abroad now, married to commoners. In general they are comfortably off, with jobs in business or farming, but not rich any more. Most of the Hohenzollern estates were in pre-war East Germany. Princess Oskar told me that after she and her husband fled from Potsdam Palace, near Berlin, in 1945, they lived for seven years in a two-room attic flat. I thought it was nice of the old lady to ask to look at Elfi's photograph, which she had spotted as I opened my wallet to take out a pencil. So it was one Prussian looking at another.

25 January 1959 : As well as reading the main book of the Christian Science religion, *Science and Health*, by the religion's American founder, Mary Baker Eddy (1821–1910), I am also reading a book attacking Christian Science, *Our New Religion* by

H.A.L. Fisher, published in 1933. I find the critical standpoint of this book reasonable.

[A central tenet of Christian Science is that as human beings, according to the Bible, were created in the image of God, they could not be subject to illness; thus illness could not be real and the 'wrong belief' of illness could be countered by spiritual means. My mother was a convinced Christian Scientist, but unlike fanatical followers of Mrs Eddy, she used conventional medicine when she thought that made sense. Later in life, although brought up in Christian Science, I rejected its central belief as nonsensical and indeed dangerous, as a number of Christian Scientists had died from simple illnesses after refusing medical treatment.]

27 January 1959 : Dr Martin Niemöller, 67, one of Germany's best-known Lutheran church leaders, was attacked by the West German Defence Ministry spokesman for allegedly saying at a meeting that training soldiers in this nuclear age amounted to running a high school for professional criminals. Niemöller, a submarine commander in the First World War, was an opponent of Hitler and was imprisoned in concentration camps between 1938 and 1945.

On the phone I asked Niemöller about his reported remarks and he told me, a little testily, that he had been misreported. He stated that he had said that training troops as commandos amounted to training them as criminals. However four reporters who were at the meeting had put out almost the same version, to the effect that using nuclear weapons amounted to crime. I tend to agree with that.

29 January 1959 : Adenauer spoke at the tenth anniversary meeting of the West German Federation of Employers' Organizations, held in the modern Ufa-Palast cinema in Cologne. There was much talk about freedom for enterprise, but also some references to taking the worker's point of view into account. Without doubt the West German worker today has a much better place in the scheme of things than 30 years ago. Real wages, for instance, increased by 50 per cent between 1949, when the West German state was founded, and 1957.

2 February 1959 : It now looks as though Alfried Krupp will be able to hold on to his coal and steel empire, which (under duress) he promised the Western allies in 1953 he would dispose of by 31 January 1959. He is to be given a year's extension, after selling less than a quarter of his holdings and already arranging to buy some of them back again. The present Krupp appears a decent enough chap. But this is a case, I think, where the allies should have made sure that the same family did not hold on to so much economic power.

7 Soviets hinder US traffic

3 February 1959 : Big news. Four American army trucks, bound from West Berlin along the 110-mile East German autobahn to West Germany were halted yesterday at the Soviet checkpoint near West Germany. I started the story in the office with a short 'snapfull' – a priority marking for hot stories which causes our teleprinter operator to make bells ring all over our London head office. That 'snapfull' was sent back from London to European clients within a minute or two.

Several of us expanded this story, writing in background about the last incident of this type, last November, shortly after the Russians announced they intended to hand over their control of the Western allied access routes to Berlin to the East Germans. It emerged later today that the Soviets had demanded, contrary to established procedure, to inspect the insides of the four trucks, each of which was loaded with an old jeep. The Americans refused this and also refused to return to Berlin. They were surrounded by a number of Soviet and East German soldiers and police. The Americans protested to the Russians, both in Berlin and at the Western allied checkpoint in Helmstedt, at the western end of the East German autobahn. The protests brought no result.

As the Americans were still being held this afternoon, I was sent off to Helmstedt, nearly 300 miles to the east, by car. I arrived there around midnight. On the way I practised Russian by reading Russian poems, line-by-line, from cards fixed onto my dashboard.

4 February 1959 : The Western and Communist checkpoints near Helmstedt are separated by about 200 yards of 'no-man's-road' where the East–West autobahn passes over what used to be united Germany's Reich Highway Number One, leading from Cologne to Berlin. At this point that onetime highway is a largely overgrown road, blocked by two lines of East German frontier wire, and a trench, also on the East German side, dug to stop vehicles trying to make an escape attempt. On the East German side, too, there are foxholes and watchtowers, and a ploughed strip to catch footmarks of would-be escapers. Hardly any come this way nowadays. Nearly all go via Berlin, which is of course one reason why the Russians want to seal off West Berlin.

On the Western side there is no barbed wire, but there are patrols and vantage points for frontier guards to spot possible East German infiltrators. It is, however, no offence under West German law for any German to cross over to the West from East Germany. In the reverse direction the step is punishable.

In the dark I walked along the 'no-man's-road' to the Communist checkpoint and asked an East German soldier, armed with a carbine, to let me speak to the officer in charge of the Soviet checkpoint where, in the waiting-room of a wooden building, there are coloured prints of not only the expected Lenin, but also of Stalin, in spite of the partial 'destalinization' undertaken by Khrushchev since 1956. The East German soldier just said a word and a khaki-uniformed fur-hatted Soviet soldier, pistol in holster, jumped out of a shadowy sentry box. I told him – much fun to use my Russian – what I wanted and he said, '*Pozhaluista*' (please) and escorted me to the Soviet hut some 20 yards further into East Germany.

As I stood in the dimly lit waiting-room, a Soviet captain emerged from a back room. He looked slightly Mongoloid and not too welcoming. We talked for a few minutes in Russian. I found I could understand him quite well, though I had to ask him to speak slowly and to repeat one or two sentences. He confirmed that the Americans were sleeping in their trucks, parked a few yards from the hut. He would say no more.

After returning to the Western side of the border and phoning a few paragraphs to Bonn, I ensconced myself for a night watch in the Western allied checkpoint – the last building in West Germany. Here I sat on a rackety chair, alternately dozing, chatting to a British and an American soldier who were manning the checkpoint, and keeping an eye on the American trucks, parts of which I could see beyond the Soviet checkpoint hut. For a while the soldiers were listening to music and propaganda from an East German radio station, which was making a big thing out of a planned ten-minute protest in Dortmund tomorrow against the intended stationing there of a British unit equipped with 'Corporal' tactical nuclear missiles. Other journalists from rival agencies were keeping watch from their cars.

Around 08.00 Bill Long, chief of the United Press Bonn bureau, and I walked over to the Eastern side again to talk to that same Soviet officer. In the daylight he was friendlier, gave us one or two useful quotes and let us watch as an American military police captain arrived with breakfast for the American truck drivers – hot coffee and sandwiches. Then we saw an empty American truck, bound for Berlin, enter the checkpoint from the West. It was the first American military vehicle to try to pass through East Germany since Monday's hold-up. The Soviet soldiers just looked into the open back of the empty truck and passed it through within about ten minutes after checking its papers in their hut. The Soviet officer turned to me, grinned and said, 'That's how it's done.'

I chatted with the Soviet soldiers about the cold (about -2° C) and made one or two of them laugh by telling them the cold was all right for them, because they were Russians, but not for me because I am English. All were polite and quite friendly.

Later this morning the Soviet captain came across to our side and had a five-minute private talk with the American military police captain. An hour or two later I visited the Soviet officer in his hut. He told me he had asked the Americans to speed matters up. He then allowed me to speak to the American truck drivers. They had been thoroughly brainwashed by their military police captain and said very little. However, even the little they said was worthwhile, for no other journalist, I believe, had been able to talk to them today.

This afternoon negotiations took place in the Soviet hut between a Soviet colonel and Mr Finlay Burns, cherubic bespectacled deputy political adviser to the American Commandant in Berlin. Around 18.00 Burns came into Helmstedt after the talks and said he thought the trucks would come westwards in a few minutes. This they did, illuminated in the dark by photographers' flash bulbs. Burns would tell us only that the Americans had not submitted to the Soviet demand to inspect the trucks. After clearing up loose ends on the story, I managed to get to bed about 22.00, for the first time in 48 hours, but was woken twice in the night to be told the Americans, blast them, were to give a press conference at 04.30.

5 February 1959 : It was announced in London yesterday that Britain had protested on Monday because a Soviet soldier at the Helmstedt checkpoint had got into the back of a British truck to inspect it. That had happened at around the time that the American trucks arrived from Berlin. Two of the Americans said they thought the Helmstedt incident involving them had been planned at a high level. They said no force had been used on either side and the Americans had been allowed to use a Russian latrine. (An increase in cultural contacts?)

After a few more hours' sleep, called on a British military intelligence officer based in Helmstedt, who told me that the American military had brought up a mobile radio unit from their zone and had been in constant touch with their European headquarters in Heidelberg. They had been looking for a suitable landing-strip for helicopters and scout planes, so that if the Russians had moved the American trucks inside East Germany, they could have seen where they were.

This British intelligence officer also told me that the Americans had not consulted the British, in whose zone Helmstedt lies, and that the British authorities were critical of the

American attitude towards the Soviets. He said that if it had been a British truck convoy there would have been a protest, but the convoy would have been taken back to Berlin. He added that the British, instead of just saying 'No' to the Soviets, would have talked to them to try to find out whether they were just being bad-tempered, or whether there had been higher orders.

In his view the incident had been ordered by Moscow as a demonstration during the European visit of the United States Secretary of State, John Foster Dulles, to coordinate the Western answer on the Soviet Berlin moves. The incident, he thought, had been intended to demonstrate what the Soviets, or the East Germans, were in a position to do to Western allied communications. I'm not sure that I agree with this assessment, as the West already knew well enough what the Communists could do.

I was pleased on this assignment to have been able to use my Russian successfully. A final conversation with another Soviet officer, a handsome dark-skinned character, went like this:

Me: 'Where were you born?'

He: 'In Russia.'

Me (grinning): 'I know, but whereabouts?'

He: 'In the Urals.'

Me (grinning): 'What town? Is it secret?'

He: 'No, it's not secret – Sverdlovsk.'

Me: 'Oh yes, I have seen it.'

He (excitedly): 'You've seen it?'

Me: 'On a map I mean.'

He: 'Oh.'

6 February 1959 : Tonight Elfi and I attended in Bonn our first 'carnival session' – about four hours of entertainment, followed by dancing, which started around midnight. The carnival season is moving towards its climax: it ends on 10 February, Shrove Tuesday. Tonight's event was put on by one of Bonn's several carnival societies, the *Sternschnuppen* (Shooting Stars), founded in the 1890s, when many people had believed the world was about to end, because they had seen a prominent comet or shooting star.

They have smart light-blue uniforms, reminiscent of operetta soldiers or hall porters. The girls' uniforms end in short frilled skirts.

The eleven elders of the society sat enthroned at the back of the podium, while the entertainers, some paid and some amateur, performed in front of a microphone or were ensconced in a *Bütt*, or symbolic wine-barrel. Each turn was marched in from the back of the hall to catchy tunes from the band. The artists we saw included comic speakers, comic singers and singers of carnival hits – some new ones come out each year. They are usually in waltz time, encouraging the audience – merry with alcohol – to link arms and sway from side to side, or *schunkeln*.

Each artist was presented with the society's medal and also with a small bottle of schnapps (spirit) which, we were told repeatedly until we were sick of it, was presented by a local firm whose *Herr Direktor* was present. The jokes included political satire – much of it directed against Defence Minister Franz-Josef Strauss and recent corruption cases in Bonn.

7 February 1959 : US Secretary of State Dulles, pale-faced but cheerful, arrived for talks with Adenauer after visiting London and Paris. Things are moving towards a conference of the 'Big Four' *[the United States, the Soviet Union, Britain and France]*. However, few here think Adenauer and Dulles will do any real negotiating on a central European settlement. Probably what will happen is that there will be some kind of makeshift arrangement on Berlin, which may hold until the Democrats get into power in the United States and Dulles quits, and until Adenauer dies and, maybe, a younger man with some new ideas about negotiating with the Russians takes over in Bonn.

I don't think the Russians will give German reunification for less than: a nuclear-free zone in central Europe, the neutralization of Germany, renunciation by Bonn of former German territories east of the Oder–Neisse line – including Elfi's home state, former East Prussia – plus reparations. But Adenauer is obviously not willing to meet these conditions. Instead, the *Bundeswehr* grows and will soon have nuclear capability.

As I waited at the Chancellery with several colleagues, while Dulles had talks with Adenauer, an American Associated Press man, Schwab, who has just spent two years in Washington, provided this joke about what the last three US Presidents had proved:

1 Roosevelt – that the United States can be governed by a strong man, namely Stalin;
2 Truman – that any average American can be President;
3 Eisenhower – that the US can get along without a president.

8 February 1959 : Dulles left today. Agreement has been reached on holding a Foreign Ministers' Conference of the Western Big Three and West Germany, sometime in mid-March, which is expected to be followed by a Big Four Foreign Ministers' Conference before the end of May, by when the Soviets have said they will hand over their Berlin control powers to the East Germans.

We are supposed to get three days off per fortnight, one day less than many journalists in Britain, and we do not always get our entitlement. I do not see why we should be exploited just because Reuters shareholders, the newspapers, won't pay enough money for the agency to have sufficient staff, while they themselves are doing very nicely.

Elfi took the boys – Robin as a Red Indian and Chris as a pussycat – to watch Bad Godesberg's carnival procession. They returned with several handfuls of sweets each, which had been thrown into the crowd from the floats.

9 February 1959 : In the office it was like the last day at school, for today, Rose Monday, was the highpoint of the Rhineland carnival. The big carnival procession in Cologne included a papier-mâché Adenauer, aged 83, embracing Cologne's female symbol, Colonia, aged about 2,000, and saying, 'Oh to be 20 again.'

With a certain amount of alcohol circulating in the office, I danced a few steps with our veteran German teleprinter 'girl', Barbara, 35-ish. Later, at a fancy-dress carnival ball in the Press

Club, had an argument with a man who had rudely grabbed four of eight seats which Elfi was keeping for our party. He turned out to be a former mayor of Bonn, Busen. Translated, his name means 'bosom'. The name was used in a political slogan: 'Bonn must get rid of its bosom.' Which it did. In the end we compromised with Busen and, to show goodwill, I danced with a young woman, whom I thought was his daughter, but who turned out to be his former secretary; gave her a smacking carnival kiss.

As I danced with Mieke, the pretty petite Dutch wife of our news editor, John Bush, she complained that he never had a day off. I told her it was his own fault. She agreed, put her tongue out playfully behind John's back and said it was the first time they had been dancing since they were married, five years ago.

11 February 1959 : I called at the Soviet embassy, a cream-painted former hotel by the Rhine, to find out whether I could carry out a plan to drive to Vladivostok, from where I would like to go by sea to visit my father in California. The press attaché, Sergeyev, told me I could not drive to Vladivostok at present, as the roads were not good enough for tourists.

He added smilingly, 'We are building an autobahn from Moscow to Peking. By the time that's ready, perhaps the United States will have taken up diplomatic relations with People's China, so you will be able to drive to Shanghai and take a boat from there to Los Angeles.'

A tourism official of the embassy told me that the Soviet part – the north – of former East Prussia is likely to be opened up to Westerners later this year. *[In fact that did not happen until 1991.]*

Otto John, West Germany's former internal security chief, was yesterday refused permission to enter Britain to visit his wife, a naturalized British subject, so he returned to Germany by train today. *[John crossed over into Communist East Berlin in July 1954. On 12 December 1955, with the aid of a Danish journalist, Henrik Bonde-Henricksen, he slipped his security guard in East Berlin and returned to West Berlin. On 23 December 1956, after a six-week trial, John was sentenced to four years' imprisonment for treason, which he denied. He alleged he had been drugged and abducted to East Berlin. John was paroled in July 1958 by the Federal President, Dr Theodor Heuss.]* I think it was despicable of the British authorities to refuse entry to John, who took part in the July 1944 plot against Hitler. Because he was a Lufthansa official he was able to escape to Western Europe. His appointment as West Germany's internal security chief was said to have been due partly to the influence of the British occupation authorities.

I am basically unsatisfied with most of the work we have to do in Bonn. We cover so many trivialities, and usually have too little time to do a proper job on the more important stuff. This is partly due to Reuters being an agency, but it is also partly due to Germany being a near-neighbour of Britain. In places further away, such as Warsaw or Belgrade, there are fewer trivial stories which are of interest to the outside world and, therefore, more time to concentrate on the important stuff. Having said that does not mean I do not realize I have an excellent job.

15 February 1959 : Our impressive Lutheran pastor, Gerhard Sass, in his Sunday sermon today, defined faith as 'being in touch with God'. That is something that this doubting Thomas finds difficult, as it hard to know whether one is in touch or what one is in touch with.

Elfi and I saw a colour documentary film about the Soviet Union, the human side of which almost brought tears to my eyes. I think the Soviet and United States governments ought to spend half their time visiting each other's countries, instead of thinking about how to outwit each other.

16 February 1959 : Religion came up again tonight, when we spent the evening at the flat of Soviet TASS correspondent, Boris Yurinov and his wife, Inna, a former television presenter. Elfi and I agreed we could not prove there was a God and they agreed they could not prove there wasn't, though Yurinov said – apparently with more conviction than his wife – that they were approaching that stage. I made it clear to Yurinov that even leftish people like myself, who often disagree with their own governments, were firm in believing that the Western allies should maintain their position in Berlin.

We drank smooth Armenian cognac and ate Baltic sprats, and crab from Vladivostok, the town I cannot drive to. I challenged Yurinov's wife, Inna, to dance a Russian polka and found that I couldn't do it. So we tried a waltz instead and she surprised me by showing me some Russian deviations in this dance, rather like doing rock-and-roll slowly and gracefully.

17 February 1959 : It was announced at a government press conference that Adenauer had told a private Christian Democratic Party meeting yesterday that he believed there would be a four-power East–West conference early in May, and that the West's prime task would be to have the Berlin ultimatum removed. He also expressed concern about some sections of British public opinion, which favour disengagement in central Europe, and he indicated he had some doubts as to whether Britain would remain what he called 'firm' in face of the Soviet Union.

19 February 1959 : Tubby Martin Thijs, the Belgian Communist journalist stationed in East Berlin, whom I got to know recently, called on me today. I like Thijs, a Fleming, because he is not as dogmatic as some Communists. He indicated that he is not enamoured of the East German Socialist Unity Party, which, in my view, is merely a Soviet puppet and is not even representative of East German Communists, never mind the rest of the country. A relatively liberal Gomulka-type Communist Party in East Germany would be a great step forward, but Moscow apparently fears it would be the beginning of the end for Communists in East Germany. Maybe Moscow is right.

29 February 1959 : Attended the foundation meeting of *Rette die Freiheit* (Save Freedom), an officially non-party organization headed by a Christian Democratic *Bundestag* member, Rainer Barzel. It is designed to fight communism on the ideological plane. The two main opposition parties, the Social Democrats and the Free Democrats, have refused to support this organization, arguing that it is intended mainly to back up Adenauer's policies.

In one speech a Social Democratic journalist, Otto Stolz, taking part as an individual, made a scarcely veiled call for governmental action against pacifist and similar organizations, even if they were not Communist-led. He claimed that such organizations were objectively weakening the West. This is getting dangerously near to saying that any organization which opposes Adenauer's policies is subversive and must be banned. I've nothing against fighting communism on the ideological plane, but think it spoils the whole thing if, at the back of your mind, you are primarily wanting to help your own political party, rather than strengthening the democratic state which is accepted by all West German parties apart from the Communist and neo-Nazi parties, which are banned.

Main speaker at the meeting was NATO Secretary-General Paul-Henri Spaak, a Churchillian-looking Belgian, who said one should not oppose communism for economic reasons – that people under communism are worse off – but because of the lack of respect for the human personality under communism. As regards the Berlin question, he said he thought the West would win, provided it stood firm without being provocative.

Pretty girls handed out to journalists little metal badges showing the Brandenburg Gate in Berlin, symbol of German unity. But the correspondent of the Soviet trade union newspaper *Trud*, Grigoriev, twice rebuffed one of the girls by refusing to take a badge. I told him afterwards he ought to have taken it for, after all, the Brandenburg Gate is in East Berlin. He said, if he had been offered it in East Berlin, it would have been all right!

22 February 1959 : Discussed the growing power of Khrushchev with Yurinov, my TASS correspondent friend. He said Khrushchev was not like Stalin, as people could say they did not like this or that about Khrushchev, whereas no one would have dared to do that in Stalin's day. Neither was Khrushchev, for Yurinov, on the same plane as Lenin; no one was, apparently.

26 February 1959 : Gathered some feature material at a hutted refugee camp in an industrial suburb of Bonn. Interviewed members of three East German families and found that their highest common factor was happiness at being able to go to bed without fearing the 2 am knock.

One of the refugees was a taxi-driver who, several years ago, had driven a refugee family from East Germany into West Berlin. He was arrested when the man he had taken to the West stupidly wrote to his East German relatives telling them how he had escaped. The taxi-driver got seven years and served three and a half of them before being released. A few days later he, his wife and daughter fled to West Berlin.

The wife agreed with me that, if the Communists allowed everyone to move freely from East to West, far fewer people would flee in the long run. People don't lightly go to live in refugee camps, leaving their belongings behind them, except the clothes they have on and a parcel or two. It takes two or three years on average for them to get a normal dwelling in the West.

8 My first look at Khrushchev

3 March 1959 : Drove the 400 miles from Bonn to West Berlin two days ago, and today drove on about 100 miles to Leipzig to attend East Germany's main trade fair, where Khrushchev is expected. The East German autobahn looks much like the West German autobahn, except that there is usually little traffic on it or, if there is, it is mainly composed of West German vehicles.

Stopped for lunch in an East German autobahn café, which compared quite well with many West German restaurants, even in price. Some items are more expensive, such as coffee. I had a nice steak for about eight shillings *[40p]*.

An East German lorry-driver asked me if I was allowed to travel where I wanted to on my way to the Leipzig Fair. I told him, 'No.' He had apparently suspected as much. He told me he could not live on his normal wage, had to work overtime to eke out. His wife worked too. But he also told me he could make complaints about working conditions and sometimes things would be improved. I couldn't resist writing on the inside of a lavatory door, in pencil in Russian, 'Workers of the world, unite!'

Leipzig, a town of about 600,000, was chock-full of visitors. The city looked somewhat ill-kept, though not poverty-stricken. A number of new buildings are going up. Flags everywhere, and posters calling for the conclusion of a German peace treaty. I'm quartered in a decent if dowdy hotel, the Bayrischer Hof.

My West Berlin colleague, Alfred Klühs, and I attended a reception given by a London agent, Ian Stach, who is running a joint stand at the fair for several British manufacturers of aircraft

69

components. They are hoping to do business with the East German state-owned aircraft industry, which, within Eastern-bloc coordination, is concentrating on making transport planes. It is developing its own four-jet passenger plane, the 152. We had an interesting talk with the East German aircraft industry's chief designer, Professor Brunolf Baade, 54, who worked in the United States for several years until 1936, and later designed Junkers bombers – more or less against his will, he implied. Now a Communist but not, I should imagine, one of the most dogmatic.

4 March 1959 : The day I first saw Nikita Sergeivich Khrushchev, Soviet Communist Party leader and Prime Minister. He spoke for about 15 minutes on a central square, the Wilhelm Leuschner Platz, which is supposed to hold about 200,000 people when full. Today it was not completely packed. It was a fairly drab sight, as the square is surrounded mainly by bombed sites. A few thousand colourful umbrellas, put up because of light drizzle, did something to brighten the scene.

Before Khrushchev arrived, in a cavalcade of about 15 limousines, 'delegations' from factories, offices and schools had marched to the square, carrying banners calling for a German peace treaty and pictures of Soviet and East German leaders, mainly Khrushchev and Walter Ulbricht, the onetime joiner who heads the East German Socialist Unity (Communist) Party.

I stood beneath a loudspeaker near the platform to take notes as Khrushchev, a small but fat figure, began to speak. As the speech was being broadcast on television and radio, it was up to our West Berlin office to transmit its interesting passages to Bonn, for relay to London; I was supposed to be responsible mainly for the descriptive. However, things can go wrong, so I decided to put something through to Bonn after the speech. This turned out to be worthwhile, because Berlin were not sure they had correctly heard the German translation of the most important paragraph in the speech: a definite statement by Khrushchev that the Soviet Union would sign a separate peace treaty with East Germany if the West refused to negotiate on an overall

German peace treaty. It turned out that I was ahead of Berlin into Bonn with this point, and beat Associated Press too, with United Press even further behind.

From where I stood, I could occasionally see Khrushchev's bald head, with its curious semi-pointed little dome at the back which sometimes makes him look like a Martian and at other times like an oversize elf. By 1965, Khrushchev claimed, the Soviet Union would have the shortest working day in the world, and wages would have increased. The most important precondition for fulfilling such economic goals was the maintenance of peace. Thus the Soviet Union wanted a peaceful solution of international questions.

He added, 'We say to the statesmen of the Western Powers, "Let us have a peace conference with the participation of both German states, and conclude a peace treaty with Germany excluding the possibility of the rebirth of German militarism." ' That would be a great contribution towards the relaxation of international tension.

He repeated the Soviet view that Germany could be reunified only by negotiation between the two German states. He said the ruling circles of the West had rejected Soviet proposals for a peace treaty without proposing anything themselves. Those circles were now trying to threaten the use of force if the Soviet Union refused to maintain the occupation status and handed over its Berlin control functions to the East German authorities, in whose territory Berlin lay.

Declaring several times that the Soviet Union wanted peace, Khrushchev said that the Soviet Union would sign a separate peace treaty with East Germany if West Germany would not sign a treaty. There was little reaction from the crowd early in Khrushchev's speech, but there was applause when he repeatedly mentioned peace. As Ulbricht began to speak, and I left to get to a teleprinter in the nearby press centre, people were already drifting away.

This evening I took a risk by driving some 12 miles from Leipzig to the adjoining small town of Delitzsch; I knew that my visa applied only to Leipzig city. I went to visit 66-ish Olga Söhner, the widowed mother of one of our best West German friends, Fritz Söhner, a horticultural expert in the Agriculture Ministry. As I drew up outside the house where Frau Söhner was visiting neighbours, two green-uniformed policemen – rather like West German ones but not as smart – drove in front of me on a motorcycle combination and stopped. After one of the policeman had told me that I was not allowed outside Leipzig city, I asked whether, as I had got there anyway, I could visit the old lady for 20 minutes. He okayed that.

I told Frau Söhner and her neighbours that I believed Khrushchev was out to maintain peace. They made some bitter remarks about conditions in East Germany, referring to the lack of both political and economic freedoms. I tried to make a tape-recording of Frau Söhner to take back for Fritz, but failed because the current was different. As I rose to go, after about 25 minutes, one of the two motorcycle policemen knocked at the door and told me I must come to the police station.

In the police station I explained to an officer why I was in Delitzsch and told him that I had been given permission to go into the house. He asked the motorcycle policemen if this was true and they nodded shamefacedly.

'Why didn't you tell me that?' the officer asked the policemen reproachfully.

After taking down my personal details from my passport, the officer said something about laws needing to be observed by visitors as well as East German citizens, wished me success in my work in East Germany and let me go. That was one of my first experiences with the East German police state; it frightened me a little.

Tonight attended a Leipzig reception given by the East German Chamber of Trade. Had a long talk with an official of the East German Trade Ministry, Schröder, who, like many East German officials, had been in a concentration camp in the Nazi period. The more I talk to such people, the more I am of the view that the East German Communists are *trying* to do good and that one should seek to understand this, while rejecting their dictatorial methods, in the hope that these will, in time, be modified. I believe that such people genuinely desire peace and that they genuinely regard the West German army as a threat, as it is now being equipped with weapons capable of firing nuclear warheads and is commanded by generals who served under Hitler.

Late tonight the East German news agency, ADN, reported that a test aircraft had crashed near Dresden, killing the crew. We were pretty certain that this was the only prototype yet flying of Professor Baade's 152, the jet passenger plane, so I rang up Baade at his home in Dresden and he – guardedly – virtually confirmed this. Officials with Baade at yesterday's reception had hinted to us that the plane was to have flown high over Leipzig during the Khrushchev speech.

5 March 1959 : To bed around 03.00 and up again around 07.00 to be ready around 08.00 to join the chosen party of about 12 journalists who are being allowed to accompany Khrushchev on a number of his engagements. First he visited the trade fair – not as smart as West German fairs I have visited.

There was a terrific crush when Khrushchev arrived at an engineering pavilion. With him were Ulbricht and the East German Prime Minister, Otto Grotewohl, who looked weary. Four or five Soviet and East German plainclothes security men kept close to the leaders, and others sometimes formed a second row, hand-in-hand, to keep back the public or the press.

I had lots of fun trying to get as near as possible to Khrushchev, so as to hear something of what he was saying to exhibitors. He walked briskly, smiling a lot, listening intently to explanations of machines and making remarks. He briefly looked at a British machine-tools stand.

In the Soviet pavilion, where we went next, Khrushchev amused himself by getting Grotewohl to take the wheel of a beautiful blue Russian limousine – I don't think it is in production yet, but it looks like something out of Detroit – while the Soviet ambassador, Pervukhin, sat by Grotewohl and blew the horn, and

Khrushchev and Ulbricht occupied the back seat. Later Khrushchev and Ulbricht climbed onto a stand displaying models of sputniks – Soviet unmanned earth satellites – the first of which was launched in October 1957. They are the centrepiece of the Soviet pavilion.

Khrushchev said excitedly, 'Now we'll fly to the moon.'

As they climbed down from the stand, Ulbricht said in his high-pitched Saxon accent, 'Now we are coming down to earth again.' Was he being sarcastic?

Ulbricht is very stiff and normally grim-looking, though he tries to make jokes, usually rather poor ones. Khrushchev, on the other hand, has a very engaging and seemingly natural approach. He shakes hands with people with great gusto, grins a lot and puts folk at their ease.

From time to time, without losing Khrushchev, I phoned through snatches of copy to Alfred in the press centre. My big moment came when Khrushchev went through into the Indian pavilion, where I was waiting. When Khrushchev arrived, no interpreter was present and the Soviet leader did not understand what the Indian director of the pavilion was telling him in English about village handicrafts. As I was near the two, I inserted myself between them and started interpreting, slowly. I explained that the wares Khrushchev was looking at, cloth and handicrafts, were made in villages and at home. He then said something like, '*Roochnoye dyelo?*' which floored me at first, so he repeated it and, realizing he meant 'handmade', I replied, 'Da' and explained apologetically that I was not the real interpreter, but was merely trying to help out. At that moment the real interpreter arrived, which was both a relief and a disappointment to me.

When a Kashmiri exhibitor gave Khrushchev a wooden beer-mug, Khrushchev said it was for soft drinks. 'Milk,' said the exhibitor with a grin, and Khrushchev repeated in Russian, '*Moloko.*' *[One of those basic words showing the many similarities between Russian and some other European languages.]* I stayed close to Khrushchev as he viewed more Indian exhibits, but an East German plainclothes policeman tried to move me away. However,

I was able to rebuff him by claiming that, as a British citizen, I had the right to be in a Commonwealth pavilion.

After Khrushchev had lunched privately with dignitaries, he came into the vast room in Leipzig's city hall where about 800 people, including me, had eaten. The Soviet leader had officials place at his table an assorted company of guests, including two British Labour MPs, Arthur Lewis and Ian Mikardo, one Tory MP, G.B. Drayson, who represents Skipton in my native Yorkshire, an Indian or two and various persons I did not know. Ulbricht sat next to Drayson.

Before that group had been assembled, Khrushchev had had a preliminary exchange with Drayson at another table. Drayson told me that Khrushchev said he thought the Labour politicians understood the position about a German peace treaty better than the ruling Conservatives. Drayson replied that the Conservatives understood better since the recent visit to Moscow of Prime Minister Harold Macmillan.

After Khrushchev had moved to the other table, he asked Drayson what kind of peace he wanted.

Drayson replied, 'A just peace.'

Grotewohl asked Drayson for his attitude to the recent Soviet Note proposing a summit conference, or a foreign ministers' conference to precede a summit conference, to discuss a peace treaty with Germany.

Drayson replied, 'I think the foreign ministers and the heads of government will work out the basis of a just peace.'

Khrushchev said there was a Russian saying – he's very keen on trotting these out – that one did not count one's chickens before autumn. He added, 'We must wait and see whether good deeds will follow good words.'

Mikardo asked, 'What about the critical date of 27 May?' (The date on which, the Soviets had said earlier, they would hand over their Berlin control powers to East Germany – including control of allied access routes to West Berlin.)

Khrushchev replied that the Soviet Union had been in existence for 41 years and would go on, like the earth around the sun.

He added (significantly), 'Therefore we can wait.'

Khrushchev later rose and made a speech. His tubby figure looked quite appealing as he spoke to this small circle. On the left lapel of his dark suit were the medals of the Order of Lenin and Hero of Soviet Labour, and a badge showing a dove of peace.

According to the German version of the speech, translated by an interpreter standing next to Khrushchev, he said in part, 'We have come together, people of different political attitudes, different religions. But we want to speak here in a common language, the language of advantageous trade . . . I have not come here to engage in ideological disputes. I represent the business circles of the Soviet Union.'

That remark was greeted with laughter, and Mikardo chipped in, 'The Soviet capitalists.'

Khrushchev went on, 'If you know only the word capitalism, then I would say it is the capitalism of communism . . . We are for peaceful co-existence . . . Let us trade – a correct policy because that is co-existence . . . In order to guarantee peace, one must remove the effects of the Second World War . . . It is nearly 14 years [*since the war*] and still there is no peace treaty. Why do you want to maintain this war, for the good of peace? . . . If you are for war . . . such men must be put into a lunatic asylum. Let us sign a peace treaty.'

On the reunification of Germany, Khrushchev said, 'Let Adenauer and Comrade Grotewohl come together and reach agreement and we shall support what they agree on.'

Here Ulbricht commented, 'Adenauer does not want to. He is afraid.'

Khrushchev went on, 'If we made any other decision, that would be intervening in the affairs of the Germans. Comrade Ulbricht made a very correct and interesting remark. That showed the weakness of Federal Chancellor Adenauer . . . If capitalism is without fault and is strong, then create a confederation between the two states. Then try to digest the German Democratic Republic in your stomach and try to make a capitalist state out of it. Apparently the digestive juices have become somewhat weak and the stomach cannot effect this digestion . . .

'One says that the Russians are uncompromising, that we make a policy of ultimatums. That is not true. Someone says that 27 May is an ultimative date. If you want to negotiate reasonably, let us put back 27 May to 27 June or perhaps carry it over to July. We have no reason to hurry. But one must solve the question.

'Someone says, "What is that, a new Munich?" If one says that, that is exploiting ignorance. Munich was the removal of the independence of the Czechoslovak Republic. Munich gave Hitler the green light for his offensive to the East. And our proposals, what do they say? We say, "Sign a peace treaty and remove the remnants of the last world war."

'. . . Conservative and Labourite gentlemen . . . If a peace treaty is not signed with both the existing Germanys, if then the German Democratic Republic declares its readiness to sign with us and the other countries who made war against Hitler, then we shall sign this treaty . . . With the signing of a peace treaty with the German Democratic Republic, the Berlin question will also be solved. We shall not hand over our control functions, based on Potsdam *[the 1945 Potsdam Agreement]*, until a peace treaty with both Germanys or the German Democratic Republic has been signed. Then we shall hand over our control functions as an occupation power to the government of the German Democratic Republic, which will then have all the rights belonging to a sovereign state. All previous rights based on the occupation of Hitler's Germany will be invalidated at the moment of the signing of the peace treaty. One cannot threaten with war a country which wants to remove the remnants of the last war . . . We too shall not bow to pressure from armed forces.'

Khrushchev ended by proposing a long toast to peace, friendship and trade. Lewis responded by proposing, 'His Excellency's personal good health.'

Several other journalists and I had hoped to be able to compare notes before sending our stories, but Khrushchev's statement, putting back the 27 May ultimatum and saying that the Soviet Union's Berlin control powers would not be relinquished until a peace treaty was signed, was hot stuff. So I dashed to a teleprinter in another part of the city hall to get the main part of the story away. I learned later that, by using the city hall teleprinter and not going across the road to the press centre, I had beaten all opposition by at least several minutes.

I was very taken by the informal way in which Khrushchev behaved this lunchtime, and impressed by the look on his face when he spoke. He gave the appearance of both sincerity and friendliness. This afternoon I caught up with Khrushchev as he toured some East German exhibits. From time to time the spectators broke out in clapping to which Khrushchev responded by clapping himself in the Russian fashion, which the East Germans have adopted too. Coming across a Soviet soldier, I asked him in Russian what he thought of Khrushchev. He said, 'Good. A simple man. A worker. A miner.'

6 March 1959 : Today I saw the unusual sight of the top Soviet leader drinking a toast in cognac to a gentleman by the name of Alfried Krupp, head of Krupps of Essen. *[In Soviet propaganda Krupps was portrayed as a symbol of aggressive German militarism.]* Alfried Krupp was not present, as the toast to him was proposed by an official of his firm when Khrushchev visited the Krupp stand. Khrushchev looked at a model of a synthetic fibre factory Krupps are building in the Soviet Union. He was not shown the model of another type of factory. I learned this was because the Soviet Union had just awarded the contract for building such a factory to Britain.

At the stand of a Belgian pharmaceutical firm, Khrushchev accepted a few bottles of a drug supposed to counteract the effect of vodka on the liver. And at another Belgian stand he reminisced with the owner about the one day when he had worked in a Belgian chemical factory in the Ukraine, but had left because he could not stand the fumes and was not paid for his day's work.

Had fun joking with the Russian and East German plainclothes men. I told one he had the right type of long arms to hold back crowds, which amused him hugely. And I had several of them laughing by describing their antics in linking hands and keeping back the crowds as 'the dance of the policemen'. This afternoon at one stand Khrushchev was weighed on bathroom scales, registering exactly 100 kilos, while Ulbricht, taller but not so fat, registered 93. *[I was then about 70 kilos.]* Everyone admires the energy of Khrushchev, who will be 65 next month.

Tonight Khrushchev presided at a reception in the Soviet pavilion, standing with distinguished guests behind a long table. He jokingly reprimanded a West German freelance photographer, Edo König, saying something to the effect that that fellow was always snapping him when he raised his glass, that the Americans were paying him to do so, as they liked to know how much drink he could hold, but usually got tired of waiting. He said it was known that he was against too much vodka, but added enigmatically, 'A great man is great in spite of his faults.' Finally he made König have a drink with him.

9 War 'not inevitable',
Khrushchev says

7 March 1959 : With several other Western journalists, was taken
to hear Khrushchev address the 'Tenth All-German Workers'
Conference' in a large hotel ballroom near Leipzig. These conferences of trade unionists, including shop stewards – mainly
Communists and fellow-travellers – from both Germanys, take
place each year during the Leipzig Fair. There were said to be
1,100 West Germans and about 300 East Germans taking part.
When Khrushchev came in with Ulbricht, the participants stood
up, cheered and clapped for two minutes. We journalists wondered whether Khrushchev knew we were present, for he made a
very polemical speech – almost the converse of what Adenauer
tells his people about the Soviets.

Some extracts from my notes, made from an interpreter's
German translation: 'We do not believe that war is inevitable, but
that is not because the imperialists have lost their taste for fighting and war. The wolf's hunger has become still greater, but conditions are different today . . . *[In the Soviet Union]* the working
class was victorious once and for all. The Western Powers wanted . . . with the help of the German people to shatter the October
Revolution. The Soviet Union . . . barred the way against
Nazism. The Western Powers opened the Second Front only
when they realized that Soviet troops could get to Paris. Our
country was destroyed, industry laid in ruins. It seemed that the
Allies ought to help. They did not give a penny. They started a

blockade. But we broke out of the blockade with our inter-continental missile. The proletarian banner waves in the cosmos. The peace camp is stronger than ever before. If there should be a new war – one could start in a small way – that would end with the destruction of capitalism.'

After claiming that the Soviet Union was following a reasonable peaceful policy and not allowing itself to be provoked, he started shouting and said, 'To speak with imperialism, one does not need merely morale, but must be supported by strength. I think that the international situation is at present good. We did not want the Cold War. Churchill invented it. He is a worthy opponent . . . old and shaky like the social order of his party. He was a clever man. He could bring things to a crisis. He was a cunning politician and he left us this Cold War.' *[Churchill had resigned as Prime Minister in April 1955. He died in 1965.]*

Khrushchev went on, 'Let us liquidate this Cold War. The Cold War consists of:

1 the German question; and
2 the question of deterring communism.

One can frighten people with the Devil. Now one is frightening people with communism. People regard communism like new shoes – they are frightened they will nip. They say, "I will live out my days in capitalism, communism is for my grandchildren." '

Khrushchev quoted a 'high personality', evidently from a Third World country, who, after visiting Moscow, said that was not communism because the people had clothes, shoes on their feet and lived in good houses. He had added that there was communism in his country because the people ran around naked.

Khrushchev went on, 'That is communism according to his ideas. Poverty. Such a distortion has got into people's brains about communism. We are moving forward consciously to communism and communism will be victorious. We shall soon approach the level of the most highly developed capitalist countries. If you liquidated the Cold War, you could no longer use the fear of communism. If you destroy the Devil, the priest has nothing more to do. Even the blind will see that there are no two ways for the world, but only one way, the way of progress, the way of communism. The struggle of capitalism with communism is a matter for all the people in the world.

'The German question is a matter for the 80 million Germans. Can the world exist without the reunification of the German states? The world can exist not too badly. Therefore that is a secondary question, but a question that must be solved, because it is a basic question regarding peace and war. The main forces face each other in Germany. When two armies are opposed to one another, accidents are easy and this question must be solved. Why does the West not want to solve it?

'They need this question for carrying on the Cold War. If, in a week or a month, we sign a peace treaty with Germany . . . and leave the reunification of the two German states to history – without war, cold or warm – that would be the reasonable solution of the problem. The Cold War makes it possible for the Western Powers to frighten people with the Soviet Union, the terror of the Soviet army. The Cold War can weld together military blocs. Militarists can earn in this way. Therefore they are frightened to end the Cold War, frightened to sign a peace treaty.'

Khrushchev recalled some of his experiences during the battle of Stalingrad, referred to the Germans of today as friends and recalled that Stalin had spoken about a united Germany. However, the Soviet leader went on to say that he did not want the 'workers' and farmers' state' in East Germany to be liquidated by means of a 'capitalist reunification'. He added, 'We say: the German people will be reunified. It is a question of when and on what basis. If it is possible to create a confederation that would also not be bad.'

Referring to the Soviet proposal that West Berlin should be made into a 'free city' after the conclusion of a German peace treaty, he said the social order in West Berlin could remain as at present if the workers wanted that. In his view it would not be bad if the government of the German Democratic Republic were extended over the whole of Germany. 'But if one is not ready for it one must not hurry. Let two states exist, a workers' republic and a capitalist state. The honeymoon of West German workers is ending. Capitalism is beginning to limp already. Factories are being closed, workers are being dismissed. In the capitalist countries, the working classes will take the steering wheel in their hands to . . . work towards communism.' (At this point a man ran up to the platform to embrace Khrushchev.)

Khrushchev wound up with a series of Communist slogans, ending with, 'Long live the German working class. Long live communism and peace in the whole world.' Applause and the singing of the *Internationale*, as the participants stood up to give Khrushchev another ovation.

8 March 1959 : To a reception tonight given by the East German authorities in the 'red' city hall, Berlin's original city hall, called 'red' not because it is now in Communist hands, but because it is made of red brick. Khrushchev told reporters he had been hunting today. I shook hands with Ulbricht, who received guests standing on a carpet with his little grey-haired wife.

One reason why so many people are suspicious of the Soviet proposal to turn West Berlin into a 'free city' is that they remember the strong-arm tactics used by the Communists to split the all-Berlin city council in 1947. Communist 'demonstrators' marched into a meeting of the city council being held in a temporary East Berlin building, and Communist council members declared that the people had taken over.

Most members of the city council then moved to West Berlin, while the Communist members stayed in the East and set up their own separate council. Some anti-Communists, who were found in the temporary building on the day of the decisive sitting, were subsequently shipped off to Siberia. I am prepared to believe that the Russians do not use such methods at present, but the distrust remains.

At the reception there was a good supply of vodka, Rhine wine and caviare. Caviare has become boring to me by now – after all, it's only fish! And when Khrushchev is around there's no time to bother about refreshments anyway. One has to be on his tail in the crush; trying to hear what he's saying or interviewing people he's just spoken to.

Overnighted in an East Berlin hotel, the Neva (Leningrad's river), which until 1945 was the Nordland. Until about 1950 it was run by the Soviet travel agency, Intourist. I felt I was working in Moscow – one of my ambitions – as the name Intourist was on several articles in my room. And there was a bottle of real Russian ink on my bedroom table. Filled my pen with it, but it was not much good – didn't run well.

9 March 1959 : The chairman of the opposition Social Democratic Party, colourless Erich Ollenhauer, had talks with Khrushchev in the Soviet embassy. A communiqué about their meeting said they had agreed that problems should be settled by negotiation. Surprisingly, later today Willy Brandt, West Berlin's Mayor, announced that he had turned down an offer from Khrushchev to receive him. On good authority, I learned that this decision was made under American pressure. Most of the journalists I spoke to thought it a bad decision – one up for Khrushchev. One Social Democratic official told me that Brandt had been near to a breakdown by the time he made the decision not to see Khrushchev.

In another big speech tonight, made in an East Berlin sports stadium, Khrushchev made a concession to the West. He said he would not oppose the retention in the proposed 'free city' of West Berlin of a minimum of troops from all four victor powers of the Second World War. Those troops, he said, would guarantee the status of the 'free city'. Of course, there is a snag to this proposal – that Soviet troops would have an occupation role in West Berlin, even though the Soviet Union arbitrarily ended virtually all Western occupation rights in East Berlin long ago. *[The main remnant of the Western allies' original rights in East Berlin was the right of Western allied troops and officials to circulate freely in East Berlin, just as their Soviet counterparts could do in West Berlin.]*

10 March 1959 : Had a discussion in the East Berlin press centre with one of my favourite colleagues, Blake Baker of the *Daily Telegraph*, on whether East Germany should be recognized. He argued that the Communist regime should not be recognized – to make things harder for it, in the hope that it would change for the better or collapse. I felt that this was not now a realistic hope, so that one must compromise by granting recognition to the regime, in the hope of relaxing tension and thus bettering the lot of the East Germans, as their government, then more sure of itself, could drop its stupid harsh travel restrictions. I regard the frontier between the two Germanys as an unchangeable frontier for the foreseeable future. The best we can hope for is a gradual reduction in the differences between the two world systems, because changes by force are unthinkable in this nuclear age.

Western as well as Communist journalists were allowed into the heavily guarded East Berlin office of the East German Prime Minister, Otto Grotewohl, to see the start of Soviet–East German talks. East and West German cameramen fell out because the East Germans had placed a floodlight, which would have spoilt the West Germans' pictures by dazzle. The West Germans retaliated by setting up their floodlight so as to spoil the East Germans' pictures. Then the two sides compromised and one West German called out in Russian, '*Mir*' (peace). Soviet and East German ministers grinned.

Tonight Khrushchev was the host at a reception for about 1,000 in the massive Soviet embassy, built in neo-classical style out of occupation funds paid by East Germany. It stands in Unter den Linden, a short distance from the Brandenburg Gate, which marks the sector border between East and West Berlin. Just inside West Berlin is the ruin of the *Reichstag* building, being rebuilt with West German funds.

Khrushchev made his usual friendly progress among the guests, shaking hands with East German officials, Soviet generals and their ladies, and West Germans from the workers' conference in Leipzig. I decided to have a go at him. For one moment he was separated from me only by two plainclothes men barring my way. I called out in Russian, 'A question, a question.'

Khrushchev immediately turned towards me, gently smoothed the plainclothes men out of the way, shook hands with me, took me by the shoulder and asked what was my question. Telling him I was a British journalist, I began in halting Russian to ask him if he could exclude Soviet troops from his proposal yesterday that a minimum of troops from the four powers could guarantee a 'free city' of West Berlin. I had got halfway through the question, when Khrushchev's interpreter said I could put the question in German or English. But Khrushchev said I was doing all right, so I continued in Russian, but asked that the answer be translated into German so I should make no mistake.

When I had finished my question, the Soviet leader looked solemn and replied, '*Nyevozmozhno*' (impossible). He said that the four powers had been the victors, so a guarantee by all four would be symbolic. I then asked him what if the West Berliners did not want Soviet troops in their city.

He replied, 'It should be decided by the victors. During the war we did not drink coffee. We lost the most blood during the war. Therefore we must have equal rights to take part in this matter.'

As I made shorthand notes of the interpreter's translation, Khrushchev looked steadily at me, solemnly but not threateningly; almost, I imagined, like a stern but not unfriendly father dealing with a recalcitrant son. Naturally, I'd have liked to have asked him lots more questions, but many others were waiting, so I shook hands with him again and let it go at that. Then I dashed to the phone, promising to tell other colleagues what he had said after I had put it through to Alfred Klühs at the press centre.

Before leaving, managed to buttonhole Professor Baade, who told me that the crash of the 152 jet plane had been caused by pilot error.

12 March 1959 : Khrushchev left today. I had a last glimpse of him on his way to the airport, as he leaned out of the window of his black Soviet limousine while passing a large crowd waving paper East German and Soviet flags.

Chatting with East Berlin postal workers in the press centre, it was clear to me that they wanted a united Berlin again, and free elections.

Driving back to Bonn, came across a British military intelligence contact in the NAAFI autobahn roadhouse near Helmstedt. He seems more worried about what the Americans would do, rather than the Russians, if the Berlin crisis comes to a head. He told me the American army has still got at Helmstedt a mobile radio station they brought in during the February incident, when the American lorries were stopped by the Russians on the autobahn. He added that more Americans had been drafted into the little town, which is in the British zone.

This has been my most interesting reporting assignment yet; probably my most useful week on earth yet, reporting to the world about Khrushchev's doings. After meeting the man I have the feeling that he is basically a good chap, doing his best in the light of his background. *[As one of Stalin's henchmen, in a number of high positions, Khrushchev had undoubtedly been guilty of, at least, complicity in Stalin-era crimes. In office, however, he turned out to be a limited reformer, who ended Stalinist terror and paved the way for the later far-reaching reforms of Gorbachov.]*

Before I left Berlin, I asked Stephanie Roussel, veteran correspondent of a leading French newspaper, *France-Soir*, whether there was any comparison between Hitler, whom she knew well, and Khrushchev. 'None at all,' she said. 'Hitler was a madman. Khrushchev is a great man.' I hope she is right and that I am right in my assessment of Khrushchev the human being.

16 March 1959 : West German miners are to get a five-day week, it seems, from 1 May, due partly to over-production. We have been able to buy some furniture with the proceeds of English–German translations done by Elfi.

17 March 1959 : Big news about Reuters: Sir Christopher Chancellor, general manager (chief executive) since 1944, is to go to Odhams Press, big publishers of newspapers and magazines, as vice-chairman, and Walton Cole, Reuters editor, is to succeed him. As Gerry Long, our chief correspondent, is well in with Cole, we tip him for some big post too in the fairly near future.

Prepared background material on West German car exports to the US and Canada – about 170,000 cars were sold to those two countries last year, including about 120,000 Volkswagens. The Germans do not seem very worried at the approach of so-called small American cars which, with six cylinders, will still be quite big cars by European standards.

20 March 1959 : Wrote a story about the coming formation of the first West German army unit to be equipped with weapons capable of firing nuclear warheads. The formation begins on 1 April. The unit, equipped with American Honest John unguided ballistic missiles, the modern equivalent of heavy artillery, will be ready for action by the year-end. The nuclear warheads will be kept under American control – but for how long?

21 March 1959 : Robin, who is nearly 11, was recently shut into a cupboard at school by fellow pupils just before a lesson. Because the woman teacher on duty was one with a sense of humour, he had stayed in the cupboard until the lesson had started and had then shouted out, '*Hilfe*' (help). The teacher released him, but said she had felt like leaving him in. He seems really fond of most of his teachers, who do not appear at all like the frequently stern Germanic pedagogue of old, but are quite modern and freedom-loving, while at the same time keen on the virtue of hard work.

22 March 1959 : We have made friends with a 30-ish East German couple, Werner and Lisa John, who fled from East Berlin last summer and are living in one room in temporary refugee accommodation in Bonn. Werner, a university graduate, was on the editorial staff of an East Berlin publisher where, of course, all the important posts were held by Communists. He had been concerned mainly with documentary works, such as reports of the Nuremberg war crimes trials. He'd made no secret that he was a Christian taking an active part in church meetings, some of them held in West Berlin, to which East Berliners still have access.

Last summer, when Church–State friction in East Germany was running high, he was warned by Communist friends in the publishing house that he was to be booted out at a staff meeting and that they had been forced to agree to speak against him. They would do so to hold on to their jobs, they said. Werner said that, out of about 100 members of staff, only six or seven were diehard Communists.

At the staff meeting, he was accused of supporting Dr Otto Dibelius, the head of the All-German Evangelical (Protestant) Church, who lives in West Berlin. He is dubbed by the East German Communists the 'nuclear bishop', because he actively supported a scheme whereby the church provides chaplains for the West German forces. The church also offered to do the same for the East German forces, but this was rejected.

At the staff meeting, Werner was told that he was unfit to have anything to do with publishing in a Communist state. He was forbidden to do such work any more, given 14 days notice and pay, and told not to appear at the publishing house again. Not wanting to work in a factory, he decided to go to the West, which is quite easy from East Berlin, but means leaving behind most of one's belongings, as there is an East German customs check on the sector boundaries.

Some weeks after Werner was kicked out, on the orders of the Communist head of the publishing house, the head himself fled to the West, after fraudulently taking some of the firm's money and being about to be found out. Once in the West, this formerly fanatical Communist became a turncoat and made a speech on West Berlin radio denouncing the lack of freedom in East Germany. Werner told me that the same man had denounced colleagues who, at the time of the Hungarian revolt in late 1956, were canvassing secretly for a move to oust Walter Ulbricht, the Stalinist leader of the Socialist Unity (Communist) Party.

Werner, like me, is of the view that it is now too late to hope for any anti-Communist revolution in East Germany. Thus one will have to recognize that state and negotiate with its leaders in an effort to obtain, in return, an improvement in the relationship between the two Germanys; for instance, the lifting of East German travel restrictions and the formation of all-German institutions to handle such unpolitical things as posts and telegraphs.

23 March 1959 : I expressed to our news editor, John Bush, my discontent about our staffing situation which, it appears, will prevent us having any day off for Easter – a statutory holiday in both Britain and Germany. Reuters does not give us enough staff, so sometimes there are not enough correspondents to provide us with our normal days off: three a fortnight here compared with four a fortnight in London. On top of this, our working day is often longer than the regulation eight hours and, unlike our colleagues in London, we are not paid overtime.

John is really a good sort, but can be said to be 'married to Reuters', while most of us consider that Reuters can well afford more staff for our office. John repeated the official Reuter attitude to such complaints: that if one does not like the situation in Germany, one can always go back to London and work eight hours a day in head office, something which is not a pleasing prospect to any of us. However, John did indicate that our complaints would be looked into.

Elfi attended a farewell concert given by the six-year-olds, including Chris, who are leaving the local Lutheran kindergarten in a few days. We have been fortunate that Chris has been able to attend kindergarten for some three years, for we are told that children who go to kindergarten settle down at school more quickly.

Had some discussion with a Herr Cornelius, 50-ish, who does a propaganda job for the Ministry of All-German Affairs and the Foreign Office. Cornelius told me he had been the editor, under Russian supervision, of a newspaper of one of the East German satellite parties, the Christian Democrats. He had refused, along with other Christian Democratic officials, to change the party on lines ordered by the Russians, and later came to the West. He argued that the West must be firm and strong because, he said, one cannot negotiate with Communists, for if one does so, one always comes off worst. However when I pointed out that negotiations with the Soviet Union had resulted in Austria being granted the status of an independent (though neutral) Western democratic state, he agreed I had a point.

I told him of Werner John's view that it would be necessary to recognize East Germany, but Cornelius said the East Germans would feel let down if the West recognized their dictators. After he had downed several whiskies – I was drinking orangeade – Cornelius said that he felt Adenauer did not understand anything about communism and did not try to. He agreed it was time Adenauer went, but thought the resultant situation might be chaotic, for want of a suitable new leader. He's got a point there.

24 March 1959 : Gerry Long called me into his private office and told me that both Cole and he had been very pleased with my work on the Khrushchev job. Originally Gerry had been ordered by London to cover the Khrushchev visit, but had fallen ill with a stomach complaint. He told me he knew his own limitations and felt he could not have done as good a job on that assignment as I did. He said I was to be given a bonus of 120 marks (about £10).

I told Gerry I thought our staff too small for the work we have to do. He took note of what I said, but added he could do nothing at the moment. He went on to say that we in Bonn would shortly be taking over coverage of Czechoslovakia, as Reuters has withdrawn its correspondent from there. We shall be receiving the service of the Czechoslovak news agency, Ceteka, in English and Russian. That'll be interesting anyway.

10 Adenauer's bid
for the presidency

24 March 1959 : Gerry told me in confidence tonight that
Reuters is intending to appoint a correspondent in East Germany,
based in East Berlin. Reuters believes this could be a great advantage, for we would then have a direct teleprinter line from East
Germany to the West, something no other Western agency would
have. In view of the conditions in East Berlin, it was considered
that a bachelor would be the best man for the job, but they needed an experienced man to open the new office if the East Germans
approved the scheme. It would take two or three months. Would
I like to do it? I said I would be very pleased. The East German
authorities had been asked to let Reuters know soon if they
approved the scheme and then Reuters would put forward the
name of a correspondent.

*[Some days later Gerry told me that, should the Berlin crisis blow
up during the period I expect to be in East Berlin, it might be the most
important Reuter job in the world.]*

4 April 1959 : The German papers were full of reports about
Anglo–German disagreements caused by Adenauer's apparent
refusal to agree to Prime Minister Macmillan's proposals for a
limitation of armaments in central Europe; something to offer the
Russians at the conference of East–West foreign ministers set for
11 May. Adenauer, it seems, is also unwilling to agree to any kind
of confederation with East Germany or to the tabling of a

Western draft for a German peace treaty. In other words he is not ready to do anything except to say, 'We stand fast in Berlin.'

I agree with standing fast in Berlin, but I disagree with not trying to improve the situation in other respects through, for instance, arms limitation in a zone on both sides of the Iron Curtain, without trying – unreasonably in my view – to couple this with a demand for German reunification. Gerry, in an interpretative story, suggested that Adenauer was hoping that Khrushchev's position might be shaken if the West remained firm. I asked Gerry what he thought Adenauer hoped to gain by that. He replied that, firstly, he could not understand how Adenauer could hope to shake Khrushchev's position and, secondly, what he could hope to gain from that anyway. 'I think the old man's going gaga,' he said. Gerry and I agreed that Adenauer is behaving like the typical old man, who will not budge from an attitude he has maintained for years.

7 April 1959 : I was in the 'slot' (the editing desk) when the West German news agency, DPA, put out a 'flash' – the rarely-used highest priority for news – saying: 'The CDU (Christian Democratic party) wants Adenauer as Federal President.' At first I thought it must be 1 April instead of 7 April, so startling was the news. Luckily I'd been told earlier that 63 senior Christian Democrats were meeting today to consider proposing a presidential candidate to succeed Professor Theodor Heuss in September in this formally highest but mainly symbolic office. But it had been stated then that no decision was to be made today and there had certainly been no inkling that Adenauer would be the choice, as he had made it clear he wasn't going to be pushed upstairs, in spite of his 83 years and a fair amount of dissatisfaction with his present obstinate policy.

After putting out a priority story, quoting DPA, and failing to get official confirmation by phone, I rang Gerry at his nearby home, so he could come in and take over the desk while I ran to the parliament building 300 yards away. There Professor Hans Furler, the Christian Democratic chairman of the *Bundestag*

Foreign Policy Committee, told me there was no doubt that Adenauer would accept the party's request.

A press conference was shortly to start and the atmosphere in the committee room where it was to be held, with some 60 journalists present, was like the last day at school, with lots of joking and shouting. It was obvious that the reported decision was popular among journalists. I said to one or two colleagues who, like me, have been in Bonn for several years, 'I never thought we would live to see this day.' They laughed heartily. But even we still thought there might be some catch. However, after a delay of about 45 minutes, Dr Eugen Gerstenmaier, Speaker of the *Bundestag* and a deputy chairman of the CDU, told the press conference that Adenauer had accepted the wish of the party's leaders after considering it for two and a half hours.

According to Gerstenmaier, himself tipped as a possible future chancellor and a left-wing Christian Democrat, by no means always in Adenauer's good books, the outcome of today's meeting was a complete surprise. For while many had had the idea of a presidential candidature by Adenauer at the back of their minds, no one had thought of proposing it, as Adenauer had rejected the idea some months ago at a meeting of the party executive. However, when the 63 'king-makers' had reported to the party's parliamentary group, it had emerged suddenly in informal discussion that there was a strong feeling that Adenauer would be the best candidate.

Gerstenmaier said he had told Adenauer outside the meeting, 'You are 83 years old. There is the matter of the loss of prestige that would be caused by a sudden exit from this office (the chancellorship) rather than if one does it in a planned way.' Gerstenmaier then returned to the meeting, made a speech analyzing the pros and cons of an Adenauer candidature, and the meeting voted unanimously in favour.

Adenauer was told of the vote, returned to the meeting and accepted in a short speech, making it clear that he was not withdrawing into old age. The meeting expressly endorsed that but, as Gerstenmaier added, 'in the full consciousness that we thereby uphold the constitution: comma, full stop and semi-colon'. (There had been questions raised at the press conference as to whether Adenauer, as President, would, in spite of the constitution's apportionment of real power to the Chancellor, would be able to exert considerable power from his new post.)

No one doubts that Adenauer will be elected when the Federal Convention, the body which elects the President and which is composed of the *Bundestag* members and representatives of the states, meets on 1 July in West Berlin. He will take over as President on 15 September. Back at the office, was glad to see that my priority report had beaten the Associated Press by 20 minutes.

I left the office after about 12½ hours on duty, not very keen to go at that. This has been a good day for Germany, and the world, I think. Adenauer, who did a great job in his first few years of office, in helping to lead a democratic West Germany back into the comity of nations, should have left the stage earlier. I had feared he was going to last quite a time longer. Gerry laughed when I recalled he'd said the other day that the old man had gone 'gaga'. I suggested Adenauer must have taken Gerry's remark into account when deciding on his acceptance.

8 April 1959 : In a speech today Adenauer made it clear, by stating that the power of the presidency had been under-rated, that he was going to do his best to pull quite a lot of strings when he became President. Constitutionally the presidency does not offer much power, but in Adenauer's hands it certainly will be more powerful than in the Heuss era. In his speech Adenauer also expressed annoyance at British press attacks on him.

9 April 1959 : Chris, who was six last month, started at school today – a day he'd been longing for. Equipped with school bag, slate, sponge, chalks and pencils, and his *Schultüte*, a large cone-shaped cardboard container full of sweets, chocolate and other goodies – like every German child starting school – he was driven to school in state. There a local Protestant pastor spoke of the need for the children to have Christian teaching, and said a prayer expressing the hope that God would take care of the children during their lives. (Naturally I do not want anything negative to happen to our children, but I do not believe that the Power behind this universe allows us all to go through life unscathed. The facts speak against this.) When we came home Chris insisted on doing 'homework' – some scribblings.

11 April 1959 : A story I had covered last night was the main front-page item in several British national papers today: an incident near Hanover, when a British army convoy was met by two bursts of automatic fire when it strayed into a farmyard during manoeuvres. A German who fired the bursts told police he had thought the convoy was a gang of motorized chicken thieves known to be in the locality. One soldier was wounded. I was surprised this story made the lead in several British papers. I imagine this is partly due to anti-German feeling in Britain at the moment, after Adenauer's speech the other day attacking his British critics, whom he called 'wire-pullers'.

14 April 1959 : Gerry told me that Reuters editor, Walton Cole, was a friend of the Egyptian leader, Gamal Abdel Nasser, who had wanted to be a journalist. Nasser has a Reuter teleprinter in both his office and villa and, Gerry has been assured, took decisions in the 1956 Suez crisis on the basis of Reuter reports. Gerry also outlined Cole's view that it is Reuters role to make satisfactory agreements with all news agencies, regardless of politics.

We have long had an agreement with TASS, the Soviet agency. The other day Pravda carried a large lump of our stuff from Bonn on Adenauer's decision to stand for the presidency. Gerry said that while Communists, on the basis of their theory, ostensibly looked down on so-called Reuter objectivity, they actually respected it to some considerable extent, knowing that we do try to give the facts and are not trying to bang a capitalist, socialist or any other kind of drum.

To a Foreign Press lunch with Ludwig Erhard, tubby, cigar-smoking Economics Minister and strongest contender for the job of Chancellor, though said not to be Adenauer's favourite. Erhard hinted that if he were to become Chancellor, there would be tactical but no basic changes. I found his attitude to the Communist world somewhat more positive than Adenauer's. While saying there could be no arithmetical mean to be reached between the two worlds regarding social systems, he held out the hope of some cooperation, particularly in the economic sphere. Not for the first time, he expressed his conviction that there should be a free trade area to supplement the Common Market – something on which he has clashed with Adenauer, who has bowed to the French until now and allowed them, for the present, to stop the free trade area from coming about.

Elfi, who does some freelance translating, got a sudden commission tonight, so I stayed up with her until 02.30, helping her with ticklish points and making her a cup of tea when she drooped. She should get about £9 for about five hours' work, which is excellent pay.

16 April 1959 : Spent most of the day at the Labour Ministry, obtaining information on a reform bill for West Germany's health insurance, which is to be presented to parliament shortly. At present about 80 per cent of the population are members of various independent, but state guaranteed sick funds (*Krankenkassen*), administered jointly by employers and workers, offering different benefits for different classes of citizens. (For instance, civil servants get more benefits than manual workers.) The result is that a minority of doctors, in spite of their oath, tend to give lower-class patients lower-class treatment.

One important reform proposal is that the payments made to doctors will be same whatever the class of patient. Doctors will still be able to charge what they like to the 20 per cent of privately insured patients. The reform will also increase benefits all round. They will be paid for by charging patients for doctors' services, towards the cost of prescriptions – which at present carry an almost negligible charge – and hospital treatment. Existing benefits are financed by an average of 8.7 per cent from gross wages, of which the employer pays half. The new charges will be fairly small, will be limited to the first six weeks of any illness and will be waived for poor people. The government view is that the charges will bring home to patients the costs of their treatment and that the fact that they know they are paying something directly for treatment will be a factor in their recovery and will also prevent people from going to the doctor when they are not ill at all.

The government decided not to unify the various sick funds, on the ground that this would be a step towards socialized medicine. I think they made a mistake there, for the different funds are bastions of class interests, as between manual and white-collar workers and between ordinary workers and officials. I am not against the imposition of some charges, because I think our experience in Britain has shown this is necessary in order to dissuade a minority from using doctors unnecessarily.

17 April 1959 : We've carried several stories this past week or so about a couple of American air force flights into Berlin which were 'buzzed' (approached dangerously closely) by Soviet fighters, because the American planes had flown at over 10,000 ft, which has not normally been done in the past. I say normally, as there is no firm rule on the matter – even the Russians admit that, but claim that the practice had become accepted – and British planes have, in some periods, also flown above that height. But, judging by reports from London, our government is concerned about the Americans sticking their necks out on this issue when the West is trying to enter into negotiations with the Russians. I think that one flight, if that was necessary at all, should have been enough to make the Western point.

20 April 1959 : My American-domiciled father, who runs a school bus company in Los Angeles, had pointed out one of my grammatical mistakes, so I retorted that he had described a male friend of his as a widow. I did not mention that in the same issue of his diary, which he sends to me, he had referred to a young man speaking Welch (which is not a language but a regiment).

As part of my efforts to learn Russian, begun early in 1957, I today started translating into English, from the Soviet government newspaper, *Izvestia*, a Reuter story from Bonn nearly a column long about Adenauer's decision to stand for President. This was under Gerry's byline but partly written by me. It also appeared in the Communist Party organ, *Pravda*. This is unusual.

An extremely busy evening shift at work. I wrote more than 30 'takes' (a take is about half of a double spaced A4 sheet) of the 100 or so written today by myself and three others.

24 April 1959 : We took delivery of a television set, bought for 250 marks (£22) at a discount store. Elfi decided she wanted one. Although I can do without TV, I was quite pleased really. *[We first had TV in the house we rented for a year in London in 1954, with a nine-inch screen made to look larger by means of a magnifying glass placed in front of it.]*

Read *Our Red Rivals*, an excellent booklet about the Soviet Union by Harold Mansfield, public relations officer of Boeing Aircraft, sent to me by Dad. This sober analysis of the Soviet Union emphasizes that the average Russian thinks he is free – because of job opportunities for those with ability – and refers to the economic challenge to the United States from a country which, ten years ago, was pooh-poohed as backward. Mansfield also suggests that the economic developments in the Soviet Union may bring it closer to us. He does not say that we also need to make changes. For instance, he bypasses the problem of unemployment.

25 April 1959 : In Hanover I followed Sir David Eccles, President of the British Board of Trade, around the second post-war annual exhibition of the (West) German Aircraft Industries' Association, which has about 100 exhibits compared with about 60 last year. The industry has reached the stage of producing its own light planes and making some military fighters under licence. A spokesman said they hoped next year to be able to show an aircraft engine designed and built in Germany. Professor Ludwig

Erhard, the Economics Minister, in a speech stressed the need for international cooperation in this sector. I believe the Germans have realized that they cannot be autonomous in their arms industry in view of technical developments.

27 April 1959 : At the big Hanover industries fair – 4,600 firms represented, including 87 each from Britain and the United States – I wrote about xerography, a process invented in the United States for the dry copying of documents, including out-of-print books. *[This is what we now call photocopying.]* Outside the United States the process is being exploited by a subsidiary of the British Rank company, Rank-Xerox.

Had a heart-warming chat at dinner with a German a little older than I who had been a *Luftwaffe* pilot on the Russian front. He told me that, although he'd not known of Nazi atrocities until after the war, he now felt – on behalf of Germans as a whole – somewhat guilty when he went abroad. I told him that I admired him for feeling this, but said I did not think he ought to. He spoke good words about friendship between peoples.

28 April 1959 : About 100 taxis in Hanover have been fitted with electric shavers for busy fair guests to use on their way from the city to the fair – a 20-minute trip. I had my first electric shave the other day in my hotel after misplacing my razor. The shave was not so clean. I think I'll stick to the old method. It seems somehow fresher.

At the aviation industry show, I quickly interviewed representatives of Messerschmitt, Heinkel, Focke-Wulf and BMW. Some of these manufacturers show pictures of planes they made in the Nazi period – good advertisements, no doubt, because they were good planes. Focke-Wulf even had an ashtray in their reception alcove showing a picture of their pre-war Condor transport, complete with swastika.

A pleasant Heinkel representative showed me a picture of himself with Ernst Heinkel, the firm's founder, who died last year. He told me Heinkel had been kicked out of the firm in 1943 after falling out with Hitler's policy – he didn't say in what way – but had got the firm back after the war.

On the train back to Bonn, dined with two French business-men returning home from the Hanover fair, which had greatly impressed them (me too). They were apprehensive of the possibility of the dynamic Germans getting us into another war. I said General de Gaulle seemed to be helping them in that direction by backing Adenauer instead of Macmillan on the question of arms limitation. They agreed. One of them agreed with me that de Gaulle was perhaps doing this because he wanted money from West Germany and assistance in making France's atomic bomb. One of them said, however, that de Gaulle's attitude had been prompted by Britain's action in persuading the Americans not to give the French the know-how on the latest atomic and hydrogen bomb technology.

Gerry told me on the phone tonight that I am to leave for East Berlin early next week to set up the Reuter office there, which will later probably be taken over by a single man. Gerry told me, however, that they'd wanted an experienced man to set up the office and to be in East Berlin during the coming crisis months, which might put Reuters one up on other Western agencies. I am very pleased at being given this task, but sorry it means leaving Elfi and the boys for about two months.

11 Reuters first correspondent in East Germany

1 May 1959 : A brass band woke me in Hagen, an industrial city south of the Ruhr, where I had overnighted. The band was leading a May Day (Labour Day) procession. For part of the train journey back to Bonn I sat with Count Baudissin, a West German Foreign Office official I know by sight, and two of his colleagues. They were returning from Berlin to Bonn after being members of a four-power working group which drafted the Western negotiating position to be put to the Soviet Union at the foreign ministers' conference beginning in Geneva on 6 May.

Naturally they weren't talking about what they'd drafted, but I had an interesting discussion with Baudissin about the pros and cons of recognizing East Germany. He argued that if Bonn recognized East Germany, the East Germans would lose the hope of reunification. He claimed that to accept the idea of a confederation between the two German states would lead to the neutralization of Germany and its swallowing up by the East – the old line. He would not say what positive move should be made, on the ground that he would be revealing what the working group had been talking about.

I argued that, sooner or later, barring the collapse or change of communism, we would have to recognize East Germany in one way or another. Therefore we ought to do it in the course of negotiations and try to get a *quid pro quo* for it, for example the establishment of all-German institutions for technical matters – such as the postal service and railways – and freedom of movement within Germany for all Germans.

He replied that, if the East were to agree to such points, we could not trust it to implement them and, although we could then break off diplomatic relations, recognition would still remain in international law. He added that freedom of movement would enable Communists more easily to infiltrate into West Germany, to which I retorted that if West Germany were really afraid of that it must not be very strong politically. I said that I personally did not believe there was a danger in that respect.

Told Robin that it was Labour Day. He commented – it's a public holiday here – that he didn't understand, as it seemed to him to be a day of no labour.

Gerry, giving me preliminary instructions on the East Berlin assignment, said I've to do an absolutely straight reporting job. That is, to rely in the main on official sources and give a balanced selection of the stuff which is put out by them. I shall not be in the position of a special correspondent who goes into a country, talks to all and sundry and returns home to 'take the lid off it', but shall have to watch my p's and q's, so as not to give an excuse for my expulsion. Gerry told me, for instance, that one of our blokes in Eastern Europe had been expelled partly because, according to the Communists, about the only things he reported were trials. I shall have to assume that all my moves are watched and that my post, telephone and telex – the teleprinter equivalent of a telephone – are being monitored the whole time, and my documents looked at when I'm out of the office.

3 May 1959 : Elfi and I went to our local Lutheran church, where prayers were offered for divided Germany and for the success of the foreign ministers' conference. A basic theme of the sermon was that, whatever happened, the true Christian need not worry. I'm not sure whether that is enough. I think I'd prefer it if the Church worked out a political programme, based on Christian principles, for the reunification of Germany.

4 May 1959 : Gerry told me that it is apparent, from letters Reuters has received from the East German authorities, that they regard the setting up of our office in East Berlin as part of the relations between our two countries, whereas the view of Reuters is that we are out to get news and not to make politics. I was interested to hear Gerry's judgement on a number of East German and Czechoslovak news agency executives he had met: namely, that they were sincere but misguided. That is, they were not devils in human form, as some would have us believe. Gerry said that while Communists, who believe in being partisan in what they consider to be a good cause, look down on the 'bourgeois objectivity' of Reuters, they nevertheless respect it to some extent because it goes some of the way with them (i.e. does not suppress facts favourable to them).

5 May 1959 : A West German radio station [*my diary does not identify the station*] reported that Reuters was opening an office in East Berlin – the first non-Communist Western news organization to appoint a correspondent accredited by East Germany. I left for East Berlin in our Volkswagen Beetle this evening, overnighting in the Ruhr mining city of Bottrop, where my refugee East Prussian parents-in-law live. Books I took with me included *Science and Health*, the basic treatise on Christian Science; *Marx and Engels on Religion*; *The American Language* by H.L. Mencken; and a Labour Party pamphlet. That's ideological coexistence for you!

6 May 1959 : A drive of about four hours along the eastward autobahn brought me to the West German frontier post near Helmstedt. Although this is in what was the British occupation zone, the Americans have strengthened their detachment at the frontier here in view of the possibility of a new blockade.

It was much easier to leave West Germany than to pass through East Germany on my way to Berlin. A West German customs official noted the number of my car, and another official looked at my passport, which I handed to him as I stayed in the car. Then

I was waved on, and a third official raised the red-and-white barrier pole so that I could drive across the 100-yard-long autobahn bridge over what used to be Germany's main East–West highway, the Reichsstrasse 1. The frontier runs across the middle of the bridge.

At the far side, an East German official opened a similar pole barrier. Then I had to park my car and do the following:

1 go into a small office to obtain a transit visa, for which I paid five East marks, which I had to obtain from an East German state bank official in exchange for five West marks *[about 40p in today's currency]* – a rate unfair to me;

2 queue up to have my visa stamped;

3 queue up to obtain a form for the autobahn toll, which cost five more West marks;

4 queue up to have the autobahn toll form receipted and pay the five marks to the bank official;

5 obtain a form from another official to declare what currency I had with me and obtain his OK to set off.

My luggage was not looked at.

As there were quite a lot of people passing through at the time, the procedure took nearly an hour. I commented smilingly on this delay to an official who lifted the barrier pole at the end of the frontier post. He said with a grin, 'Things that are good take a long time.'

I replied, 'Not necessarily.'

About 500 yards down the road, I had once again to show my papers and, some 20 miles inside East Germany, I was stopped by a police patrol and ordered to show them again. All the officials were courteous.

The fields in East Germany, to my untrained eye, looked no different from those in the West, but there were weeds on the edges of the autobahn in many places, which one rarely sees in the West. Traffic was mainly of Western vehicles travelling between West Germany and West Berlin or vice-versa. Occasionally there were East German cars and lorries, usually older than the West German ones, and here and there a Soviet army vehicle. Some people at the side of the autobahn or on bridges or in fields waved and I waved back. Some of the bridges over the autobahn bore fading slogans calling for a ban on the atomic bomb.

The East German check at the other end of the autobahn (about 110 miles from Helmstedt) took only about a minute. Then I passed quickly through the West Berlin checkpoint and within about 15 minutes was in our West Berlin office.

It turned out that East Germans were about to start a two-day holiday: tomorrow is Ascension Day – still observed in East Germany as in the West – and 8 May recalls the 'liberation' of East Germany by Soviet troops in 1945. I drove quickly into East Berlin to obtain temporary accreditation documents from the Foreign Ministry before it closed for the holiday. Initially I am staying in the Hotel Johannishof – said to be the best in East Berlin. State-owned, it is used both for guests of the government and normal customers. It is up to the standard of a good West German hotel, though not as luxurious as some of those. The staff are courteous and friendly. My room ticket tells me I am not allowed to take anyone to my room.

7 May 1959 : Set up my temporary office in my hotel room. Hotel prices are similar to those in a hotel of the same class in West Germany. A few years ago East German prices were astronomical in comparison. Some items, such as wines, are still a good deal dearer than they are in the West, especially wines from West Germany.

My hotel is just off the Friedrichstrasse, not far from Unter den Linden (under the lime-trees), which just now is looking well, with all its trees in leaf. Today I wore a suit Dad had sent me from California, with a zip fly. It reminded me of the apparently true story of a chap who had forgotten to zip his fly shut. He went into a café where a friend pointed out his omission. He then zipped it shut as he sat at a table. When he left the table, he took the whole tablecloth and its contents with him – caught in the zip.

I receive the news service of the official East German news agency, ADN, three times a day in duplicated form, delivered to the hotel, until I get an office and teleprinter. The main coverage of East German stories continues to be done by Bonn and West Berlin, who get the ADN service by teleprinter. One cannot telephone from East to West Berlin, as the East Germans cut off the lines some years ago. They offer to restore them if the West Germans will negotiate with them, but the West Germans refuse, saying that the East Germans have no democratic mandate. I can phone West Germany, but there are sometimes delays of several hours. Quickest communication is by telex (public teleprinter) to Bonn – one is connected in a minute or two. Bonn can then phone West Berlin. Waited several hours for a call to Elfi to come through last night without success. Had it put back until 09.00 this morning, when it came through immediately.

8 May 1959 : Had the thrill of sending my first story as Reuters first accredited correspondent in East Germany *[and the first non-Communist Western correspondent based there]*. My story was about the departure of the East German delegation for the conference in Geneva of the foreign ministers of the 'Big Four', and the foreign ministers of the two German states.

The delegation was headed by the Foreign Minister, Dr Lothar Bolz, a senior figure in the National Democratic Party of Germany (NDPD), one of the smaller 'satellite' parties in the bloc called the National Front.

[Bolz, born in 1903, was a Communist lawyer who fled to the Soviet Union after the Nazis took power and was active there in the 'National Committee for a Free Germany', which conducted Communist indoctrination among German prisoners of war. He returned to Germany in 1946. Bolz died in 1986. The NDPD was known as the party of little Nazis, intended to give such people a new political home under the Communist umbrella.]

The National Front is led by the Communists – here called the Socialist Unity Party (SED), because of the fusion in East Germany in 1946 of the Communist Party with the Social Democratic Party *[on the orders of and under pressure from the Soviet occupation authorities]*. There are ten parties in the bloc.

107

The nine smaller ones all recognize the 'leading role' of the Communists.

I suppose that, in line with Communist theory, the smaller parties will one day be declared no longer necessary, as the Communists will consider that the country has passed through its transitional stage as a 'people's democracy' and has become a socialist state like the Soviet Union, embarking on the road to communism, in the course of which, eventually, the organs of the state are destined to wither away. *[In fact the smaller bloc parties survived until the East German regime collapsed in 1990.]* The smaller parties also include the East German Christian Democrats, the Liberal Democrats and the Farmers' Party. They all back socialism *[they had to]*, but have differences of emphasis on detail. Votes in the *Volkskammer* (parliament) are, so far as I know, always unanimous, at least in the public sessions. The admission of this East German delegation to the foreign ministers' conference, by agreement between the 'Big Four', marks a real East German incursion into world diplomacy.

Tonight I attended a function held in a vast old East Berlin music hall, the Friedrichstadtpalast, to mark the East German–Soviet friendship week. I came across several of the East German plainclothes bodyguards who had shepherded Khrushchev in Leipzig, and told them I was now working in their country. Uninteresting political speeches were followed by entertainment, which included an amusing sketch, put on by young East Germans, illustrating the advantage of growing maize *[an idea pushed by Khrushchev]*, instead of root crops. The star turn was the State Volga Choir from the Soviet Union, who both sing and dance. The classical beauty of their colourful peasant costumes and the slightly Eastern strains of their music made me imagine at times that I was in a Russian Orthodox church.

Chatted with an East German actor, who told me that late last year there was a hardening of official policy on what plays may be put on. No longer are theatre directors allowed to work according to the premise of Bertolt Brecht, the famous Communist playwright, who died in 1956. Brecht had said something to the effect that it was permissible to put on all types of plays except those expressing fascist, militarist or racist ideas. The actor told me that since about last August there had been increasing restrictions. The basic principle now was: 'That which helps the cause of socialism is art.' That was a premise the actor did not accept, though he said he did not oppose socialism.

9 May 1959 : Had another, though minor, thrill today: used my power of attorney to the Reuter bank account and drew 1,000 East marks (about £88) – not really a lot of money. *[The Reuter account in East Berlin, containing a large amount of blocked East marks, was built up in respect of Reuter news services provided to the East German news agency, ADN. The existence of this account was one reason why the Reuter management decided to open an East German office, as the East marks could only be used within East Germany.]*

Called at the Foreign Office to meet the head of the Press Department, 63-year-old veteran Communist, Ambassador Stefan Heymann, formerly ambassador to Poland. This greying man, with a friendly face and manner, sported the clasped-hands buttonhole badge of the SED, whose executive is the real government of this country. I learned from Heymann that my arrival here was causing somewhat of a stir in the West Berlin papers. He showed me one which, in a rather unfriendly tone, suggested that Reuters must have been led up the garden path if it thought it could report objectively about East Germany. Heymann told me I shall be able to travel anywhere in East Germany except in the five-mile forbidden zone near the frontier with West Germany. (There is no such zone in West Germany.)

An elderly doctor who, unlike many of his colleagues, had not left East Germany for the West, told me that socialism was on the march throughout the world. But he complained that in East Germany things were being done too radically. He himself was not under political pressure, he said, but from time to time he went to West Berlin to read what he wanted and to 'charge up my accumulator'. For two years he had been refused permission to visit West Germany, but was hoping to be allowed to go this year, as travel restrictions for the professional classes had been somewhat relaxed.

I put to this elderly doctor my view that the type of socialism being imposed on East Germany is the result of history and not the personal fault of SED officials who, like us all, are creatures of their environment. I expressed the hope that, with economic progress, already evident, there would be political liberalization as well. *[I did not record the doctor's response.]*

A foreign Communist journalist I know, who has lived for some years in East Berlin, considers that this political liberalization has already started, if on a small scale. I cannot judge that, having only just arrived, but there are clear signs of its having started in the Soviet Union, and that usually has repercussions in East Germany.

10 May 1959 : Had dinner with jolly, attractive Phyllis Rosner, Sheffield-born East Berlin correspondent of the British Communist Party organ, the *Daily Worker*. She is espoused with Peter Gellert, correspondent of the Austrian Communist paper, *Volksstimme*. Peter was in Vienna, casting his vote in the Austrian parliamentary elections, in which the Communists were wiped out of parliament by failing to get the necessary minimum vote. After our meal Phyllis took me to their pleasant rather old-fashioned flat for some cups of English tea made in an earthenware oriental pot.

A sports trainer, working for one of the People's Police sports clubs, told me he earned about 750 East marks (£66) a month, which enabled his wife to stay at home. The teleprinter girls at the main telegraph office get around 350–400 marks (£31–35). The pages in my hotel get 220 marks (£19). Tipping is not called for, because wages are supposed to be sufficient, but a waiter told me he thought a tip was a sign of appreciation. He took mine anyway and no one has refused one yet. I'm against people fawning to get tips, as a lot of waiters in West Germany do. Here they are polite without overdoing it.

Had a glorious swim in the outdoor – but heated – swimming

bath in the People's Park stadium in the inner East Berlin suburb of Friedrichshain. Was whistled at furiously by an attendant for not wearing the obligatory bathing skullcap. Had to hire one. Each day I read several batches of the ADN news service, sent to my hotel, as well as East German papers.

11 May 1959 : Was received by Frau Deba Wieland, plump, middle-aged but quite good-looking head of ADN, an SED member. We discussed technical details of the Reuter operation in East Germany. Like all the other officials I've met so far, she seems to want to do all possible to make our cooperation work, which smoothes things for me. *[I learned later that Frau Wieland, born in Moscow in 1916 into a Jewish family, grew up in Riga, Latvia. Between 1933 and 1939 she was a Communist journalist in France and Belgium. She spent the Second World War in the Soviet Union. After her return to Germany in 1946, she held a number of journalistic and political posts. Frau Wieland remained head of ADN until 1977. She joined the Party of Democratic Socialism, the successor party to the SED, in 1990. She died in 1992.]*

In arranging the printing of office stationery, learned I had to obtain authorization for this from the local authority – a security measure, I imagine. Security is tight here. Officials say this is due to the division of Berlin. Perhaps they fear the use of force by the West, though I do not think they need to. Even a postal official on duty at night in the main telegraph office had a pistol in his belt. At ADN a policeman sits in a booth at the entrance, examining passes. In the Foreign Ministry there are blobs of some soft plasticine-like stuff near the outer edges of the doors and on the adjoining doorframes. The ends of a piece of string can be pressed into each of the blobs and a seal is then imprinted on the blocs. If the door is opened, it damages the seal.

Felt rather depressed tonight, mainly due to tiredness and being away from my better halves. That feeling had been reinforced by an early morning phone call to wish Robin many happy returns – he was 11 today – and hear all about his boisterous birthday party.

12 May 1959 : Transmitted a story on East German official jubilation expressed in the SED party organ, *Neues Deutschland*, at winning the first round in the Geneva foreign ministers' conference: achieving the right for both German delegations to be present all the time and to speak when they want, according to the East German version of the arrangement. An American spokesman said the Germans would be able to speak if all four Big Powers agreed, but there appears to be some Big Four gentlemen's agreement that if the Germans want to speak they'll be allowed to. The West German Foreign Minister, Heinrich von Brentano, made a weak figure in my view by refusing to enter the conference room and sending in his deputy instead, for fear of making it seem that West Germany was recognizing East Germany. It seems to me that East Germany is being recognized by being invited to the conference.

Spoke to a joiner who had served in the *Wehrmacht* and had been taken prisoner by the British. He was bitter about the evils of German militarism, said he did not oppose socialism, but wished to remain an independent one-man business. He explained that if he joined one of the 'production cooperatives' which, according to the wishes of the SED, are being formed in increasing numbers, he would earn only about 450 marks (£39) a month for an eight-hour day and would not be his own boss. At present he was earning about 600 marks (£53) by working a longer day than members of the cooperatives. He was able to take a month's holiday each year to go camping and boating, his hobby.

He said he was worried about his daughter, who wanted to become a teacher. During their training, teachers have to study Marxism–Leninism, with its atheist basis, whereas his daughter belongs to a Protestant church youth group. This is a difficult problem, because the Communists believe that religion is merely a cloak for capitalism, because of the role played by the Russian Orthodox Church before the Soviet revolution and the behaviour of some other churches, while churchgoers argue that one can support the economic basis of socialism without losing one's belief in God.

Am now typing on the East German typewriter, bought today, of Reuters East Berlin office. To buy it, I had to show a special pass, which everyone living in East Berlin has to show in making purchases – except books, records and similar things in the cultural-cum-propaganda sphere. The pass tells the shopkeeper that the buyer is entitled to be using East German money and is not someone from the West, who has obtained the money by changing at the artificial free-market rate of about four East marks to one West mark prevailing at the West Berlin moneychangers. It is generally accepted that a fairer overall rate would be nearer two East marks to one West mark, with parity or even a greater value than that for the East mark for some items. The typewriter, for instance, cost 420 East marks (£37) – about the same sum as it would have cost in West marks over there.

Attended my first press conference as the first accredited Reuter correspondent in East Germany. Was warmly greeted by an East German official, Communist journalists and officials of the North Korean embassy, which held the press conference. The ambassador interrupted the proceedings several times to call on us to drink a toast in ginseng liquor, made from a rare Asiatic root supposed to make you young again. At the press conference it was claimed that the Japanese were being recalcitrant in the question of the proposed repatriation to North Korea of about 400,000 Koreans living in Japan who had requested to go to the North.

12 'You will not be censored'

13 May 1959 : Making the round of East European embassies, I took a cup of coffee and a glass of vermouth with the friendly press attaché at the Czechoslovak embassy, Dr Vojtech, a former journalist on a satirical publication. Had another cup of coffee and a glass of *zubrowka*, yellow Polish vodka with a bison on its label, with the Polish press attaché, Janusz Rachocki, who illustrated what he claimed to be the atmosphere of free speech in Poland by telling me that, when a Pole was in a meeting, he did not know what he would say when he stood up, but would be certain to oppose the other speakers. Not always a good quality, Rachocki said.

I made my first call at the Soviet embassy last week. Shall try to make contact with all the foreign embassies, so as to be put on their mailing lists. *[In 1959 there were only about a dozen foreign embassies in East Berlin, all of Communist countries.]*

Called on the head of the Government Press Office, 36-year-old Kurt Blecha, who warmly expressed the hope that our cooperation would be good. *[Blecha, a former Nazi from the Sudetenland, served in the Second World War as an army lance-corporal. Aged 20, he was made a prisoner-of-war in Russia and was active in the Communist-run 'National Committee for a Free Germany'. After his return to Germany, was trained as a Communist journalist. In his youth in the Sudetenland, he was an acquaintance of a fellow Nazi, Erhard Eckert, who became a journalist working for the West German Social Democratic Party, and one of my close friends. The East German Press Office licensed and supervised news-*

papers, periodicals and the ADN news agency. Its premises were in the former building of the Nazi Propaganda Minister, Joseph Goebbels, near the ruin of Hitler's Chancellery.]

Blecha told me there was no question of censoring my dispatches. I said, I'd be glad if he'd tell me of anything I had written which they didn't like, and why, for one could easily get wrong impressions. He commented that one correspondent who had been invited to take pictures of East Berlin's show street, the Stalinallee, had concentrated on dustbins. I replied that he knew Reuters was not like that, and he agreed.

I asked a man sitting at the next table in my hotel tonight if he were speaking Russian. He came and sat at my table and asked me why I had asked.

I said, 'As an excuse to start a conversation with you.'

He turned out to be a Polish art professor working as a designer on two films. One is a joint East German–Polish production based on a space novel by a Pole. At the East Germans' suggestion the period of the action, which was originally many years ahead when all frontiers had gone, has been changed to some years ahead when existing frontiers remain. An internationally owned space rocket in the original version has been replaced by a Soviet rocket. And an incident has been inserted in which a big American firm at first refuses to release one of its rocket pilots to fly to Venus, even though that might be vital for the future of the world, as the Venusians are believed to be planning to attack earth.

The other film this man is working on is being made jointly by Poland and a West Berlin firm – quite an example of the Poles' readiness to cooperate all round. One reason for this cooperation is that the Germans are paying in hard currency for using Polish facilities to do some of the filming. The story is about German country people in East Prussia before the First World War, or just after. It is written by the famous East Prussian author, Hermann Sudermann (1857–1928). I was pleased to hear this Pole say frankly that he knew Germans had been living since about AD 1200 in parts of what are now usually called 'Poland's western territories'.

[Nearly a quarter of Germany, within the frontiers of 1937, was placed under Polish administration in 1945 on the basis of a decision of the 'Big Three' victor powers, the United States, the Soviet Union and Britain, at the Potsdam conference in August 1945. The 'Big Three' stated that final decisions on the territories to be administered by Poland were to be made in a peace treaty with Germany. No such treaty came about.

The East German regime, as a Soviet satellite, formally recognized Poland's incorporation of the territories in a treaty with Poland on 6 July 1950. Successive West German governments refused to recognize the loss of the territories until the centre–left coalition, led by Chancellor Willy Brandt, did so in a treaty with Poland on 7 December 1970. Finally, as part of the compromise with the Soviet Union bringing about German reunification, the centre–right government of unified Germany, under Chancellor Helmut Kohl, recognized the new frontier in 1990.]

The Polish professor added that the frontiers were too complicated before the Second World War *[when, for instance, East Prussia was separated from the rest of Germany by the 'Polish Corridor']*. He pointed out that there had been large Polish communities in the former German areas, particularly in Masuria, part of East Prussia.

14 May 1959 : Drove out of East Berlin into East Germany proper, crossing what amounts to a frontier on the edge of East Berlin. This is to prevent West Germans, West Berliners or foreigners who, in various legal ways, have access to East Berlin, from entering East Germany proper without permission. East Germans – unless suspected of wanting to flee – can enter East Berlin freely by showing their identity cards at this 'frontier'.

[Under 'Big Four' agreements, East Berlin continued to have a different political status from East Germany proper. This was shown, for instance, by the fact that military and diplomatic personnel of the United States, Britain and France had the right of free entry into East Berlin, though not into East Germany, and equivalent Soviet personnel had the same right to enter West Berlin. Furthermore the

RIGHT *Peter Johnson (centre) at a press conference in Germany on 2 October 1958 with Private Elvis Presley (Photo: Associated Press)*

ABOVE *Peter and Elfi on their wedding day, 31 May 1947, in Bradford, Yorkshire*

ABOVE *Peter, Elfi, Robin and Chris at Bad Godesberg, 1 November 1958*

LEFT *Chris and Robin at the Ratzenbergers' farm, 1 November 1958*

LEFT *The checkpoint at Helmstedt on the border between East and West Germany, April 1961 (Photo: German Federal Press Office)*

RIGHT *Peter Johnson, in conversation with a Russian officer, walks from the allied post at Helmstedt during negotiations for release of the American convoy, 3 February 1959 (Photo: Sphere, 14 February 1959)*

BELOW *Stalinallee, the East Berlin show street*

RIGHT *Konrad Adenauer,*
Federal Chancellor from
1949 to 1963 (Photo: Inter
Nationes, Bonn)

BELOW *A West Berlin car*
passes the Western allied
checkpoint at Zehlendorf,
West Berlin, and joins the
East German autobahn to
West Germany, 1959
(Photo: German Federal
Press Office)

YOU ARE LEAVING
THE AMERICAN SECTOR
ВЫ ВЫЕЗЖАЕТЕ ИЗ
АМЕРИКАНСКОГО СЕКТОРА
VOUS SORTEZ
DU SECTEUR AMÉRICAIN
SIE VERLASSEN DEN AMERIKANISCHEN SEKTOR

YOU ARE ENTERING THE
SOVIET ZONE
Achtung!
Sie verlassen nach
30 m
West-Berlin

LEFT *Walter Ulbricht and Nikita Khrushchev discuss exhibits at the Leipzig Fair, 5 March 1959 (Photo: ADN/Zentralbild)*

BELOW *Report on my encounter with Khrushchev* (Bradford Telegraph & Argus)

ABOVE *Walter Ulbricht at a press conference in the late fifties (Photo: ADN/Zentralbild)*

WITH KRUSCHEV

AN important assignment recently for Mr. Peter B. Johnson, a Reuter's correspondent in Germany who is a former member of the "Telegraph and Argus" reporting staff, was to cover Mr. Kruschev's visit to Leipzig. For a week he was in close touch with the Russian leader, hearing him make nine speeches and watching him at the Leipzig Fair and at several receptions.

Mr. Johnson, who has been studying Russian, "had a lot of fun" translating for Mr. Kruschev at the fair's Indian pavilion for a few minutes while the official interpreter was delayed. He translated from English several sentences about village handicrafts When there was a hitch he had to explain to Mr Kruschev he was not a real interpreter.

His closest contact with the Russian leader came when he got an opportunity to interview Mr. Kruschev at a reception at the Soviet Embassy.

After being cordially greeted, Mr. Johnson began a conversation in his imperfect Russian, but when an interpreter invited him to speak in either English or German Mr. Kruschev asked him to carry on as he was doing "well enough."

ABOVE *Khrushchev talks to Leipzig Fair visitors, including, seated far right (right to left), G.B. Drayson, Conservative MP for Skipton, Walter Ulbricht and Ian Mikardo, Labour MP for Bethnal Green and Bow, 5 March 195. (Photo: ADN/Zentralbild)*

ABOVE *Horst Sindermann (left), President of the East German* Volkskammer, *in discussion in Bonn with the West German Chancellor, Dr Helmut Kohl, 18 February 1986 (Photo: German Federal Press Office)*

LEFT *Sanssouci, Frederick the Great's palace at Potsdam, 28 May 1959*

Bad Liebenstein
Heinrich-Mann-Sanatorium
11th August 1959

Mr. P. B. Johnson,
Reuters Correspondent,
Hotel Johannishof,
Berlin N.4
Johannisstr. 20/21

Dear Mr. Johnson,

I understand that the annpuncment concerning my appointment will be made by the Presseamt beim Bureau des Ministerpraesidenten, although I am not certain, when the announcemnt will be made.

Concerning your request for an interview, I am sorry that at present I can not comply with your wish. The Director of the Institut, in which I shall be working, is unfortunately on holiday, and I think it would not be proper on my part to grant an interview, before I have had an opportunity to mention it to him.

However, I have no objection, if it is of any use to you, to state that you have been in touch with me and that I declined an interview for the reason given above.

Yours truly,

K. Fuchs

LEFT *Letter to Peter Johnson from Klaus Fuchs, the friendly atom spy, 11 August 1959*

BELOW *Dr Heinrich Lübke (left) in conversation with Willy Brandt, Mayor of West Berlin, on the eve of the presidential election, 30 June 1959 (Photo: Inter Nationes, Bonn)*

ABOVE *The entrance tower at Bartoszyce in Poland (formerly Bartenstein in East Prussia), 23 July 1959*

RIGHT *The main square in Bartosyzce*

BELOW *Peter Johnson pictured in the ruins of Schönbruch dairy, where Elfi was born …*

ABOVE *… and in a neighbouring town square*

ABOVE & LEFT *East German police guard the Brandenburg Gate and the border between East and West Berlin, on the day when construction of the Berlin Wall was started, 13 August 1961 (Photos: German Federal Press Office)*

'Big Three' powers, until the seventies, refused to recognize that East
Berlin was part of East Germany.]

A pleasant 150-mile drive to the Baltic Sea port of Rostock, first through flat, then slightly hilly country, with glimpses of several lakes. A little of the land looked rather neglected, but as a layman I did not notice much difference from West Germany. However, the roads were bad, recalling roads I knew in West Germany in 1946. Some buildings in towns needed a repaint but, on the whole, streets did not look depressing. And at times – apart from the slogans on banners with red backgrounds, on houses and shops, and the red flags hung out – I could have been in West Germany.

Over a good lunch, main dish veal, for which I paid no more than in West Germany, 2.80 marks *[about 20p at the official rate]*, I chatted with a 35-ish cattle expert from a collective farm *[called officially an 'agricultural production cooperative']*. He said the farm had been formed by joining some land formerly controlled by the local authority and the holdings of a number of farmers who had been allocated their land in 1945 when several big estates were broken up in the land reform *[ordered by the Soviet occupation authorities]*.

Until 1955 those farmers had been allowed to go on farming as individual small farmers. Then the collective had been formed – voluntarily, according to my informant. He said there had been teething troubles and the collective was not yet producing as much as the individuals had done before. But it was producing more per hour worked – the normal working day in a collective is eight hours, while private farmers work much longer. He added that collectives could use machinery much more effectively by joining fields together. He said he was earning about 700 marks (£61) a month.

The people around Rostock speak a *plattdeutsch* (Low German) dialect, which has similarities with English. They say *Dag* instead of *Tag* for 'day' and, like the English, they say *go* instead of the High German *gehe*. Near Rostock I gave a lift to two women aged about 35. One said she earned 320 marks (£28) net in a dairy,

117

while the other said she had 400 net (£35) as a shorthand typist in a municipal office. When I asked them to tell me how they felt about socialism, one of them said, 'I'm keeping quiet.' After a little while she added, 'There are certain things which are not right.' Both said that the standard of living had improved considerably in recent years and that they were able to manage quite all right, as single persons, on their incomes.

I had come to Rostock to report on the 'parliament' (conference), of the Communist youth organization, the blue-shirted Free German Youth, which claims 1,700,000 members, about 60 per cent of the youth in its age-groups – between 14 and 25. Its last 'parliament' was held in 1955. When formed after the war, this organization was not avowedly Communist, but has gradually been made so.

An interesting change in its statute to be made during this conference is the deletion of the obligation of members to 'struggle against superstition' – meaning religion. In addition a clause has been added to the statute welcoming the membership of youth with religious ties. At the same time the statute retains the obligation to study Marxism–Leninism, which among other things, includes an atheist view of life. In essence this means that the Communists do not want to frighten Christian youth away from their youth organization, but want to persuade them in time that the Marxist – and atheist – view of life is the correct one.

One speaker today made it clear that the organization did not want to be nasty to Christians who, he suggested, might be doing just as much to 'build socialism' as their atheist colleagues. My view is that one can believe in socialism without being atheist. Indeed, some Christians would argue that certain parts of Christian teaching are calls for a socialist order. In discussions with Free German Youth members I did not find one who could offer proof that there is no God.

15 May 1959 : East Germany's top leader, Walter Ulbricht, First Secretary of the ruling SED and a deputy premier, spoke to the conference today. He contested claims by some West German bishops that East Germany was denying religious freedom. He said there were four times as many churches in East Germany *[a mainly Protestant territory]*, as Communist 'houses of culture'.

He went on to suggest that there ought to be as many faculties of Marxism–Leninism in West German universities as there were religious faculties in East German universities, which is quite a number. He attacked those West German clerics who had supported nuclear armament *[partly a reference to West German armed forces' chaplains]*. They were misusing the Church, he said, and amounted to being officials of the West German Defence Ministry.

Ulbricht claimed that the presence, at the Geneva foreign ministers' conference, of the two Germanys amounted to the *de facto* recognition of East Germany. He once again called on West Germany to sign a German peace treaty. He said East Germany was becoming stronger in all respects and could afford to wait for recognition, but was prepared to negotiate now. He proposed competition between the two German states in what he called an 'open territory' which, I suppose, means some relaxation, in time, of the Communist-imposed restrictions on movement between the two Germanys, providing the West agreed, in some form, to the idea of a confederation between the two states, which has been put forward by the Communists.

At the final conference session, to the crashing strains of a brass band, about 150 smart young men of the East German forces marched in, headed by soldiers in field grey uniforms modelled on those of the wartime *Wehrmacht*, but wearing shallow-looking Russian-style steel helmets, followed by sailors, air force men, green-uniformed riot police and khaki-uniformed frontier guards. Major-General Heinz Kessler, Deputy Defence Minister, made a speech claiming that East Germany wanted peace, but adding that any aggressor would not survive an attack on East Germany for 24 hours, for the whole 'socialist camp' would reply to such an attack. His main target of attack, as is usual in East Germany, was the West German leaders.

[Kessler, a pre-war Communist, born in 1920, deserted from the

119

German army on the Russian front in 1941 and was one of the founders of the pro-Communist 'National Committee for a Free Germany'. After the war he became a leader of the Free German Youth and later an officer in the barracked police, which became the nucleus of the new army. Kessler, who was Defence Minister in 1989 and a Politburo member when the Communist regime collapsed, was put on trial in unified Berlin in 1992, because of his membership of East Germany's National Defence Council. Along with five other former members of the Council and the Politburo, he was charged with manslaughter in connection with the fatal shootings by East German border guards on the Berlin Wall and the East–West German border, and in connection with fatalities caused by mines and automatically discharged weapons on the East German border.

On 16 September 1993 Kessler was sentenced to seven and a half years' imprisonment – a sentence which was confirmed on appeal. Altogether Kessler spent nearly four and a half years in custody, including pre-trial arrest, before being paroled. He was the only one of the six defendants, who included East Germany's former top leader, Erich Honecker, to be convicted in that trial. Proceedings against the others were dropped for health reasons.]

Among about six Communists and non-Communists, I was taken around the Warnow shipyard – East Germany's largest – in the Rostock suburb of Warnemünde. We were told that it had been developed from a tiny firm which had employed 100 in 1945, now employed 7,800 and was short of about 600 workers. The yard produces 10,000-ton freighters and 7,500-ton coal-and-ore transporters. It has launched ten of the former, of which eight are in service: six of them for East Germany, plying to China; one for Poland and one for Czechoslovakia. The transporters have been ordered by the Soviet Union. A two-shift pattern produces a working week of 45 hours, normal in East Germany.

The average wage of manual workers at the yard, we were told, was 314 marks gross in 1951 and is 526 gross now, which means take-home pay of about 440 marks (£39). I'd estimate that this is ample for a single man. For a married man it would be hard to make ends meet, but most wives work in this country. Top wages for the yard's manual workers are 650–800 marks (£57–70) gross. A shed with an area of 20,000 square metres (215,000 sq ft), where ship parts are prepared, was stated to be the biggest shipyard workshop in Europe. Two women crane-operators were manning each of 12 cabins controlling cranes which moved along cables over the yard's four slipways. At present a ship leaves the slipways every four months on average. By next year it is planned to complete one ship per month.

One way to increase production has been to hire about 90 Dutch shipyard workers, many of whom had been unemployed. The men are obtained through a Dutch agent, who is paid 400 guilders a fortnight, of which he gives the men half. The rest pays his expenses, profit and the cost of transporting them to Rostock. The men also get 40 marks [£3.50 at today's rates] pocket money, plus free food and accommodation, four to a room. At their own request, they work 11 hours a day instead of the eight hours worked by the East Germans. One of them, a coloured man from Surinam, said that if he were not married – his wife and children are in Amsterdam – he would stay at the yard permanently, for, unlike his experiences in capitalist firms, he was treated as a human and not as an object. He did not mean from the colour point of view, but regarding the manager–employer relationship. The Dutchmen's wages compare roughly with those of the Germans.

The chief of the welding section, Walter Krinetzki, 47, told us he became a Communist because of what he had seen under Hitler. He had been unemployed for five years under capitalism. He praised the wage increases and price reductions made in East Germany in recent years. Another welder spoke of the free holidays and medical care. We also discussed the question of how working norms – the amount of work to be done to receive the standard wage – are fixed. We were told this was done by means of modern assessment methods and consultation with the men on the job. No one was asked to do too much, they said. However, if a norm was too easy, someone on the job would suggest that it should be corrected. This, we were told, was done because the

121

workers realized that increased efficiency benefited them and not some capitalist.

Normal annual holiday is 12 days, plus up to 12 days for particularly unhealthy work, such as welding, and a few days more for staying at the same workplace for a number of years. The men we spoke to were in working clothes, with flat caps or nebbed caps like yachtsmen. All seemed to be keen on 'their' shipyard.

Later we were taken out in a motor launch to see work on Rostock's new harbour, which will come into use next year. To build the necessary mole, which was finished last year, stones were collected 'voluntarily' from all over East Germany. Lorry drivers returning to Rostock used to pick up stones at special collecting places. I asked a harbour engineer, Fritz Jung, 30, who is not in a political party, if he felt that East Germany was democratic. 'Yes, altogether,' he said. Did he feel the lack of any political rights? 'No,' he said firmly.

16 May 1959 : After watching the launch of one of the ships for Russia at the Warnow yard, I was told by a boilermaker overseer, Otto Reichardt, that he earned 1,045 marks (£92) a month. 'We are very satisfied in our state and it gets better from year to year,' he told me. He, too, said he was not in a political party. Referring to the development of the shipyard, he said, 'We have done all this ourselves. It belongs to us. We are the state.'

Another man, a 28-year-old mechanic, an SED member, earning 600 marks (£53), told me, 'Our workers don't need to worry about what will happen tomorrow. We always have work.' Workers' suggestions for improving output brought them in bonuses up to 10,000 marks (£876), I was told.

At lunchtime I had the unusual pleasure of bathing in the Baltic – virtually no tide – from the silvery sands of Warnemünde in beautiful sunshine. It was cold, but bearable for a short time, and I did not want to miss the experience.

Later I was shown round a large diesel-engine factory in Rostock by Johann Dvorak, 43, a Viennese Communist who intends to join the SED when he takes East German citizenship shortly. He said his prospects in East Germany were better than in Vienna. He had been able to build up his household more quickly – he's married, with two boys – and had no fear of the unemployment he had suffered in Austria earlier. He trains apprentices in marine engineering. 'I could not have a more beautiful job,' he said.

Another man I spoke to, when we went round the works, told me he spent about 200 of his roughly 450-marks-a-month (£39) wage on beer. His foreman had sought out this man to show me he had enough money to spare.

My general impression so far, from talks I have had with people in East Germany, is that they are full of hope for continued economic progress and have now reached a standard of comparative well-being in which the troubles of an economy in which everything is scarce are beginning to disappear. Life is much more normal than I knew it to be in East Berlin three or four years ago.

17 May 1959 : My stay in Rostock was justified in terms of hard news today when Ulbricht, in a speech to a crowd of about 50,000 Free German Youth members, invited the United States Secretary of State, Christian Herter, to visit East Germany to convince himself that the 1945 Potsdam agreement – calling, among other things, for abolition of militarism and fascism in Germany had been carried out in East Germany.

Ulbricht, whose goatee beard and spectacles made him look fatherly, gave his speech a dash of humour. He spoke from a platform in front of Rostock's unusual town hall, which is half baroque and half Gothic. When Ulbricht issued his invitation to Herter, I did not think anything more important would come – I was right – and dashed to the post office at one side of the square. I was able to beat both my opposition colleagues, from DPA and United Press.

Later I was shown round a state-owned trawler, where the seamen earn an average of about 600 marks (£53) a month. They are paid a basic wage plus a sliding scale according to catch, a similar system to that in fishing fleets in the West, I believe. I was told they had better living conditions aboard than in some capitalist fishing fleets, and was shown a two-man cabin which was as big as the officers' wardroom which another officer and I occupied in a Royal Navy motor torpedo boat during the Second World War. This high-seas fishing industry is an East German development, as previously such fishing boats were all based at West German ports. There are now about 50 vessels in the East German high-seas fleet, fishing as far away as Labrador.

The Communist official who was conducting us deprecated developments in Yugoslavia where, he said, capitalism was being partly restored. I told him that in the West, nevertheless, the Yugoslav Communists were still regarded as Communists. I asked him whether, in East Germany, if it were shown that a family could continue to run a farm economically, as in some parts of the USA, such a farm could be left uncollectivized on the ground that no one was being exploited. He said he did not know enough about the circumstances in the USA to answer that one, but he did not think it possible for family farms to remain economic in East Germany.

Spent a short time in a cinema showing a film in which, during the Second World War, some officers and soldiers were shot for taking part in an anti-Nazi plot involving Communists. I didn't really grasp the story, but a Communist was one of the heroes.

18 May 1959 : Back to the Warnow shipyard again for a youth forum said to be attended by about 1,100 West Germans and about 200 East Germans. Ulbricht, sprinkling his words with humour, called for an end to what he called militarism in West Germany. He said East Germany was not demanding that West Germany be made socialist, but merely that militarism and fascist elements should be rooted out. Whether West Germany went socialist depended on the population, he said. He expressed confidence that East Germany would beat West Germany economically. (East Germany has said it plans to equal or overtake West Germany in the per head consumption of 'important consumer goods' and food by 1961.) Ulbricht forecast that East German socialism would produce an 'economic miracle' – an allusion to West Germany's 'economic miracle' in recent years.

I buttonholed the pleasant-faced sturdy Commander-in-Chief of the East German navy, Vice-Admiral Waldemar Verner, 44, who readily confirmed a story I'd heard that a Rear-Admiral was doing a month's service in a frigate as part of a programme decided on by the SED to improve 'class solidarity' and the relationship between superiors and subordinates. Verner told me that the Rear-Admiral, Schaeffler, a worker's son from Hamburg, West Germany, and a former Merchant Navy seaman, was enjoying his period in the ranks. I understand that this principle of higher-ups working temporarily in the ranks is being introduced in all sections of the economy and society. I think it is a good idea. Verner said he would be taking his turn later.

Have visited two exhibitions in Rostock: one showing how East Germans are contacted by Western espionage organizations in West Berlin and another claiming that Western comics and crime books encourage some East German young people to become criminals. *[East Germans have easy access to West Berlin.]* It was alleged that such literature was a weapon of NATO. I asked a police officer in charge of the second exhibition if the authorities had any proof that NATO encouraged such literature. He said he personally had not, but suggested I put the question to the press section of the Ministry of State Security in Berlin.

Driving back to Berlin I passed a Soviet jet-fighter base and a tank barracks both surrounded by planked fences. Also saw a number of collective farms and state-owned machine and tractor stations, from which the farms lease machines. My room in one of Rostock's best hotels cost under four marks a night *[35p]*. Most items in restaurants were as cheap or cheaper, in marks, than in West Germany.

19 May 1959 : Wrote a story based on an official announcement that Moscow and East Berlin would have a television relay link by 1961. To make the story more interesting for Western readers, I said this meant that a Moscow–London link would be possible by the same date, as West Berlin is already linked to the Western European 'Eurovision' network. An East Berlin radio spokesman, while confirming that a Moscow–London link would be technically possible, pointed out that whether it came about would depend on political factors.

Buttonholed man I heard speaking English in my hotel. He turned out to be Desmond Flower, chairman of Cassell, the London publishers, on his first visit to East Germany. He told me he had been struck by the fact that everyone here seemed happy. Of course, he had not had to go round East Berlin like me trying to buy office equipment and meeting, here and there, quite a number of disconsolate shopkeepers who had not got this and that, owing to the sort of shortages we had in Britain shortly after the war.

At an East Berlin cinema, saw an East German–Bulgarian co-production, *Sterne* (*Stars*), a reference to the yellow stars Jews had to wear on their clothes in the Nazi era. It was about a German army NCO, stationed in a Bulgarian town, who tries to help some arrested Jews who are waiting for a train to take them to Auschwitz. The film is very well done and is not propagandist, at least not for communism as such, but is against Nazism and brutality.

21 May 1959 : Dr Johannes Dieckmann, President (Speaker) of the *Volkskammer*, East Germany's rubber-stamp parliament, told a questioner at an East Berlin press conference today that East Germany had proposed all-German elections in 1951 and 1952, but Adenauer had erected a barrier to these by deciding to take West Germany into NATO. I don't believe that East Germany would have agreed to all-German elections if West Germany had not gone into NATO. But I agree with opposition criticism of Adenauer for not even testing this, and I also think that it is a bad thing that Adenauer did not try for a neutral Germany. *[Dieckmann, a Protestant churchman, was the leader of one of the pro-Communist satellite parties, the Liberal Democrats.]*

126

23 May 1959 : After a swim in a now-warmish East Berlin lake, the Weissensee, chatted with a railway labourer's son who is a law student. He disapproves of his father's relief that his son, thank goodness, is now getting out of the workers' class; the son believes in the 'classless society'. This young man, not an SED member, said he believed there was democracy in East Germany and that, after Stalin's 'infringements of party democracy', people would take jolly good care that there would be no repetition of that. He said that people who felt wronged by a legal decision had the right to appeal and that many appeals were granted.

I've acquired a stapler for my office, after failing to find one in about half a dozen shops, being told they had gone out of production. Mine was given to me by an official of the Foreign Ministry press department, Mai, together with a box of staples made in Shanghai.

24 May 1959 : Was provisionally allowed to join an East Berlin tennis club belonging to a gasworks. They asked me to obtain a certificate from the Foreign Ministry authorizing them to accept me, a foreigner from the West. *[This I did later]*

Spoke to one member, the owner of a small private optical-equipment business, employing about ten men, which is to be nationalized at a time not yet fixed. He will remain as manager and will receive what he described as reasonable compensation for his capital. He said he did not much mind the proposed change. He would be earning rather less and his deputy, who is just as qualified as he, but has no capital, would get rather more than before. He thought this would not be unjust. I imagine that, in taking that view, he must be in the minority of small businessmen. Membership of the sports club costs about one mark a month, compared with five or ten times as much in West Berlin.

13 Reuter bosses visit East Berlin

25 May 1959 : Together with Gerry, met Reuters more-than-bulky editor and general manager-designate, Walton Cole, who arrived by train at East Berlin's main station after a 1½-day journey from Yugoslavia. He was accompanied by George Bloom, a grizzled 49-year-old, the head of Comtel, Reuters economic services. Cole is to attend a conference in West Berlin of the International Press Institute.

26 May 1959 : I was invited – mainly as interpreter, I imagine – to a lunch given for Bloom by the ADN chief, Frau Wieland, with several other ADN executives present. We lunched in one of East Berlin's top restaurants, the Budapest in the Stalinallee, starting with hors d'oeuvres and shark's fin soup (Chinese, of course), and followed by a main course of asparagus with, I think, veal, rounded off with an ice-cream about 10 inches high, which I know Elfi would have loved, but which took a real effort for me to consume. Finally a cup of mocha. In between, sips of cognac and gulps of wine. My poor old tum, suffering for business reasons.

The head of the ADN department responsible for the agency's services to foreign countries, Grenz, took Bloom and me for a tour of East Berlin by car. We saw lots of ruins and also lots of new buildings now going up, including many blocks of flats being constructed from large concrete panels instead of bricks.

I told Bloom as we drove over Marx-Engels-Platz, the big square used for Communist parades, that the royal palace which had stood there had been razed by the Communists for ideological reasons. Grenz denied that, saying the palace had been so badly damaged that it was decided not to restore it, as it was artistically not so worthwhile. *[Other sources later confirmed my version.]* Grenz pointed out that the Communists had restored some other historic buildings, including the circular Roman Catholic church of St Hedwig. Bloom was impressed by the Karl Marx bookshop in the Stalinallee, which indeed has a big selection. *[A selection that was politically screened.]*

27 May 1959 : Two taxi drivers I spoke to the other day told me their pay was a percentage of their takings. They earned about 500 marks (£43) a month for evening and night work and about 400 for day work. One of them said he bought things like shoes in West Berlin, even though the Communist authorities forbade this. For 35 West marks, he said, he could get a pair of shoes costing 135 East marks in East Berlin. He also bought foreign fruit in West Berlin, because it was so scarce over here. Both agreed that in general food prices and amounts were reasonable. The abolition of rationing a year ago had brought some advantages, but prices of formerly rationed goods had risen.

Badly dirtied my ticket this morning by being 25 minutes late to pick up Gerry to take him from East to West Berlin. This happened partly because my watch had gone slow and partly because I got involved in an interview with Lieutenant-Colonel Odintsov, Deputy Soviet Commandant of Berlin, on the question of when, as Khrushchev has threatened, the Soviet Union would hand over to the East German authorities its powers over Berlin and the access routes to the West. It was also my inaugural visit to the Soviet army's Berlin headquarters. Gerry was understandably furious, saying I'd overestimated the importance of talking to the Soviet officer and underestimated the importance of being on time for Cole. Actually I had tried to fulfil both duties.

Today was the day, originally set by Khrushchev, by which the Soviet Union was to hand over its Berlin control powers to East Germany, but Khrushchev modified that threat later, saying he was not insisting on any particular date if genuine negotiations took place. Colonel Odintsov told me that there was no change for the present and that the Soviet Union wanted a peaceful solution. He spoke to me in a small conference room in the Soviet army's Berlin headquarters in the suburb of Karlshorst; the building, I was told, where the capitulation of the German forces on the eastern front was signed in May 1945. I accepted a glass of wine and a Russian sweet, declining a *papirossi* cigarette, and we both expressed the hope of good cooperation between Reuters and the Soviet army. He said he hoped I would write objectively, and I said I hoped he'd tell me if he thought I wasn't doing so.

28 May 1959 : Accompanied Bloom and the deputy head of ADN, Müller, on a trip to Potsdam, former summer residence of the Kaisers. It's just outside West Berlin but, as is usual for East Berlin cars, we drove all the way round the south side of Berlin to reach Potsdam, so as not to pass through West Berlin. On the way we passed the spot where, a year or two ago, the Americans tunnelled about 300 yards from their sector into the Soviet sector to tap underground telecommunications wires leading to the Soviet headquarters. Eventually the American tunnel was found. *[It had been betrayed to the Russians by the British double agent, George Blake, who was an official in British Military Government in West Berlin. Blake was unmasked in 1960 and sentenced to 42 years' imprisonment in 1961, but escaped from prison in 1966 and went to the Soviet Union, where he died in 1994.]*

In Potsdam we first visited Cecilienhof, a large Tudor-style country house completed in 1916 for the wife of the last Crown Prince. It was the scene of the 'Big Three' Potsdam Conference in 1945. It is now an East German national memorial, intended to stress the Communist viewpoint on the Potsdam decisions, including the claim that these decisions are being flagrantly infringed by the West German state.

The little SED man who showed us round told us he had been in a concentration camp together with Müller; he spoke emotionally about the brutality of the guards, some of whom are living unpunished in West Germany. Felt at home in the Tudor house, which includes a room modelled on a ship's cabin for the sailor prince. Under the floorboards there used to be machinery which reproduced the noise of a ship's engine.

On to Potsdam's greatest showpiece, the palace of Sanssouci (carefree). No one knows why Frederick the Great, who had the palace built between 1745 and 1747, had a comma inserted between *Sans* and *souci* when the name was engraved on the façade. Sanssouci, designed by Georg Knobelsdorff, is a rococo gem. Built at the top of a rise above terraced glassed-in vineyards, its decorations have a Bacchanalian theme, and the whole place has a jolly air. In Potsdam itself is the ruined Stadtschloss (town palace), another of the imperial residences. It was blasted in an air raid in April 1945. On the ruin is huge hoarding with the words, 'That is war.'

29 May 1959 : Cole and Bloom left today. It was interesting having them around, but I can't say I'm sorry the tornado has passed us by.

Met Konni Zilliacus, a left-wing Labour MP whom many regard as a fellow-traveller. He and two other MPs today had a 90-minute interview with Ulbricht. Zilliacus told me Ulbricht had said he would allow the Social Democratic Party to operate again in East Germany if a German peace treaty, as proposed by Moscow, were signed. However, he added that the SED, which is banned in West Germany, must be allowed to operate in West Germany as a *quid pro quo*.

30 May 1959 : Drove out to the village of Schönow, about six miles northeast of East Berlin proper, to visit Elfi's uncle, 40-ish Fritz Engler, his wife and two of his three young daughters. Fritz, a dairy expert, is a shift leader at a large state-owned milk-processing station in East Berlin. He earns 800 to 900 marks (£70–79) a month, a good wage in East Germany. They own a pleasant small detached house standing in an ample garden. The house is well furnished and they have radio, TV and tape-recorder.

131

Fritz told me he was a non-party man, but from some of his remarks he seemed reasonably satisfied with things, and he attacked the 'capitalists' for this and that. Fritz said the Berlin situation could not remain as it is and I agreed. The question is, how to change it. Some people in Schönow still work in West Berlin, though the authorities discourage this. Some young men go to West Berlin and work for a few days, because they can earn more in West Berlin. These things tend to disrupt East German economic planning, I suppose.

31 May 1959 : Around 11.30 my twelfth-wedding-anniversary phone call to Elfi was on the line. 'I'd been waiting for you,' she said. She had not, by then, received the bouquet of roses I'd asked a colleague to take round to her. She told me she had fixed one each of my passport photographs by the boys' beds, so they don't forget their Dad! All three are cheerful which makes a lot of difference to me too.

This afternoon drove about 120 miles to Leipzig. On the way I stopped at an autobahn hotel, which was packed with people eating and drinking, and included – horrors – a jukebox just like the ones I know in West Germany. I don't think that would have been allowed in East Germany a few years ago.

A ruddy farmer told me that people were no longer being threatened with arrest if they refused to join collective farms, but that other types of pressure were being used. For instance, he said, the machine and tractor stations, which have most of the machinery for doing large-scale jobs, were neglecting the private farmers, who thus got behind and lost money. He said his brother-in-law had joined a collective farm after being forced – he did not say how – to sign up at a meeting in his village at which party officials and local councillors were present. His brother-in-law was not too happy in the collective, he said, because the spirit was not right. In some collectives, farmers who had earlier been tending their own land well, were having to work on other people's land and were neglecting their own to some extent. In some cases they were having to look after land whose owners had left the area.

This man said his brother-in-law was in a Type I collective, in which the land is worked in common, but the individual farmers retain ownership and control of their own cattle. In the other main type of collective – Type III – the farmers look after both land and cattle collectively. In both types, each farmer can keep a couple of acres of land for growing things for himself or for market, and for keeping chickens and pigs. My informant said it was planned that his village would be collectivized by October this year. He added with a grin that he would keep out as long as he could. He said that some collective farm managers, elected by the members, tended to be bossy and to treat the former independent farmers as employees.

This farmer said his farm covered about 10 hectares (about 25 acres) and he did not need to employ outside labour. But owners of larger farms, say twice the size of his, who were classed ideologically as 'large farmers', were finding things difficult, as labour costs were heavy.

I don't think one can say that a small farmer like this man is exploiting people, except perhaps himself, his wife and his sons, by having them work too hard to earn more than the collective farmers, who work a normal working week of 45 hours. A big argument for collectivization is that small farms are becoming increasingly uneconomic in the era of mechanization. This farmer, indeed, mentioned this argument to me spontaneously and said he agreed with it. The Communists argue that it is better to form collectives than that the small farmers should be squeezed out, or made into tenants or farm labourers on big estates owned by large landowners, as is happening to some extent in West Germany.

Booked in at East Germany's largest and poshest hotel, the Astoria, where a handsome large single room cost only about ten marks *[about 90p at the official rate]*. One Russian and two East German radio programmes on tap. I had come to Leipzig partly to report on two concerts of the two-centuries-old Gewandhaus orchestra to be conducted by 77-year-old Leopold Stokowski, the first American to conduct the orchestra since the war.

The Communist administrator of the orchestra, Zumpe, aged 35, told me that the orchestra, which received an annual subsidy of more than two million marks (about £175,000), continued its triple tradition of giving concerts, playing at the Leipzig opera, and performing Bach motets and cantatas in Leipzig's Thomaskirche.

Stokowski, white-haired and ascetic-looking, with delicate expressive fingers, was given a great reception by the audience at tonight's concert, where he was clapped for nearly ten minutes at the close. He is on a short visit to East Germany, partly to see some of the places where Bach worked, including Eisenach and Leipzig. Dripping with sweat in his dressing-room after the concert, Stokowski described the Gewandhaus as a splendid orchestra including some young and enthusiastic players. In a day or two he is to conduct the Berlin Philharmonic in West Berlin.

2 June 1959 : On my way back to Berlin, after attending the second Stokowski concert, I passed through the old town of Wittenberg, where Martin Luther did much of his preaching during the Reformation and where he nailed his 95 critical theses onto the church door of the Schlosskirche. *[Luther, a miner's son who became an Augustinian monk, was made a professor of theology in Wittenberg in 1512. He published his theses, attacking misuse of 'indulgences', in 1517.]*

Underneath a crown-shaped Gothic turret of the church are imprinted the words from Luther's famous hymn, *Ein feste Burg ist unser Gott (A mighty fortress is our God)*, but they are peeling off somewhat. A Luther statue in the main square badly needs cleaning and some of the metal letters on the side of this monument, giving quotations from Luther, have fallen off or have been torn off. In a quotation to the effect that what God makes lasts, but what men make withers away, the word 'men' has been removed, and also Luther's name at the bottom. (Back in Berlin I read in a West Berlin newspaper that the East German authorities were seeking to change the character of a Luther museum to make it follow the Marxist line, which regards Luther as to some extent progressive, but accuses him of having betrayed the farmers who revolted against feudal landlords in that era.)

3 June 1959 : Attended a *Volkskammer* session. Main business was the final reading of a law designed to strengthen the collective farms. It clarified the legal position by assuring farmers who join collectives that they retain ownership of their land and the right to pass it on, in some form at least, to their heirs. On the other hand it gives legal force to provisions already operating in most collective farms for fining slackers or people who negligently cause damage to collective property or seriously affect production.

About half of East Germany's farmland is now collectivized or state-owned. The only one of seven speakers not to use a text, a collective farmer called Paul Pflock, made a jolly speech, talking about that sign of prosperity, television aerials, springing up in the countryside, and saying it was no longer necessary to marry the ugly daughter of a farmer if you had no land. Instead you could join a collective and have some given to you. *[Pflock, a farmer's son, was a member of the national executive of one of the satellite parties, the Liberal Democrats.]* Wages in the collectives depend on their profits; they can be twice as high in prosperous collectives as in poor ones.

14 To colourful Hungary

5 June 1959 : Flew to Budapest to report on a visit to Hungary by Nikita Khrushchev, the top Soviet leader. At East Berlin's airport, Schönefeld, which is being extended to take jets, I had to deposit all my East German money, as one cannot export or import it. The customs and passport checks were efficient and friendly. The East German and West German Lufthansa airlines have similar symbols and each claims to be the real one, or at least to have as much right as the other. The West German Lufthansa argues it has the sole right to the name, as it patented it. The East Germans do not accept this, but in West Germany one can be sued for referring in a publication to the East German Lufthansa.

I flew in a Soviet-designed partially East-German-built Ilyushin 14, a 26-passenger plane of the Hungarian state airlines. On the first 90-minute leg of the flight, to Prague, I sat by a West German professor of physiology, Pichotka, who had recently accepted a chair at the East Berlin Humboldt University, originally Berlin's only university. *[West Berlin's Free University was founded in 1948 after the Communists split the city administration.]* Until then he'd been at Freiburg University in southwest Germany.

He told me he was a Catholic and had not gone to Berlin for political reasons, but because the Humboldt University is an important centre for physiology. From what he told me, the job also offered him higher pay. He said he wanted to increase mutual understanding between East and West Germans. He was of the view, like me, that in their propaganda about each other both sides

136

exaggerate. He shared my opinion that at the moment it is up to the West German Government to do more to try to reach a compromise on the question of armaments in central Europe.

Shortly after we took off from Prague airport, the pretty Hungarian stewardess pointed out the Czechoslovak capital about 15 miles away. I spotted a castle on a hill and asked if it were the *Hradschin*, the traditional seat of government. It was. Later I was allowed in the pilot's cabin as we flew over southern Czechoslovakia. Soon we could see ahead of us the silver ribbon of the Danube, which turned grey-green (not blue!) as we passed over it; at this point it marked the Hungarian frontier. A few minutes later we could see the hills around Budapest.

It was fun trying to translate the Russian names of the plane's instruments. The pilot frowned on the aircraft's slow speed – about 200 miles an hour. He was obviously full of hope that he would one day be allowed to fly a jet. The purchasing power in Hungary of his wage amounted to about £13 a month; he said that was not very much.

At Budapest's imposing airport I was amused by an Austrian, of all people, complaining about the *Schlamperei* (sloppiness) of the Hungarians, because we had to wait about 20 minutes to start the entry formalities – normally it is Germans who complain about Austrian *Schlamperei*. An old airport bus – the Austrian complained about that too – phutted us the eight miles or so into the city. I was alternately intrigued and annoyed by the signs in Hungarian, which I can't understand except when they are words like *frisör* or *amatörfotokopie*. I saw a moderate amount of damage in the streets, partly dating from the war and partly from the abortive 1956 uprising.

We drove to the old but good hotel Duna (Danube), on the Pest (eastern) side of the river, facing the beautiful mainly wooded heights of Buda, dotted with the odd castle or palace and many villas, with styles mainly looking rather Italianate. Down by the river, with its several handsome bridges and the dignified impressive official buildings, mainly dating back to Austro-Hungary, there is more than an echo of London. The Danube here is about as wide as the Thames in London. It was a particular thrill for me to stay at the Duna, as it was here that my Reuter colleague, Ronnie Farquhar, sat it out during the revolt. Two hotel rooms were destroyed by gunfire but no one was hurt, as everyone had taken refuge in the cellar. Members of the hotel staff asked to be remembered to Ronnie, now based in Peking, when I wrote to him, as I did today from the hotel.

After tapping various sources, was able to send this evening only a rather thin story about Khrushchev making a Danube trip with the Hungarian leaders, and including a denial that he was to meet Tito in Hungary. Last time Khrushchev came here – in April last year, his first visit since the revolt – this was followed some weeks later by the announcement that Imre Nagy, the liberal Communist who became Prime Minister during the revolt, had been executed along with Pal Maleter, Nagy's Defence Minister. They had fallen into Russian hands after the revolt was suppressed by Soviet troops and tanks.

I think those executions were a great tragedy, though I can see that from the Communist point of view Nagy deserved to die, just as much as the Rosenbergs, the Americans who gave nuclear secrets to the Russians, deserved to die in the view of the United States Government. I personally don't think that any of these people should have been killed.

6 June 1959 : Was at the airport to see Khrushchev leave for Moscow. He was loudly clapped by a few hundred, after he'd shaken hands along a long line. I was behind the line, but he smiled at me, put out his hand and I shook it. I said, 'Good day' in Russian, probably not quite the right thing, but the first thing that came into my mind. I wonder whether he remembered me from Berlin or Leipzig. Later I wished I had asked Khrushchev to say something, but was afraid I would not understand his reply, which would have been more agonizing than not asking him anything. He waved and smiled from the top of the gangway before getting into the Tu-104 jetliner as the plane's designer, Andrei Tupolev, filmed from the tarmac with a cine-camera.

I found myself quite near Janos Kadar, the Hungarian Communist leader, an unassuming pale man who did not seem very cheerful. He declined to comment on the talks, but the Prime Minister, bespectacled, elderly Ferenc Muennich, said the visit, which had earlier been billed as a holiday for Khrushchev, had been spent in eating, drinking and chatting. I got my story away by dictating it in German to a Hungarian woman teleprinter operator in the Duna and she teleprinted it to our Vienna office, which has a leased line to London.

7 June 1959 : A Budapest taxi driver told me he didn't think much of his Soviet Moskvich car. Using broken German he told me that this, that and the other had had to be replaced. Then, with admiration causing his voice to throb, he repeated the magic words: 'Opel Kapitän, Opel Rekord, Mercedes Benz.'

Was told that ordinary Hungarians are discouraged from making contacts with Western foreigners, and sometimes visit them only at night. People I saw on the streets were poorly, if adequately, dressed – not by any means as well as in East Germany – and few of them looked cheerful. The economy is in a rather better state than at the time of the revolt in 1956, but, I hear, the atmosphere is not as optimistic as in East Germany.

On my direct flight back to Berlin I talked with an elderly East German engineer and inventor, Grosch, who had won a national prize for designing machine tools. He said he was a keen Protestant churchman and had refused to join the SED, telling the Communists they would get more out of him if they let him be. He added that he had 'regrettably' been a member of the Nazi party, but had refused to leave the Church at the behest of his local chairman, saying that one needed a God to pray to. He had once written to Prime Minister, Otto Grotewohl, explaining his Christian convictions, which had been respected.

8 June 1959 : Up at 05.00 to go to East Berlin's Schönefeld airport to report on the departure for Moscow of a top-level East German delegation, headed by Ulbricht and Grotewohl. In the

25-minute departure ceremony, the leaders first inspected a guard of honour, three companies and a band of the National People's Army, with uniforms similar to those of the Nazi-era *Wehrmacht*. Then there were handshakes along a line of party officials, with workers' delegations standing behind and ordinary sightseers looking on from the airport restaurant. The guard and band then goose-stepped past. I think this was the first time I'd seen the goose-step in the flesh; I don't believe the West German army does it. It brought back unpleasant memories of wartime newsreels.

In a send-off speech Dr Dieckmann, President of the *Volkskammer*, praised the delegation as the representatives of peace-loving Germany. He then referred to the big story which has been making the headlines in West Germany: Adenauer's surprise decision not, after all, to stand for the presidency, but to remain as Chancellor. Obviously the East German leaders would have preferred Adenauer to take the less powerful position of President. Dieckmann said that Adenauer had decided to remain Chancellor in order to maintain his 'policy of strength'. *[A major reason for Adenauer's change of mind was that he did not believe that his party's favourite to succeed him as Chancellor, Economics Minister Ludwig Erhard, was fitted for the post.]*

Two friendly detectives came round after I'd reported that my Volkswagen Beetle had been broken into and the spare wheel stolen. They told me how much they had enjoyed a recent British film about Scotland Yard; 'Somewhat pokey in there though,' one said. They tried to find fingerprints by dusting with a silvery powder. No luck. The last time I came to Berlin I had a couple of hubcaps stolen – in West Berlin.

9 June 1959 : After buying a new spare wheel in West Berlin, was able to obtain a tyre and tube in East Berlin. The mechanic who put on the tyre and tube said the East German tyres were not as elastic as the Western ones. I helped him to get it on.

I bet I could solve the Berlin problem nicely if I were a dictator. Both sides would have to climb down somewhat. Things are certainly stupid as they are.

10 June 1959 : After the American news agency, UPI, had reported that there were missile bases at three places in East Germany, the East German Foreign Ministry press department invited me to visit these places where, it claimed, there were no such missile bases. In response to this invitation, I told the head of the press department, Ambassador Heymann, I thought it unlikely Reuters would allow me to accept the invitation, as it would make it seem that we were contesting another agency's story, almost at the behest of the East German government.

I also pointed out that it is hardly possible for one reporter to find out whether in fact missiles are stationed in a certain area. To do that one needs a whole arms control system, as these weapons are mobile. Heymann saw my point, but added that East Germany was ready to accept an arms control system. Gerry told me to tell Heymann we were declining the invitation, since any story we put out would be purely a throwdown of a story which, anyway, we did not carry. (We had put out the official denial.)

An American correspondent in West Berlin told me he had met a British airline pilot who said his plane had been 'buzzed' by a Soviet air force jet some weeks ago and that he had a picture of the jet. He refused to sell the picture, because it showed:

1 a river indicating that his plane was about 16 miles out of the air corridor;
2 his girl friend (he is married) sitting in the cockpit – she had been piloting the aircraft and had put it off course; and
3 an easily recognizable window aperture typical only of the planes his firm operates.

Told by the correspondent he could have started the Third World War, he grinned and said, 'I know.' This seems to support the Soviet view that the Berlin situation must, in some way, be defused. But the West must insist that this is done without placing the West Berliners under the rule of a regime that most of them abhor.

11 June 1959 : Called on Georg Hansen, 56, deputy editor of *Neues Deutschland*, the SED party organ (a daily), a white-haired man with delicate features who displayed a sense of humour. He appeared to have much respect for Britain's political system and forecast that Britain would be the next country to go socialist.

[Hansen did not tell me that, according to his semi-official biography published in West Germany, he had been a Soviet spy in Britain in about 1933, was unmasked and was sentenced to nine years' hard labour, but was expelled to Russia in an exchange deal in 1941. He returned to Germany with the Soviet army in 1945 and became a leading SED journalist.]

Hansen told me it would be unwise to assume that the majority and, in particular, the majority of workers, were against the government as they had been some years ago. He argued that the workers were increasingly realizing that they were working for themselves and were seeing the fruits of this. He insisted that pressure was no longer being used to force people into collective farms or craftsmen's cooperatives. This had been the case two or three years ago when, in certain cases, a planned percentage for collectivization was laid down and people were forced accordingly. He said that method had been rejected as a 'left-wing deviation' and agreed with me that the former methods had caused production losses instead of increases.

Hansen claimed that people were increasingly realizing that collectivization was an economic necessity, and emphasized that workers were being encouraged more and more to take part in improving their own factories, instead of being bossed from above all the time. I think that is true and I'm that glad it is so, because it is an element of democracy – an element missing in most capitalist firms.

12 June 1959 : Intriguing to be living in a hotel mainly housing Russians, Chinese and other Communist countries' citizens, mostly members of delegations. I practise Russian with the night porter, who was born in Bartenstein, the nearest town to Schönbruch, Elfi's home village in East Prussia, but is the son of ethnic Germans who had lived in the Soviet Union. Another porter bought me a drink to celebrate the start of his holiday – the first time this has happened to me in a hotel. I reciprocated by giving him a large tip.

An absorbing 2¼-hour interview in the onetime Air Force Ministry building of Hermann Göring, along the border with West Berlin, now housing several East German ministries. I interviewed Slawik, chief press spokesman of the State Plan Commission, the supreme economic planning body. The Commission is headed by Bruno Leuschner, a Politburo member born in 1910. *[Leuschner, a shoemaker's son who became an office worker, joined the Communist Party before the Nazi era. Because of his anti-Nazi activity after Hitler came to power in 1933, he served sentences in prison and concentration camps between 1936 and 1945.]*

As in the Soviet Union, some industrial ministries were abolished last year. Their functions are now carried on partly by the Commission and partly by new bodies called Associations of State-owned Firms (VVB) – one association for each branch of industry, such as heavy engineering, light engineering, chemicals and so on – and partly by the economic committees of East Germany's 14 regional councils. When the industrial ministries were abolished, the regional councils were given increased economic powers, and local municipal councils were given such powers for the first time.

Slawik said the old system had caused dualism because, while the Commission had to produce the plan, the ministries had to carry it out. Now, in the most important sectors, planning and direction is in the hands of the Commission. Results had been positive. Last year's reorganization transferred about 600 factories from central to regional control, but the more important factories were still directed by the Commission through their VVBs – in particular, heavy industry. More than half consumer goods production is under decentralized direction.

East Germany, I was told, is now the fifth industrial power in Europe, after the Soviet Union, West Germany, Britain and France – measured on total production. East Germany's economy in 1945 was very unbalanced. For example, it had only 2.7 per cent of Germany's hard coal production, 1.6 per cent of its pig

143

iron and 6.6 per cent of its steel. But it had a strong chemical industry and produced 70 per cent of Germany's lignite, 60 per cent of its electrical equipment, 55.5 per cent of its textile machinery and 50 per cent of its machine tools, though it had only about two-fifths of Germany's total population.

In the early years after 1945 strong efforts were made to build up heavy industry. Now, thanks to increased economic coordination between Communist countries, they had realized it was cheaper, say, to let the Soviet Union produce most of the required iron and steel and ship this to East Germany, rather than shipping the ore. Under East Germany's seven-year plan, which started this year, it was planned to increase industrial production by nearly 90 per cent, Slawik told me. In 1958 industrial production had risen by 10.9 per cent. (Although the increase in West Germany has been between 3 and 4 per cent, the absolute production figure per worker is still much higher in West Germany.)

Supply of citrus fruits, which had been very poor, was improving. Lemons were now freely available and they were hoping to achieve that for other citrus fruits which, at present, were scarce, owing partly to shortage of foreign currency.

In the past, lack of coordination between Communist countries had resulted in much investment to build up, say, a factory making lathes, which then could not sell its lathes. But in the last three or four years coordination had been increasingly effective. Recommendations made by the Soviet-bloc Council for Mutual Economic Aid (known in the West as 'Comecon') set up in 1949, were without legal force, but were being increasingly regarded as binding.

The spokesman said that a more enthusiastic atmosphere in the workforce had enabled plans to be speeded up. There was 'a growing realization that the result of better work is direct or indirect benefit to the worker, either through increases in wages and bonuses, or cuts in prices, or through better cultural and social services'.

By 1950 production had reached the 1936 level, before Hitler's arms production had got into full swing. Under the first five-year

144

plan, between 1951 and 1955, industrial production had just about doubled. However, part of this increase had gone in reparations to the Soviet Union *[ended in 1953]*. When I said that this production increase had not been very apparent in living standards, the spokesman said that a lot of increased wealth had gone into social services and education, and into subsidies for the public services (such as transport), and for basic foods and rents, which were kept low. I would add that much money went to subsidize socialized agriculture which, in its early years, was largely uneconomic.

Slawik referred to East Germany's goal, mentioned by Ulbricht in his Rostock speech, of overtaking West Germany in the per head consumption of foods and important consumer goods by 1961. It had already done this in regard to butter, sugar, meat, vegetables, bread and potatoes, cameras and bicycles. It was about to overtake West Germany in motorcycle production – partly because West Germans are buying more cars. East Germany would not be able to overtake the large West German car industry by 1961, having neither the capacity nor the raw materials. The planned production increase between 1956 and 1960 was to have been 36 per cent, but would in fact be about 50 per cent.

Slawik said that, in the first five-year plan, the emphasis had been on heavy industry, including the iron and steel works of Stalinstadt *[later renamed Eisenhüttenstadt]*, the Lauchhammer cokery where, for the first time, coke suitable for smelting was being made from lignite, and heavy engineering. In the second five-year plan the emphasis had been on coal and power. In the current seven-year plan the emphasis was on the chemical industry, in order to produce consumer goods from plastics, artificial fibres and the like. (In this period a pipeline bringing oil from the Soviet Union is to be completed. More oil will come by sea to Rostock.)

Slawik said that in the planning process, targets were not just decided from above, but there was a lot of discussion, with plan proposals going back and forth. Sometimes there were 'heated discussions'. Planning had become much more exact than a few years ago, he added. When I referred to a recent case when a number of milk-tankers were made without having outlets, Slawik smiled and agreed that such things happened. But he added, 'There were many more mistakes a few years ago.' In the past, economic mistakes had sometimes been kept secret, but now they were publicized, so they could be publicly condemned and to show the plants concerned that they were hurting themselves by making such mistakes.

In East Berlin I saw a well-made West German film, *Das Mädchen Rosemarie* (*The Girl Rosemarie*), which is an incisive exposure of some aspects of the West German economic miracle, spotlighted in the career of a call girl, Rosemarie Nitribitt, who actually lived and whose murderer is still being sought. The film shows up some of the material excesses of West German society. The Bonn government tried *[unsuccessfully, I believe]* to stop its showing at the Cannes film festival, and I understand some cuts were made when the film was shown successfully in West Germany. It is, of course, a 'natural' for East German cinemas.

15 A fearsome parachute jump

13 June 1959 : Drove to Leipzig. Over lunch in the Ratskeller, a restaurant in the basement of the city hall, chatted with an East German man who'd been a prosperous importer and was now earning less in some other trade post. He said that people of his class had gone down in the world, which made it seem he was not exactly a supporter of the regime. However, he criticized Adenauer's decision to stay on as Chancellor and his unwillingness to negotiate.

At Markkleeberg, a small town south of Leipzig, I attended the opening of the seventh annual East German agricultural fair, quite an impressive event. I was put off by the loud voice and humourless manner of the Agriculture Minister, Hans Reichelt, who, however, gave some interesting figures. He said that in 1958 the collective farms – covering about 40 per cent of farmland – produced on average 18 'crop units' per hectare, compared with about 17 on private farms. (The actual weight of the crop is different for differing crops.) However, the private farms were sending 7.7 units per hectare to market while the collective farms were sending only 7.35 units, as they consumed more themselves. The shortfall of 0.35 units, of crops sent to market by the collectives, compared with a shortfall of 1.40 units in 1957. That shows that the collective farms, with their big fields and large degree of mechanization, are catching up on the small private farms. Large private farms were either nationalized – turned into state farms – or brought into the collectives earlier. It is planned that there shall be no more uneconomic collective farms by the end of this year.

With Lothar Sobczak of the West German news agency, DPA, I travelled some 20 miles eastwards to attend a workers' festival of music and drama in the industrial city of Halle.

14 June 1959 : After listening with Sobczak to a rather boring concert in a park, I saw East German soldiers doing an obstacle course, one of them wearing a radiation suit with gas mask. Soviet soldiers and their wives were enjoying a Sunday afternoon walk. Nearby was a 240-ft-high tower used for captive parachute jumps. After being told that 14,000 people aged between eight and sixty-seven had jumped from it without accident, I asked several khaki-uniformed young men, members of the Society for Sport and Technology, which provides pre-military training, if I could try it. I could.

While Sobczak stayed on the ground and grinned evilly, I was fitted with a parachute harness over my suit. I then climbed up the tower, step by step, stopping to get my breath occasionally and thinking how it would feel if something did not work properly. I consoled myself by thinking that one has to die sometime and then remembering that 14,000 had gone before me without mishap. One of the two lads acting as launchers at the top of the tower asked me if I was scared. I said, of course I was. He admitted that he, too, had been scared the first time. He said he was going to make his first jump from a plane soon, which gave me fresh courage.

The parachute, held open by a metal ring, was hoisted to the top of the tower by means of a wire fastened to the center of the parachute, and running over a crane pulley at the top of the tower. On the other end of the wire is a counterweight, which moves downwards inside the tower structure to pull up the parachute after each jump. When the parachute had reached the top again, after the previous jump, the two lads took hold of the shrouds and had me stand between them on the edge of the tower, between an inner railing, to which they were fastened with canvas belts, and an outer railing with a gate in it. They fastened the shrouds to my harness. The 20-ish, commanding woman who was in charge on the ground had told me that I should step off with my hands on my stomach as, in a real jump, there's nothing to hold onto until the parachute opens. I didn't like that idea at all, just stepping out into space not holding on to anything, so I asked if I could hold on to the strap connecting my harness to the parachute ropes. That was okay, they said.

The gate was opened and I stepped off. The first split second was the worst, as the slack on the ropes was taken up and the parachute was braked by the air filling it. Then it was pleasant, just hanging there and floating down quite slowly – 3 metres (10 ft) a second instead of 5 metres (16 ft) a second, as in a jump from a plane. I looked around a bit, really enjoying the view now, as I was no longer frightened. I looked down and saw Sobczak standing there, holding his notebook, probably still grinning. Soon I was down. The impact was like jumping off a wall, say 4 ft high. Just bent my knees like in gym at school, and did not fall over like the previous jumper. Someone in a queue waiting to have a go asked me how I'd felt. I said, fine, once I had got into the air.

Sobczak and I drove south from Halle to nearby Merseburg, passing the giant Buna (synthetic rubber) works formerly owned by I.G. Farben, the big Nazi-era combine. It is now state-owned – a good thing, I think, in this case. Slave workers from Eastern Europe and the Soviet Union suffered rotten conditions there during the war, just as they did at the neighbouring, and even bigger, Leuna chemical works, which also belonged to I.G. Farben. Leuna, now also state-owned, like all large plants in East Germany, was our destination. We attended a concert by chemical workers, trained partly by professionals, in which works by Goethe and Beethoven alternated with dances attacking West German nuclear armament and illustrating East Germany's seven-year-plan. Quite well done and some of it was even entertaining.

We were able to talk to Dr Wolfgang Schirmer, the 39-year-old director of the Leuna works, which has 30,000 employees, the largest number of any plant in East Germany. Schirmer is both a Communist and a man with industrial and scientific experience. He made a friendly impression and gave us lots of production figures from his head. He said Leuna intended almost to double its annual turnover by 1965, compared with 1958. To do this, it is making big investments to build a second plant to be sited nearby, to produce basic materials for plastics and artificial fibres. Schirmer gave us a good story: that Leuna executives leave on 18 June for Britain to negotiate with ICI on the very likely purchase of plant worth two or three million sterling.

15 June 1959 : A young woman student, to whom I gave a lift on my way back to Berlin, told me there were still traces of 'bourgeois ideology' in East German universities, particularly among some older professors who, for instance, did not want to join in what she called voluntary work on the land. They said their job was to be professors, which was hard enough. This woman laughed as she told how a lorry driver, who had earlier given her a lift, said that she could be honest with him, meaning that she could tell him frankly that she was going to Berlin, to flee from East Germany by way of West Berlin. In fact she was just going from one East German town to another during her holidays.

Did she believe all the Marxist–Leninist theory she had learned at university, I asked. 'Some of it,' she said. 'It's been proved.' She praised the government for doing a lot for the students financially. Some of her professors had gone West, she told me, one of them because his son failed to get into the equivalent of a grammar school in East Germany – often a cause for academics to go West in the past. It has meanwhile been made easier for the sons of such people to get higher education.

16 June 1959 : Made my first call on the Yugoslav embassy press attaché, ex-partisan Veselin Lazovic, smallish, tough looking, but humorous. He thinks things are getting better economically here, and that Khrushchev has made quite an improvement politically in the Communist bloc which, however, still exerts pressure on Yugoslavia because of its independent policy. He said that while the Communist Party remained the boss in Yugoslavia, it was seeking to work by means of persuasion. That was why it had left it to farmers to decide whether to continue in collectives or to dissolve them, and was helping them in other ways to increase production. He added, however, that it was desirable that more collectives should be formed, as big fields were an economic necessity in the long run. Yugoslavia should this year exceed the 1939 harvest, he said.

17 June 1959 : I had a happy, if quiet, 34th birthday. Cards had come from Elfi and the boys and other family members. And flowers, ordered by Elfi's two West Berlin aunts from the other side of the Iron Curtain, arrived early. This tipped off the hotel staff, who congratulated me and shook hands. I responded by buying several of them drinks – coffee, beer, cognac or apple juice – with ice cream for the pages, cheerful helpful lads. Later I was surprised with roses by the hotel manager, Leo Heim, and his protocol chief, a younger man who particularly looks after the needs of the many foreigners who stay here.

Had hoped to have colleagues over from West Berlin for a meal this evening but, as my birthday falls on the anniversary of the abortive East German uprising of 1953, which was easily crushed by Soviet troops and tanks, they were busy covering a function held in West Berlin in memory of the uprising. By chance, late tonight, I came across an elderly social insurance official and Communist, whose birthday also falls today. He was celebrating it with his wife and three friends in my hotel. We had a two–hour discussion of the political situation, which we broke off at 01.30.

I had spent much of my birthday morning in the headquarters of the SED Central Committee, whose inner Politburo is the top ruling body of this country, superior to the government. The SED headquarters is housed in a large severe-looking Nazi-era building which, until 1945, was the Reichsbank, the German central bank, where Dr Hjalmar Schacht, the Reichsbank President, laid the financial basis for German rearmament from 1933 until 1939, when he broke with Hitler.

I went there to make my first call on Horst Sindermann, my most important official contact, head of the Central Committee department concerned with press and propaganda. Sindermann, who has a friendly manner, was pushed into journalism in 1945 on the ground that his father, a Social Democrat, had been a journalist. He has edited two regional SED newspapers and is generally regarded as being an able journalist, out to brighten up East Germany's mainly stodgy press.

[Sindermann, born in 1915, was arrested by the Nazis as a young Communist and spent most of the Nazi era in prisons and concentration camps. He became a major political figure in the era of Erich Honecker, who succeeded Ulbricht as SED chief in 1971. From 1971 to 1973 Sindermann was a deputy Prime Minister, and was Prime Minister from 1973 to 1976. He was then demoted to be President of the rubber-stamp parliament, the Volkskammer, *a post he held until the regime collapsed in 1989. He died in 1990.]*

Sindermann told me his department's job was to instruct, encourage and improve the SED newspapers throughout the country. He said he did not give orders to the newspapers of the other parties in the Communist-led National Front, but had good contacts with them. (The other newspapers all follow the basic Communist line with certain special emphases for their intended readership – such as the Christians, the middle class and so on.)

As today was the anniversary of the 1953 rising, I asked Sindermann to tell me how he thought things had changed in East Germany since then. He said that in 1953 East Germany was concentrating on building up heavy industry, leaving few resources for other things, and was also continuing to pay reparations to the Soviet Union, which he thought was justified. He said that the uprising was caused by economic discontent, intensified by Western propaganda. (An increase in working norms without an increase in wages was the immediate cause.) He recalled arguing with discontented chemical workers in the Leuna area at the time of the uprising, and said these same workers now had a much different attitude, because they could see what had been achieved in the meantime. He added that the campaign to encourage workers' initiatives in industry was showing such great results that the difficulty was to turn the many suggestions made into practice without unbalancing the state plan or running short of capital.

I complained to Sindermann about the poor quality of an East German razor-blade I'd bought and which did not give me a decent shave even on the first day. I had to use a four-day-old Gillette blade to finish my shave. He said they were working on such shortcomings, and told me with a smile that he had bought 40 packets of razor-blades in Austria.

When I mentioned the razor-blade problem to another East German, he said he bought West German ones 'under the counter' in an East Berlin shop. However, I understand from the hotel barber that there is a reasonable East German razor-blade on the market. I shall try to track some down.

Was told at a big store that they had only 1958 tennis balls in stock, which did not bounce well. They did not know when the 1959 ones were coming in. Such shortages are typical. Most basics are available at prices becoming increasingly reasonable, but there are shortages of this, that and the other from time to time. Sometimes improvements in income cause shortages: if people have more money they try to buy more tennis rackets, which makes them scarce, even if more are being produced. An official at my tennis club, where I played tonight, called me '*Der Sportfreund Johnson*'. *Sportfreund* may be translated as 'sports-man' or 'player' – it is an East German term.

18 June 1959 : Called on Wang Ping, Chinese embassy first secretary who deals with press matters. Drank three cups of aromatic weak (thank goodness) Chinese tea as we talked near several beautiful painted screens – the most tasteful embassy waiting-room I've come across here. We argued about whether Marxism explains everything and Mr Wang finally agreed that it could not explain where the universe came from, or why. But he asked whether this was a reason for believing in God. I said it was not, but added that the Marxists could not disprove God's existence. This Chinese diplomat said an East German bishop had told him that he (Wang) could not live without God, but Wang said he was managing to do so.

Wang, aged about 40, has a friendly face, greying hair and a typical polite Oriental smile. I liked him, and also the young cultural secretary, Wang Hsing Yang, who translated my English for the press secretary, who knows only a little. We also argued about the June 1953 uprising, I maintaining it was caused mainly by widespread dissatisfaction with the regime, even among socialists, and he claiming it was something whipped up by the Americans.

Played tennis with an elderly master plumber, who remains self-employed. He told me he was under no pressure to join a craftsmen's collective, but was, of course, subject to persuasion. He wants to stay on his own. His work is mainly repairs and I do not see how it would be more efficient if he joined with others, for they would then have to employ office staff and each plumber might not work as well as the others. This would cause trouble if total earnings fell, through the slackness of one or another.

19 June 1959 : Attended the press view of an exhibition put on by the Ministry of State Security depicting espionage and sabotage allegedly being carried out in East Germany by organizations from the West. Asked an officer who showed us round whether the Communist countries weren't spying against the West. He said he had no knowledge of any such thing. Told him this seemed incredible to me. When I asked what sabotage was being carried on against East Germany, he said there had recently been the firing of crops instigated by Western organizations.

I know from other sources that sabotage had been carried on against East Germany for some years, but had thought it had been given up, now that most people, even on the extreme right, realize that one cannot subvert the East German state by that kind of tactic. I think sabotage is a crime but to continue with it is not only a crime, it is stupid.

20 June 1959 : I was the only non-Communist at a party held by Belgian Communist journalist, Martin Thijs, in his flat, once the home of a doctor who went West. We talked much politics and culture, and in the end I had them playing English party games.

An old pro-Communist historian, Gabriel Bruegel, one of the guests, described Rosa Luxemburg, an early German Communist leader who was murdered by right-wingers in 1919, as a 'regal' person, who had made a great impression on him. That right-wingers in Germany could murder a Communist shows how different political conditions were here in 1919 compared with those in Britain.

[After German reunification in 1990, I noticed that a metal street sign on a wall in the Rosa-Luxemburg-Strasse in Magdeburg was hanging on by but one nail – probably due to neglect rather than for a political reason. I managed to appropriate it, and it now has a place of honour in our home. The name of that Magdeburg street has not been changed.]

16 Klaus Fuchs, friendly atom spy

21 June 1959 : I interviewed the East German Foreign Minister, Dr Lothar Bolz, on his return from the Geneva foreign ministers' conference, which has adjourned for a while. He blamed West Germany in the main for trying to make the conference fail. I agree. West Germany is determined not to give diplomatic recognition to the East German state. It still hopes that, in some undefined way, as West German strength grows through nuclear armament, the East German regime will collapse or the Russians will grant reunification on Western terms. This, I think, is nonsense.

The conference has brought some progress on Berlin. The Russians have agreed not to hand over their control powers for an interim period, while the West has expressed readiness to accept the East Germans as controllers on the access routes, depicting them as agents of the Russians. Further, the West has agreed not to equip its soldiers in West Berlin with nuclear arms, not to increase its forces in the city, or even to reduce them, and to go into the question of mutual espionage. Most important, I think, has been the comparative absence of polemic and bitterness in the conference.

I think it is time the West took up the Communist proposals for a thinned-out military zone in central Europe, something which should be of value to both sides if accompanied by an arms control system – to which the East has agreed. Up to now Adenauer has blocked those proposals, because they would mean the end of nuclear armament – and first-class power status – for West Germany.

While waiting for Bolz, I came across Sindermann and asked him if, should East Germany become as strong economically as West Germany, the travel restrictions imposed by East Germany – particularly on its own citizens – would be dropped. He replied that the restrictions were not imposed for economic reasons (that is, to prevent a drain of population to the West), but were part of the efforts of the East German government to have its sovereignty recognized.

I suppose this implies that if East Germany obtains diplomatic recognition from the West it will drop some of the restrictions. I told Sindermann I did not think it was doing the East German authorities any good to stop old ladies from visiting their children in the West because one or other member of the family had fled to the West at some stage. An East German woman I know, who is married to a Communist, had two requests to be allowed to visit relatives in West Germany turned down. Only when her Communist husband – evidently more trusted by the authorities – put in a request for both of them to go was permission granted. Sindermann asked me how I thought things would have developed had Britain been split like Germany. I did not have time to answer, but he has a point. It is not easy when your country has been split between two world systems, neither of which is prepared to let go.

Sat squinting in hot sunshine to report a Portugal–GDR football international, which East Germany lost 2–0. The Portuguese, some of them black, rang rings round the Germans. The away team stayed in my hotel and I heard from some of the staff that they were also trying to play games with the chambermaids and lift girls. But here, I was told, the German defence was firm and the Portuguese lost.

An example of what can still happen in divided Berlin was given to me by a father and son working as heating engineers. The father, who owns the small private firm, lives in East Berlin. The son lives in West Berlin and comes across to work in East Berlin, having a special pass and being paid part in East marks and part in West marks. The East Germans have offered him a lucrative job as a flying instructor, for which he has the necessary qualifications. He is not keen. He told me he feared there might be war between the two Germanys. I replied that in that case it would not matter much to any of us which side we were on.

Another craftsman, who installs tiled stoves, lives in East Berlin and employs four men – the largest number allowed for the lowest business tax bracket. If the firm employs more, taxes on it rise steeply, unless it is state-owned. This man said he was content with the way things were improving and because of the prospects of continual improvement.

23 June 1959 : I had learned that the world-famous 'atom spy', German-born Dr Klaus Fuchs, who had served nine years in prison in Britain for passing nuclear secrets to the Soviet Union, was expected to fly to East Berlin today after his release from Wakefield prison in Yorkshire.

[Fuchs, a Communist born in 1911, was a brilliant physicist. He emigrated from Nazi Germany to Britain in 1933 and became a British citizen in 1942. From 1943 to 1945 he worked in the United States on the top-secret project to produce atom bombs. In 1946 he became head of the theoretical physics division at the British nuclear research centre, Harwell. It was evidently while he was in that post that he supplied the Russians with plans for the uranium and plutonium bombs.]

I expected Fuchs to go first to his father, Professor Emil Fuchs, a Quaker and socialist, who is a theology professor at Leipzig University. But I did not know where Emil Fuchs lived. I'd been told that he had booked in at an East Berlin hotel, but that turned out to be false. After various inquiries, someone gave me the address of Professor Fuchs' weekend house at Wandlitz, a lakeside village and tourist spot just north of East Berlin, some 20 miles from the centre of Berlin.

I drove up there and managed to have a quick look at the rambling wooden house behind a fading green fence in the Karl Marx Strasse. I did not go in, partly because I did not want to bother the old professor at this stage and partly because I'd learned by phone from my hotel that Klaus Fuchs was due at Schönefeld airport, about 20 miles south of central Berlin in about two hours' time. It was a rush to drive south through Berlin, picking up, at my hotel, money and frantic messages from our Bonn office – telling me to get out to Schönefeld quickly. Made it to the airport two minutes before the plane was due to land, but found – what a relief – that it was about 25 minutes late.

The main body of Western reporters, about 15 when I drove by, were standing frustrated at the checkpoint on the Berlin boundary about three miles from Schönefeld. At the airport were only Phyllis Rosner, East Germany correspondent of the London Communist paper, *Daily Worker*, who like me can travel freely around East Germany, and an unidentified Belgian man carrying a camera. Orders had been issued to keep us off the tarmac.

As Fuchs got out of the plane, the Belgian managed to slip through the police cordon. Phyllis tried the same, but failed. I had gone to an office on the first floor, from where I saw Fuchs walk a few yards from the plane to a big black Russian-built limousine, as three or four photographers took pictures: one, I think, from the East German agency, ADN, and others who had come in the plane from London. I dashed to a teleprinter in a neighbouring room, which I'd already had connected with our Bonn office, rattled out a couple of paragraphs and then rushed back to my car to pursue the black limousine as it left the airport. Phyllis did the same in an old East Berlin taxi which, however, dropped out after a few hundred yards, while I just managed to keep the limousine in sight, doing between 50 and 60 mph.

After a drive of about ten minutes, the limousine was stopped at a level crossing. Ahead of the limousine was a grey car, containing a driver and a khaki-uniformed officer of the frontier police, which had led the way from the airport. I asked the officer if I could speak to Fuchs. He said, 'Not yet,' Fuchs had to go through the formalities first. I continued the chase, but when the limousine entered East Berlin through a checkpoint – not the one where the Western reporters were waiting – I had to show papers, so lost the limousine.

I drove into Berlin, sent my story on the Reuter teleprinter, which only started operating today in my hotel telephone exchange, then drove out to Wandlitz again. It was nearly ten at night as I reached the house. An elderly woman in the garden, who said she was a friend of the family, asked what I wanted. I asked if I could see Dr Fuchs. (I did not know whether he was there.) She said, 'Sorry, no.' He was asleep. I said I'd come back tomorrow. She laughed when I told her I bet I was more tired than Fuchs after pursuing him all day.

24 June 1959 : After about six hours' sleep, to Wandlitz again, for 08.00. When I rang the bell fixed on a metal letterbox by the gate, the woman I had spoken to yesterday came out in her dressing-gown and told me that Fuchs was still asleep. But shortly after-wards he came out, still wearing the brown suit and light-coloured striped shirt in which he was released from Wakefield prison yesterday – a few miles from my hometown, Bradford.

Fuchs is of medium height, slight build, partially bald with some thin grey hair. His face looked pale and he had not yet shaved, but he did not look drawn or bitter, rather ascetic and tranquil. His features are delicate, with smallish brown eyes and a rather precise mouth, but with a pleasant, perhaps rather shy, smile, which somehow reminded me of the oriental smile of Mr Wang of the Chinese embassy. He was wearing the steel–rimmed spectacles which had made his face famous at the time of his trial nine years ago.

Fuchs was stated (I think at the trial) to have passed the nuclear weapons' secrets to the Russians for idealistic reasons – mainly, I believe, because he thought it dangerous that the West should have the atomic bomb and the Soviet Union should not.

He came to the gate and apologized for not opening it as, he said, he had no key. I told Fuchs there was terrific interest in Britain in anything he wished to say. He replied that he had had discouraging experiences with the press, but that yesterday in the plane he had got on quite well with the men from the London papers who travelled with him and had agreed to answer them

160

two questions. They had asked if he felt any resentment against Britain and he told them he did not. He had also said he was happy to be in the German Democratic Republic and could not say yet what kind of job he would take.

At first he did not want to say more than this to me either, but as we talked he opened up a little. All the time he was polite, quiet-spoken and friendly, smiling many times. In answer to a question, he said he intended to become an East German citizen. When I asked him if he remained a Marxist, he first replied by saying I could draw my own conclusions from the fact that he had come here to 'build up the new society'. Questioned further, he said, 'I am a Marxist.'

At one stage in our interview, I told him I wanted to say something to him 'off the record'. I said that, though I am not a Communist, I had sympathized with his reported motives. He seemed pleased to hear this. We spoke in English, he with a slight German accent. As we talked, his 85-year-old father appeared, in dressing-gown, at a window. When Fuchs said it was time for him to get ready for breakfast, I asked if I could ask one final question. He agreed. I said, 'Why did you pass the atomic secrets to Russia?' He said with a slight smile that he did not wish to say anything more about that. We shook hands.

By shortly after 09.00, I was sending the story from my teleprinter in the hotel. I knew my story had every chance of being exclusive and it turned out to be so. I think it made the splash in the two London evenings, the *Evening Standard* and the *Star*. After the lack of sleep and the dashing around – I drove 125 miles yesterday, almost all inside Berlin – I was fagged out.

Was called in this evening to see Kurt Blecha, head of the East German government press office. Blecha offered me the first chance for any Western journalist to visit a unit of the East German 'National People's Army', which I was pleased to accept. He also offered me an interview with the Defence Minister, Willi Stoph, a veteran of the Spanish Civil War: another 'first', which I did not accept. I told Blecha this was against Reuter practice. We do not interview politicians when we could appear to be merely acting as their mouthpieces for something they want to put over, rather than being a news agency issuing what we consider to be news.

Dashed from Blecha's office, opposite the ruins of Hitler's bunker, to drive to East Berlin's main station, the *Ostbahnhof*, where a few minutes later my family rolled in joyously to spend a holiday with me. Elfi assured me that Robin and Chris had been washed about five times on the 420-mile train journey from Bonn, but they looked like filthy imps to me.

Although the East German frontier check had been friendly, an official on the train had confiscated several Western magazines, which Elfi had placed on the rack. These included a pleasant West German children's publication, *Rasselbande (Gang of little Rascals)*. How stupid can the authorities get? Even if they want to keep 'bad' Western literature from their population – just as the West German authorities try to do with Communist-inspired publications – they ought to have enough sense to leave out the trains, if only for cosmetic reasons. Robin nearly cried when his magazine was taken away, but Elfi promised to get him another in West Berlin. The boys noticed there were far more police about in East Berlin than in Bonn. That applies to West Berlin too, but to a lesser degree.

25 June 1959 : Called on Klaus Fuchs and his father again today and found them lunching outside. Gave Fuchs a print of a picture I had taken of him yesterday, with his permission, and which was put out by the Press Association-Reuter photo service. Also gave him a copy of *The Times*, with an item describing his departure from Britain. Fuchs invited me to join them at the table for dessert, strained apple purée. Told him I wanted to do another story today, to say what he was doing, and he agreed.

Fuchs' father, Emil, greying and moustached, was, I understand, the first Protestant pastor to join the Social Democratic Party after the First World War. He tries hard to claim that Christianity and Marxism do not have to be antagonistic. He's now a Quaker, of whom there are only about 50 in East Germany.

He said the Quakers, unlike some other religious organizations which had fled West, had retained their original office and meeting-place in East Berlin after the city split. This had paid off. He said their relations with the State were good, because they were always open about their views and did not indulge in plots. I told them I had thought of becoming a Quaker myself.

Had been told by a colleague – had not seen it myself – that at the airport Fuchs had been met, among other people, by a woman. I asked Klaus Fuchs if this was true. He said, off the record, that it was. It was a Frau Keilson, with whom he had worked in the Communist underground as Hitler came to power. She now has some kind of official position here.

26 June 1959 : Chris, six, who is beginning to recognize individual letters as well as words now, notices the big 'H' and 'D' in lavatory signs saying *Herren und Damen*. When he sees the 'H' he says, *'Hase'* (hare), which is the word starting with 'H' which he knows best. For 'D', he says, *'Dora'*.

Fuchs gave me another beat today when I called on him; he told me he had now received East German citizenship.

27 June 1959 : Have found an East German razor-blade with which I can get a decent shave. It lasts me, though, only for a couple of days at the most. Still, an advance, and I have not had to resort to buying foreign ones, like some Communists I know. *[An obvious jibe at Sindermann. I had no doubt that he could have access to my diary, thanks to the State Security Service.]*

The family came with me to the Baltic port of Rostock, where I am covering the 'Baltic Sea Week', organized by the East German regime to popularize the idea of neutralizing the Baltic. At the opening meeting, Ulbricht argued that the Social Democrats ruling some of the countries around the Baltic should have more in common with the SED leaders in East Germany, with whom they had fought against the Nazis, than with the 'Hitler Generals', etc., who are back in power in West Germany. He invited Norway's Prime Minister, Gerhardsen, who was in a

Nazi concentration camp, and others who had suffered in such camps, to come and see East Germany for themselves. Later Ulbricht, unusually, gave a press conference, attended by about 220 journalists, mainly East Germans and Scandinavians. He did it quite well, with many a dash of humour. I understand he has much more confidence for that kind of thing these days than he had a few years ago.

28 June 1959 : On our way back to Berlin we came near an air-field at Ribnitz where Elfi, as a civilian cashier, was briefly stationed in 1945 with a *Luftwaffe* rear unit, fleeing from East Prussia just ahead of the Russians. As the unit's lorries were full, she sat at times on the mudguard of one of them. She recognized a bridge which, she was told as her unit passed through, was about to be blown up.

29 June 1959 : Elfi alternates between telling me I've been 'indoctrinated' during my stay here, and realizing that East Germany is not as bad as it is depicted in Western newspapers.

17 Inspecting the East German army

30 June 1959 : The East German Foreign Ministry gave me details about an East German Note protesting to the Western allies about the holding in West Berlin tomorrow of the West German presidential election. East Germany regards this event as a provocation, because West Berlin, though closely linked to West Germany, is not a constituent part of it. I had a good beat on this story.

[The West German President was elected by the Federal Convention, a body convened only for that purpose. It comprised the members of the Bundestag (Lower House) and an equal number of members elected by the state parliaments. The new President, elected on 1 July, was Dr Heinrich Lübke, a Christian Democrat, formerly the Agriculture Minister. He succeeded Professor Theodor Heuss, a Free Democrat, who had held the office since 1949. The President, whose duties are mainly representational, holds office for five years and may be re-elected once.]

1 July 1959 : To Hermann Göring's onetime Air Ministry building, near the border with West Berlin, to report a meeting of the National Council of the Communist-led National Front of political parties and mass organizations. This always follows a broadly Communist line, with some concessions on detail to the various parties representing such people as private farmers, small capitalists, craftsmen and the Christian community. The meeting, this morning, was obviously held to coincide with the presidential election in West Berlin, which began an hour later. About 500

165

persons present included, according to a spokesman, about 140 West Berliners and West Germans.

The main speaker, Dr Lothar Bolz, the Foreign Minister, asked what value could be placed on the words of the Western Powers who, at the Geneva foreign ministers' conference, had stated that West Berlin was not part of West Germany. In spite of that, the West German presidential election was being held there. He attacked that step as being part of West Germany's irredentist and cold war policy. I think he is wrong there, for in fact it was Eugen Gerstenmaier, Speaker of the *Bundestag* and a moderate Christian Democrat, who pressed for the election to be held in West Berlin, as at the last election in 1954, when Heuss was re-elected. I am sure Gerstenmaier did not want to provoke, but did not want to retreat in the face of Communist moves directed at altering the status of Berlin.

2 July 1959 : Today I became the first Western reporter to be taken round a unit of the East German National People's Army. Two majors in uniform, an official of the Government press office and an ADN photographer, who said he'd been told I'd requested him – I hadn't – drove with me in two badly-sprung *Sachsenring* (formerly *Horch*) limousines, East Germany's most luxurious home-produced car, which is going out of production soon as part of the Communist countries' specialization programmes. (East Germany will concentrate on smaller cars.) We drove to Stahnsdorf, near Potsdam, to the former Hitler-era barracks, now housing the 2nd Motorized Infantry Regiment.

Each barrack block bears a stone relief showing one of the types of helmets used in German military history. They have not added one of the present East German type, which is Soviet-style. They have retained the memorial stone to a few soldiers of one of Hitler's reconnaissance units who were killed in the 1939 invasion of Czechoslovakia and are buried beneath the memorial.

I was received at the entrance of one of the four-storey barracks by the regiment's commanding officer, Major Karl Firla, bald, cheerful and 30 years old, wearing his *Wehrmacht*-style uniform which, I was told, is not the old field grey, but is called stone grey. He took me to an office upstairs, where about 15 officers were waiting. I shook hands with some, and the others took their seats at a table. Their faces had none of the traditional arrogance of the Prussian officer, nor did they talk in the clipped style affected by such. In fact, they looked like an average, decent lot. Most of them appeared to be in their thirties.

I started by interviewing Firla. At first he was secretive about numbers, but then told me there were about 1,000 men in the regiment. Firla, born near Magdeburg, East Germany, said he had left school at 14 and become an apprentice mechanic. As a 16-year-old he had been conscripted to help defend Berlin from the advancing Russians. On 20 April 1945, on the advice of older men, he had deserted and joined his parents, farm labourers, in their village near Magdeburg. When, after the war, a large estate was nationalized and split up among 'new farmers', he was given 7 hectares (about 17 acres). He went on, 'It was the first time that the workers themselves had ruled, and it became clear to us young people who were in the Free German Youth that we must protect our state.' He had therefore joined the frontier police in May 1949, and was taken over into the army after its formation in 1956. That had been a matter of course for him.

Firla said that none of the soldiers under the rank of sergeant in the regiment had served in the old *Wehrmacht*. Only 1.5 per cent of the officers and NCOs had served in the *Wehrmacht* for more than a few weeks; that 1.5 per cent amounted to two officers and two NCOs. I was told that both these officers had realized during the war that they were 'fighting on the wrong side' and – evidently as prisoners of war – had joined the Communist-run National Committee for a Free Germany.

Major Horst Franke, 31-year-old 'political worker' – this sounded like a new word for political commissar – said, 'Our army is an army of workers and farmers. The commanding officer has to educate the soldiers, NCOs and officers so that they represent the interests of the working class, the working farmers and progressive democratic forces. Therefore the commander cannot just stand still and give orders, but must give the reason for them, and tell the servicemen in whose interests they are standing to attention.'

Outside on a parade ground, I was shown 23 members of a 120-millimetre battery, in grey fatigues and jackboots, doing drill, armed with sub-machine-guns. The commands, I was told, differed little from those in the *Wehrmacht*. The men, all volunteers, serve initially for two years, but about half of them volunteer for a further two years. Their pay after deductions is 264 marks (£23) a month.

When I disingenuously asked if the sub-machine-guns were German, Firla said, 'Only sporting rifles are produced here. These are weapons from our friends – Soviet weapons.' In addressing each other the soldiers use the word 'comrade' before the rank, for instance, 'Comrade Lieutenant'.

I asked Firla if there was any of the traditional *Wehrmacht* (or British Army) chicanery by superiors in the National People's Army. He replied, 'There can be no chicanery in our army because there is open discussion. A soldier has the right to say, after duty, to his NCO, "I want to have a discussion with you." If his NCO does not listen to him he can go to his platoon commander (usually a second lieutenant) and talk to him.' A soldier had the right to take a grievance right up the hierarchy to the Defence Minister.

Major Karl Koegler, the 29-year-old SED secretary of the regiment, interposed to say that the soldier had the right, if he got no satisfaction through military channels, to take up matters through social organizations such as the SED or the Free German Youth. Another officer put in, 'He has the duty to do so. The party would reprove him if he did not.'

The squad which had been drilled marched off singing. The song, I was told, had been struck up in response to an order. On long marches the men were allowed to sing when they wanted, but in barracks they had to wait for orders. An officer told me that the song was about the soldiers being on guard for peace and carrying out the orders of the working class.

From the parade ground we went to a 'recreation room'. On a wall, as well as photographs of East German leaders, there were pictures of industrial progress, with the caption: 'Our progress in socialist construction. Socialism is winning. We defend its victorious march forward, under the leadership of the SED, by increasing the fighting readiness of our battalion.' There was a pictorial map illustrating the armies of other Communist countries, with the caption: 'Socialism has good soldiers.'

Also on the wall was a framed text about the life of a Communist worker, Arthur Ladwig, who organized an anti-Nazi resistance group in a Daimler–Benz factory during the Nazi era, and was executed. The battalion I was visiting bears his name. It has a link with a state-owned plant at Ludwigsfelde, near Berlin, which makes jet engines for East Germany's airliner, now undergoing tests, as well as motor scooters. The text ended: 'Let us learn from the struggle of the simple worker, Arthur Ladwig, and his comrades.' As part of the official practice, under which officers have to do a period of manual work, some officers from the battalion had worked in the Ludwigsfelde factory for several months. Koegler commented, 'In the first two months it was too hard for them, but in the third, fourth and fifth months they overfulfilled their norms.'

Another framed text on the wall was the oath of the National People's Army: 'I swear always to serve faithfully my fatherland, the German Democratic Republic, to protect it against all enemies, on the order of the workers' and farmers' government, by staking my life; to give unconditional obedience to my military superior and to maintain always and everywhere the honour of our republic and its National People's Army.' A photomontage on the wall showed soldiers carrying out the 'Ten Commandments of Socialist Morals', which were outlined in a party decision a year or two ago. On one wall there was an oil painting of *Sanssouci*, Frederick the Great's palace at Potsdam. That was virtually the only link with the previous German military tradition in the room.

In corridors and barrack rooms I saw, here and there, red banners or placards with the usual slogans. I was shown a bedroom with about eight bunks in two tiers, each with a flock mattress, two sheets and two blankets. Each man also had a stool and a cupboard. No pictures on the walls, but an officer said they were allowed to fix photos of their loved ones there, though pin-ups were 'frowned upon'. I raised a laugh by saying that in the British army the walls of barrack bedrooms were often covered with pin-ups, usually nude. As we moved from one barrack block to another it was raining, so I was given a khaki cape to fling over my shoulders. Behind me came the 15 or so officers in stone grey. I felt like Napoleon. In an attic room I was shown a model of countryside on which a model Soviet T-34 tank could be moved by a man sitting in a replica tank cockpit, connected to the model tank by a wire. The device, they told me, had been built by a sergeant in his spare time.

When I asked whether East German soldiers got drunk, Firla replied diplomatically, 'That does not happen often.'

We sat down to lunch in an officers' mess – officers and men eat separately. I sat at the head of the table with Firla on my left and Major Heinz Japp, one of the two Defence Ministry officers who had accompanied me, on my right. Firla started things off with a toast in cognac. We drank wine, beer and coffee, with a good solid meal. I asked whether they always drank so much. No, only when guests were around.

I made some quip about letting my sons join the National People's Army, which prompted Japp to say, 'We are learning the art of war only to ensure peace. All education in the People's Army is directed towards friendship between peoples, not only the peoples of the socialist camp. You will hear from the soldiers that they recognize the achievements of the British people.' He went on to attack 'certain forces' in West Germany which, he claimed, had 'not learnt from history'.

Major Alfred Palmer, the regiment's deputy 'political worker', who was born in East Prussia, joined in the table talk, so I asked him how he knew that the East German army would always be used for peaceful or just purposes. He replied, 'The main point is that, at the head of our government, are workers' sons, who have struggled, politically, for years and in whom I trust.' He added that another reason was that the SED was a Marxist party, directing historical forces.

The other officer from the Defence Ministry, Major Franke, joined in, 'In the GDR the working class, the working farmers and the progressive democratic forces made the army. In the Bonn Federal Republic that army is composed of Herr Adenauer's truly devoted servants who served Hitler's dirty goals. Which class is interested in war? The working class can only lose something in war – life, health and family. Therefore the working class is not interested in war because it wants to live well, to eat well, wants all modern equipment, TV and so on, and if possible to have a car.' Such things could be achieved only in peace.

Who wanted war? Krupp, Stinnes [industrialists] and Pferdmenges [a banker and adviser of Adenauer]. He claimed that most West German army officers were 'incorrigible fascists', while many of the East German army's senior officers had fought for the republic in the Spanish Civil War. I contested this viewpoint, saying that I did not think that a man who had fought as an officer in the Hitler era was necessarily a fascist. I also said that only a madman, whether he was a capitalist or not, would think he could come through a new war unscathed. I think I made some impression with that.

I spoke about the dictatorial power achieved by Stalin in his later years and I argued that had Stalin ordered them to attack, they would have obeyed. No one disputed this, but they replied that Stalin would not have done such a thing, as he remained a Marxist, even though he had infringed Marxist principles in certain respects. If Stalin had issued an order to attack, it would have met resistance among his colleagues, they claimed. However, they agreed that the leaders around Stalin had been afraid to interfere with his orders.

Several officers referred to an alleged NATO plan to attack East Germany, but I asked how could one know if that was genuine. Japp argued that, like Hitler before the Second World War, the West Germans were saying they did not want to attack, but were doing everything to be ready to attack. He referred to irredentist meetings in West Germany and to some senior officers of the West German forces who, he said, had been condemned as war criminals by all the four wartime Big Powers at the Nuremberg trials. 'Their profession is to make war,' he said. The East German army, which had no atomic weapons, could put its cards on the table with a clear conscience, he added.

A Major Ziem mentioned the practice under which officers worked in factories when they had not done manual work for a long time. He said it was 'so that we do not lose our links with the working class'. If officers did not go into industry, they served instead in the ranks of their own unit for a month each year. Japp commented, 'It is intended that they see how their orders work out in practice. This is only possible where there are no class differences in the forces, where the soldier and officer represent the same interests.'

After the meal I interviewed Private Ernst Huebner, aged 20, a member of the SED and the Free German Youth, who was born in the now-Czechoslovak Sudetenland. None of his relatives were in the SED, he said. He had been an apprentice in a ventilator factory, but had decided to join the army to help in the protection of the republic. Only one out of 25 men in his platoon wanted to do long-term service in the army, he said. Huebner said his platoon had two political classes weekly, each of two hours. There were also discussion groups at company level, usually led by an officer or NCO. If someone was ideologically out of step, the leader of the group or his comrades tried to talk him round, not by giving orders.

Huebner said there were, in addition, many SED and Free German Youth meetings at which soldiers were called upon to express their grievances openly 'from comrade to comrade'. He instanced an occasion when they were ordered, while marching after a long hot day, to sing, and the singing didn't work out. They were then ordered to do the goosestep. The orders had to be carried out, but afterwards they had told their platoon commander he had done wrong. 'Either we must be convinced that our view is partly unjustified, or the platoon commander must admit his mistake. In this way friction is removed. Going round with a pent-up grievance rarely happens.' I asked what happened to the type who was always complaining. 'We defend our officer and ask the soldier if he could do things better.'

Huebner said they came to meet girls through friendship meetings with schools, and individually. An officer put in, 'Love is written large with us too. We do not want our soldiers to be monks.' Franke put in, 'We do not organize things to satisfy our soldiers sexually. That contradicts socialist morals. But if we have a link with a factory and a soldier gets to know a girl, has decent relations with her and they love one another and want to get married, that is fine. But if a soldier is like a butterfly going from flower to flower, we talk things over with him to educate him. We do not want to teach our soldiers to satisfy themselves with girls and then throw them away like empty cigarette packets.'

Franke said that he could not punish a soldier militarily for being promiscuous. He must try to educate him. Franke added, 'With some of them one must despair.' Japp put in, 'If he is immoral and the collective education has no effect – it rarely happens – then we must say it is better that he leaves.' Firla said there had not been such a case in his unit – 'the collective is so strong'. Franke explained they could also work through the soldiers' parents, who would be brought to the barracks. The influence of the soldier's former factory was also used.

Franke said that, if an officer decided he must impose a punishment, he had to think this over for 24 hours, so that he did not make the decision in anger. It was also his duty to discuss a proposed punishment with the appropriate SED group or Free German Youth group, so that the punishment might be reduced to the minimum necessary. A soldier could appeal against a proposed punishment, which would not be put into effect until the appeal had been deal with.

Huebner commented, 'If I get an order from an officer to carry out some task which seems unfit for humans or nonsensical, then I can say so.' He said, for instance, that he would not carry out an order to fire at civilians coming into East Germany from West Berlin. I argued with Huebner that he could not know that such an order was illegal, because it might be necessary. Japp agreed and said, 'It could be thinkable. But before such an order would be given, it would be explained politically.' I said this would not always be possible in time of war, and there were nods.

Huebner said he hoped to become a corporal in October. He had one black mark against his record. In winter, doing a job outside, he had cold hands, so he put them in his pockets to warm them. An officer passing by told him to take them out again and instead of doing so, he walked away and kept them in. Huebner said he could have worn gloves or warmed his hands at the exhaust of a vehicle. He described his own behaviour as silly and said he had received a reprimand.

I also spoke to Lance-Corporal Walter Heyer, aged 20, a former apprentice mechanic, who was nearly at the end of his two years' service; a member of both the SED and the Free German Youth. When I asked him why he had joined the army, he said, 'It is laid down in our constitution that everyone has the honourable task of learning to use weapons. I was interested to learn.'

I told him the average young Briton was not interested in joining the forces, and asked why he was interested. He replied, 'We are in the workers' and farmers' state, and what we possess, which is a lot, must be protected.'

After listening to our conversations, Major Palmer indicated that there were sometimes problems with discipline, like the soldier who came back to barracks late after going out with his girl, and did not get his hair cut. 'We do not get all angels here,' he said.

When I asked to speak to a soldier who was not in the SED or the Communist youth organization, they got hold of Gerhard Spindler, 21, a lance-corporal who is shortly to leave the army, after two and a half years' service. He had been a building labourer. Why had he joined the army? He blushed, then said, 'In order to defend the homeland.' When I asked him for further reasons, he said, 'One can save a lot of money.'

Back in the officers' mess I spoke to Captain Werner Boettger, 33, born near Leipzig, East Germany. Boettger, a battalion commander, had been a lance-corporal in the *Wehrmacht* during the last year of the Second World War. After the war he joined the SED and became a teacher. As a young man, though not in the Nazi party, he had been enthusiastic about Nazism and had been in the Hitler Youth. When the war ended, his enthusiasm for Nazism had disappeared when he learned of Nazi atrocities. He had entered the National People's Army in 1956.

Boettger said the difference between the East German army and the *Wehrmacht* was 'crass'. An officer in the People's Army had to prevent the chicanery he had been subject to in the *Wehrmacht*. There was now a new relationship between officers and other ranks. 'In the old days I would never have dared to speak to a platoon commander or even a sergeant in the way our soldiers do. We kept our distance from all superiors and were happy if we did not cross their path.' He recalled being forced to run around a parade ground in a gas mask for an hour, becoming completely exhausted. A sergeant once came across him in a corridor and had him alternately standing up and lying down as he went along the corridor.

In the *Wehrmacht* there had been much swearing, but that was now forbidden. He added, 'It can happen that, when excited, an officer or NCO uses a swearword. But if this is found out he is brought to book. A soldier has the right to complain if he feels his honour has been insulted.' Another officer corrected Boettger by saying that swearing was not forbidden by regulation, but that it was an unwritten law not to swear. When Boettger spoke of the 'corpselike obedience' in the *Wehrmacht*, another officer put in, 'We are strict.' But he added that inhuman methods were rejected on principle.

One officer recalled that, while he was in the *Wehrmacht*, for a short period he had to clean out a washroom with a toothbrush. If such a thing happened in the People's Army, the person responsible would be discharged. That officer said Hitler had fooled people into thinking they were serving a good cause. I asked how he knew he was now serving a good cause. He replied, 'In the old days I had no chance to consider problems of social development. We were kept away from that. Only after 1945 did I start thinking. And on the basis of the philosophy of our Marxist teaching I took in the social lessons.' Under capitalism his father had been unemployed for six years. 'At home there was neither butter, nor chocolate, nor oranges, which today here have become a matter of course. There was chocolate perhaps once a year.' Suits and shoes were bought in larger sizes, to last several years. 'I have experienced capitalism. It was a miserable existence.'

Our final discussion was over a cold meal of meat and salad, again with cognac, beer and coffee. My day with the National People's Army ended with another toast – in cognac, I think – a toast to peace, to which I drank heartily.

[When the East German Communist regime collapsed in late 1989, it became clear from documents obtained by the West German authorities that the National People's Army had not only feared – without reason – an attack from NATO forces, but had also prepared plans for an attack on West Germany and West Berlin in certain circumstances. The plans included one for a surprise attack on West Berlin through the city's underground railway tunnels and sewers. The use of chemical weapons was also planned.

In the event, after German reunification in October 1990, the East German armed forces, totalling about 103,000 men, were largely disbanded. Many soldiers applied to join the unified all-German forces, the Bundeswehr. *Six thousand officers and 11,000 NCOs were taken into the* Bundeswehr *for two years on trial and, of these, about 3,000 officers and 7,600 NCOs were then taken on for longer periods of service. The demise of the National People's Army took place without serious problems.]*

18 Chasing Khrushchev in a Beetle

3 July 1959 : With my family, I drove along the 110-mile East German autobahn to West Germany, and then a short distance further to the main Volkswagen factory in Wolfsburg to pick up our next 'Beetle', a used works vehicle with about 16,000 km (10,000 miles) on the clock, built in September 1958, in tiptop condition, 3,985 marks (about £350).

Owing to the unusual case of a Briton buying a West German car and taking it through East Germany to West Berlin, we had quite some headaches on our journey back. The climax came when we were told that the boys were not mentioned on our East German transit visa. An East German official wrote them in and I pointed out, rather unkindly, that anyone could have done that, as the handwriting was different from that on the original visa.

It was midnight when, after passing through West Berlin, we reached the Brandenburg Gate, one of the entrances to East Berlin, and were halted by a West Berlin customs officer who, at first, did not want to let us through, but did so when I told him we lived in the Eastern sector and intended to register the car there.

6 July 1959 : Completing car bureaucracy. Had been told by a Western official that I should not have driven the car into East Berlin using West German trade plates. The upshot was that I today left my trade plates in West Berlin and was allowed – illegally, I think – to drive a short way into East Berlin to the customs yard without plates, with policemen's eyes popping here and there. Tore around in a taxi to complete formalities.

Had a pleasant discussion with a police sergeant, who had made the obligatory technical check on the car. We discussed whether capitalism inevitably meant war. Here I pleaded for the capitalists who, I believe, are not mad enough to want war, however much they may enjoy exploiting their workers. The police sergeant, however, did not accept my simple contention that capitalists did not want to die any more than workers did.

The taxi driver I used told me that no current East German cars were fit for taxi work since East Germany had lost the licence to build old BMW cars some years ago. The driver did not think much of Russian cars either, saying they were either too expensive to run or not hardwearing enough.

7 July 1959 : Called on Klaus Fuchs' father, Professor Emil Fuchs, who told me his son was visiting scientific institutes in Dresden, near where East Germany's nuclear research institute is situated. Professor Fuchs, a Quaker *[widely seen in the West as a fellow-traveller]*, told me that though he was not a Marxist, he disapproved of the attitude of some important Protestant church leaders who, in his view, mixed politics with religion and thus made relations with the Communist state worse than need be.

He told me how, about 18 months ago, at a meeting of professors, he had in somewhat veiled, but nevertheless understandable terms, criticized the wounding statements made by some East German Communist leaders, including Ulbricht, on Christian belief and church people, and had said that these statements had not been of service to the East German state. Ulbricht, who was present, had attacked him for his speech and left, but later wrote him a friendly letter and sent his secretary to apologize for his reaction.

Professor Fuchs considers that the friction between state and Church in that period, which had been brought to a head by the offer of the still existing All-German Evangelical (Protestant) Church to provide chaplains for the West German forces, is now past. He said his views had been met with much understanding, even by Communists, and believes it is necessary for churchmen to try to cooperate with the present East German state as far as they can, and not to think that Christian morals are somehow linked with capitalism.

Professor Fuchs, a longtime socialist who moved to the East from Frankfurt in 1949, is critical of the policies of the West German Social Democrats who, he considers, have no backbone. We agreed that fanatics on both sides of the Iron Curtain are the main danger in today's world. His view is that capitalism, if it does not change, is bound to fail, because it is based on selfishness, whereas socialism is gradually working towards a society based on community effort in the interest of all.

8 July 1959 : Have been reading Professor Fuchs' two-volume autobiography. How many tragedies his family has gone through. His wife, who had suffered from melancholia, committed suicide in 1931 shortly after their happy 25th wedding anniversary. His eldest son, Gerhard, died from tuberculosis after the Second World War, partly because he had been imprisoned by the Nazis for a time as a Communist.

We know the story of his second son, Klaus. His eldest daughter, Elizabeth, committed suicide in 1939 after her husband had been sent to a concentration camp and had escaped to Prague, where she had not been able to join him. Only his fourth child, Christel, who married an American in Cambridge, Massachusetts, seems to have had anything like a normal life. And yet Professor Fuchs is a most friendly and charming old gentleman, with an acute brain – even at 85.

9 July 1959 : Tonight we were guests of Belgian Communist journalist, Martin Thijs, and his Social Democratic wife, Julia. Also present was a German Communist living in Belgium and his Belgian wife. We had a hammer and tongs discussion, in which I accused the Communists in East Germany of being less than honest by, for instance, pretending that the single-list elections held here were really an expression of the people's support for the regime, and claiming there was a multi-party system here when,

in fact, the other so-called parties are not parties in the real sense, but organizations controlled by the Communists, intended to get people who do not belong to the working class to accept the basic Communist line. I can see why the Communists do that – quite natural from their point of view – but it irks me when some of them pretend it is a multi-party system comparable to that operating in Britain.

10 July 1959 : Was asked to check a statement by a British spokesman in West Berlin that two British soldiers had been granted asylum in East Germany. I learned from Ambassador Heymann that, in fact, two more allied soldiers, an American and a Frenchman, had gone East at the same time and had also been granted asylum. Heymann gave me this information at a reception held to celebrate the 38th anniversary of the Mongolian People's Republic (Outer Mongolia) in the onetime Air Ministry building of Hermann Göring.

The ambassador made a speech, in what seemed like very outer Mongolian, which was translated into German. Outer Mongolia has an interesting coat of arms, displayed at the reception. The centrepiece is a nomad rider – now being collectivized, of course – in a cowboy-type hat, galloping across the desert, away from a snow-tipped mountain with the sun rising behind it. The food was good and we drank a toast in fermented mares' milk.

Afterwards to Wandlitz to check with Klaus Fuchs on whether he had decided to take a job – he had not yet done so. He told me his father had seemed to be seriously ill earlier today, owing to the tremendous heat: about 38° C in the shade, an all-time record for Berlin. He was better this evening, but not fit to receive visitors. Took Klaus Fuchs out to our car to introduce him to Elfi and we chatted for a few minutes, about freedom, of all things. Elfi spoke of the bad advertisement for East Germany caused by the frontier barbed wire and that kind of thing. I backed her up by saying I hoped the Communists would one day allow people who did not like living under communism to go elsewhere. Fuchs said something to the effect that there was much misunderstanding in both

180

blocs due to ignorance, to which I responded that the Americans in general had a wrong idea of communism and the Russians had a wrong idea of America.

12 July 1959 : This Sunday morning I called at the all-German headquarters of the Society of Friends, the Quakers, in an old building in East Berlin's Planck Strasse. I was too late to attend the meeting for worship, which starts at 10.00, but was cheered by a chat with a woman secretary from West Berlin, who told me something of the Friends' work in divided Germany. Admirable that they have kept together in one organization, in spite of the political division.

14 July 1959 : Set off to Poland to cover a visit by Khrushchev. About two and a half hours' driving brought me to the Polish frontier at Frankfurt-on-the-Oder, where the autobahn from Berlin peters out. Frontier formalities took about half an hour on each side. The Poles have renamed what was the Eastern suburb of Frankfurt, across the Oder, 'Slubice'. A Pole in their frontier post told me no Germans lived there any more.

The first 80 miles or so of the drive from the frontier to Warsaw – about 300 miles in all – lie in former German territory. Most German signs have been thoroughly expunged, but in one or two places I caught a glimpse of a few German words showing through a later Polish sign, such as *Schmidt*, *Schlossermeister* (master mechanic or locksmith) and *Postamt* (post office) on a building now renamed *Poczta*. Most of the towns and villages have been renamed too.

Some villages looked very dilapidated, others no more neglected than many West German ones. To a layman the land looked reasonably tilled, though the grain did not seem to be standing as high as in East Germany. Cattle and poultry were an extra road hazard – rare in East Germany. Small children were often the drovers. Many children waved as I passed – probably a begging ploy. I threw bars of chocolate to two kiddies.

A drive of about 110 miles brought me to Poznan ('Posen' in

German), a major city with university, which has changed hands between Poland and Germany several times in past centuries. *[It was Polish between 1919 and 1939 and was annexed by Nazi Germany during the Second World War.]* Soon after I had left Poznan, the scene of the 1956 disturbances which brought back to power the relatively liberal Communist, Wladislaw Gomulka, I picked up two medical students. Each carried a book marked *Autostop* containing certificates which are handed to drivers who give them a lift. Drivers send in the certificates – showing how far they took people – and the Polish driver who, in total, has transported people furthest in one year receives a free car.

One of the students told me life had improved under Gomulka, but prices were still high. The father of one of them earned 1,600 zloty monthly as a factory worker; that gives purchasing power of about £20. *[At the official rate the zloty was worth nearly four old pence (less than 2p).]* One student sang to me a snatch of *My curly-headed Babby*, which he'd heard on the BBC. I translated some of the words for him. The students and I conversed in Russian; very good practice. A policeman stopped us. To check our papers? No, he wanted a lift too. Took him along for ten miles. At about 22.45 tried to get something to eat from a restaurant, but it was closing. So the students gave me some of their bread and lard, and I bought us all coffee.

As we approached Warsaw, I spotted the red aircraft warning lights on the towering Palace of Culture and Science, which Stalin gave to the Poles after the Second World War. Flopped into my bed at the Hotel Bristol around 02.00.

15 July 1959 : Although the Bristol is one of Warsaw's best hotels, I was attacked during the night by one or more insects; I saw one creeping away this morning. Drove another 200 miles today to Katowice in southern Poland. David Sells, our lanky bespectacled Warsaw correspondent, had gone ahead to chase Khrushchev's motorcade for four hours around the mining area surrounding Katowice, which in 1939 was only about 15 miles east of the then German frontier, but is now, I estimate, at least

182

90 miles from the new frontier. During my drive, picked up two more medical students, who told me that the Polish authorities allow their people to travel to Britain, which is not the case for East Germans.

I noticed many Catholic shrines, as in the Rhineland. The countryside reminds me of Belgium, partly because, similar to Belgium, road signs have black letters on a yellow background with red surrounds, partly because the houses are smallish, quaint and redbrick in many places, partly because the roads here and there are paved with a kind of brick, as in Belgium. Very little motor traffic, less than in East Germany, but very good main roads – though with hardly any autobahns.

I failed tonight to gain admittance to a reception for Khrushchev in a workers' club. A chap told me in French that I could not come in, as I had not been invited. A frustrating day for me. Must get some sleep. A Russian-born Pole told me that the Poles are unruly and don't like saving. I have noticed they have a sense of humour; more people laugh spontaneously here than in Germany.

16 July 1959 : The Polish press agency, PAP (its name reminds me of some of its stories!), suppressed some remarks of Khrushchev to miners yesterday, when he said he did not want to hurt their religious feelings, but that, unlike the Church, the Communist Party was promising something concrete for this world, as opposed to 'pie in the sky'. Or that was the gist. In strongly Catholic Poland that would not go down too well.

The area around Katowice reminds me of the West Riding of Yorkshire – mainly coal mining and heavy industry. Some Poles I've spoken too have emphasized their strong feeling of distrust towards Germany after past events, and their conviction that the present frontiers of Poland are just. *[Between 1772 and 1918, Poland was, in succession, partly or completely occupied by Russia, Prussia (later Germany) and Austria. An independent Polish state emerged again in 1918 and regained some formerly Polish Eastern territories in a war with the then weak Soviet Union. After the Second*

World War, those territories were annexed by the Soviet Union, and Poland was compensated with the former German territories of Silesia, Eastern Brandenburg, Eastern Pomerania and southern East Prussia, about 20 per cent of Germany as it was in 1937. Poland was in effect moved westwards some 150 miles and about six million Germans were expelled from the former German territories.]

Today we drove to nearby Sosnowiec, where Khrushchev spoke to an international conference of miners, mainly from Communist-run unions. Fortunately there was a simultaneous English translation, so I could take a good note. David's translator on the tour, Leszek Jeczmyk, a young Polish graduate, helped out on some tricky bits, having done his own translation from the Russian. Khrushchev said the Soviet Union would 'never, never, never' launch a war. He added that though the Soviet Union would not foment an uprising against the capitalists, it would welcome any which might come. There were many other good quotes in the speech and I wrote about 14 takes, which were sent mainly by teleprinter to Warsaw and Bonn. Felt I had earned my keep today.

Gomulka also spoke briefly at the meeting, but there was nothing worthwhile in it. This man who saved Poland from the tragedy of Hungary is small, rather cadaverous and with piercing eyes. He has little charisma.

17 July 1959 : As Khrushchev is flying round Poland and we only have a car, we left at 02.00, taking with us ham sandwiches – Polish ham is good – and bottles of soda water. A most interesting drive of about 320 miles to the Baltic port of Szczecin (Stettin), bordering on East Germany. Except for the first 15 miles or so from Katowice, the whole drive was through former German territory.

It is a strange feeling to travel through so much territory which, one knows, belonged to another country such a short time ago. Rather eerie, especially when you set off in the dark and see the dawn come up out of an overcast sky in drizzle, as you approach the large Silesian city of Wroclaw (Breslau) which, in parts, looks like Hamburg in 1947: whole areas with little standing, mouldering ruins, damaged churches standing like islands in a sea of nothingness. Other suburbs are now returning to normal, thanks to rebuilding and repainting, most of which, I am told, has been done in the last three years.

It seems that, up to 1955, the Poles had some doubts as to whether they would be able to keep the former German territories awarded to them by the 'Big Four' at the close of the Second World War. According to some reports, many Poles who were settled in those territories did not feel they were there permanently. However, it is now clear that this frontier is permanent, at the very least in the main, as it has been guaranteed by the whole Soviet bloc and is tacitly accepted by the Western allies, in spite of what some Western politicians say in deference to the West Germans. As a result the Poles are making strong efforts to bring these territories back to normal.

[The West German centre–left coalition, under Chancellor Willy Brandt, recognized Poland's postwar frontier in 1970, and this was confirmed by the centre–right government of reunified Germany, under Chancellor Helmut Kohl, in a treaty concluded with Poland in November 1990.]

Some towns we passed through looked in quite good shape. There were others where the swathe cut by war was still clearly visible. Little motor traffic and many farm carts drawn by good horses – the Poles love horses. Old-fashioned street markets and cattle markets. People decently dressed in the main, but much of their clothing looked of poor quality and was lacking in style.

By flashing my press pass near Szczecin, I got permission for us to drive along the road towards the airport, from where Khrushchev was to come. We were parked on the roadside a few miles from the airport, when we met up with Khrushchev's motorcade. He and Gomulka sat in an open Buick Eight black convertible. We managed to nose our way into the motorcade. Part of the drive into Szczecin was along a stretch of former German autobahn, where in places grass was sprouting from cracks in the concrete, testifying to the light traffic. (Poland is really a grand country for motoring, as the main road network is excellent and the traffic negligible, except that one must look out for poultry, hares and cows.)

Szczecin made a good impression, with a quite well-dressed crowd of thousands lining the streets, which were decorated with alternate yellow hammers-and-sickles and white Polish eagles. There were boy scouts here and there – the only boy scouts in the Communist bloc and, I understand, not Communist-dominated, but pretty well non-political. Many people, though not all, clapped and waved at Khrushchev. (I imagine that for most Poles, who in the view of most Western observers are anti-Communist, Khrushchev is at any rate a lesser evil, and deserves a clap for that.)

In the city hall, on a platform decked out with potted palms, Khrushchev was made an honorary freeman of Szczecin, with Gomulka and the long-faced (literally) Prime Minister, Josef Cyrankiewicz. In his response the Soviet leader recalled that, as a young man he had learnt to count to 100, which was quite a feat in his rural community. His father had then told him he had learned enough and had added that the family would never have 100 roubles.

There was little of interest in speeches made by Khrushchev and Cyrankiewicz at an open-air mass meeting attended by about 40,000. We three were put up in the pleasant detached house of Mrs Lidia Wieckowska, a pretty woman in her late thirties who is a journalist – not a party member – on the local party newspaper, *Glos Szczecinski* (*Voice of Szczecin*). Her husband, an ex-partisan, was away having medical treatment. Mrs Wieckowska told me they bought the house, only about five miles from the East German border, from the Polish state in 1945. She had learned from books found in the house that it had belonged to a German lawyer. (I'm told that the prices paid for such former German houses in 1945 were but token ones). A friend of her husband had been commissar for that section of Szczecin and had earmarked the house for him. It stands amid pines, not far from a lake.

Mrs Wieckowska gave forth with something of a tirade, claiming that Britain went into the Second World War purely for economic reasons, which is nonsense. She said that, during the war, the Poles had expected to get East Prussia and German Silesia, but had not expected to get Eastern Pomerania (including Szczecin). This had been some compensation for the loss of territories to the Soviet Union. Questioned, she said that the Soviet Union's action in taking Polish territory had been a bad one. But she said one must accept the present situation, now that virtually all Poles were within the new national boundaries and minority problems had been wiped out.

I suggested to this Polish woman that she might try to find the German former owner of her house and invite him to spend a holiday in his onetime home, just to show him there was nothing personal about her being there. She rejected the idea. I think that if, say, my German mother-in-law were invited by the new occupants to visit the dairy, now in northeastern Poland, where she used to live when it was in East Prussia, she would be pleasantly touched. Mrs Wieckowska told me she had worked in the office of a German trading firm in occupied central Poland during the war, to avoid being sent as a slave labourer to Germany. She said the Germans she had worked with had been 'unkind'.

18 July 1959 : Our landlady apologized for getting worked up about Britain last night, so I told her I had not taken it seriously. That annoyed her – just like a fiery Pole – as she had wanted to be taken seriously! An old Pole working as a hotel porter, speaking German with an East Prussian accent, told me he had worked all over East Prussia for a German electrical firm during the Second World War and could not complain about his treatment then.

A drive of about 150 miles southwards brought me to a state stud farm at Racot, near Poznan, where a new breed of horse had been produced since the war for all-purpose work – the Poznan: a mixture of Berber, Arab, German Trakehner and others. A banner on a welcoming arch wished Khrushchev 100 years of health and happiness – a traditional Polish greeting. I joined a crowd of farm workers, including girls in traditional folk costumes with garlanded hair, beautifully embroidered bodices and full skirts;

and local officials in business suits. About 20 uniformed riders on Poznan horses waited. Several horses shied and fell into a ditch with their riders, but no one was hurt. As Khrushchev arrived and walked smiling through the crowd with Gomulka, a horse which had shed its rider dashed through the crowd and was halted only a few yards from the Soviet leader by a young man who sprang, grasped the rein and held on in spite of a hoof kick in the face. This could have caused an ugly incident – it made the lead for my story.

Shortly afterwards a plainclothes policeman ejected me from the stud farm, in spite of my expostulations in Russian that I had been given a visa to cover the visit. So I drove on to the next spot on Khrushchev's tour, a state farm, one of the relatively few in Poland. They cover only about 5 per cent of the cultivated land, I believe.

As the motorcade drove towards the state farm buildings, a plainclothes man ordered a policeman to arrest us for an hour – until Khrushchev had gone. We remonstrated that this was stupidity and would harm relations, but it was no use. I asked to see the policeman's papers, but he refused to show them, so I took his picture. He motioned for me to give him my camera, but I didn't and he didn't insist. Polish officials told us the police measures were at Russian request. Why, I cannot understand, for they were the height of stupidity.

After our release, we had a very useful talk with the state farm director, who told us Khrushchev had inspected maize being grown experimentally from new Soviet seed strains which were expected to produce 1,400 metric hundredweights per hectare (2½ acres), compared with only about 700 from previous seeds and up to 1,000 from Polish seed. Maize has not been very satisfactory in Poland, because of the climate, but the director said the results so far with the new seed were so good that he would double the hectarage from 15 to 30 next year. This would enable him to breed more cattle and pigs. The Russians had given the seed, and the necessary machines to tend and harvest it, so as to convince the Poles of the advantages, he said.

I learned later that, at a collective farm which he visited this morning, Khrushchev had expressed support for a statement by Gomulka referring to the Polish policy of persuasion rather than compulsion in getting farmers to join collective farms. Western observers here agree that compulsion is not used. There were about 11,000 collective farms when Gomulka came to power in 1956. They shrunk to about 600 when the farmers were given real freedom to leave them. They now stand at about 1,800. Khrushchev reportedly said it was no use forcing people – even to do a good thing. Those sound like the words of a true democrat and do not accord with what happened in the Soviet Union under Stalin.

19 July 1959 : While Khrushchev had this Sunday off, Leszek and I drove about 250 miles from Poznan to overnight in Cracow, a onetime capital of Poland, in the southeast. Until 1918 this was an Austrian city. Its partially crumbling buildings are a mine of history. We booked in at the Grand Hotel, where Austria's last emperor, Franz-Josef, had stayed before us. (According to the joke, Cracow people, who apparently quite liked being in the Austrian empire, are reputed to have asked Stalin to add 'Franz' to his 'Josef'.) As I went to bed I heard a bugle call. I wondered what it meant.

20 July 1959 : Leszek explained that the bugle call, played from the tower of an ancient church, is reputed – not without some doubt – to date from the thirteenth-century Mongol invasion. It is said the city was warned by a bugler, who turned in four directions and whose call was cut off by a Mongol arrow. The tune played now ends in the middle of a phrase. It is played several times a day.

Cracow is like a decrepit Vienna, and the coffee house in our hotel was much like one I have patronized on Vienna's Ring. We glimpsed an old market or exchange building on a large square, and a castle on a hill, before we set off early this morning for Rzeszow, a regional centre about 80 miles eastwards, close to the

Soviet frontier. It adjoins territory which the Soviet Union took – or took back – from the Poles after the Second World War. The city of about 60,000 has quite a hopeful air, with much building going on. The style reminded me of pictures of Russia: some neo-classical official buildings, with much use of colour washes on the façades. Around Rzeszow are many old wooden farmhouses, often attacked by beetle. A poor region. Industry was brought here before the war and more so since.

My press ticket enabled us to get into the airport, where Khrushchev was given a tumultuous welcome by a crowd of perhaps 15,000. Too few police, so people could move where they wanted. Never on any airport have I seen a plane so hemmed in by crowds as it taxied in. People on either side had to duck to avoid being hit by the wings of Khrushchev's propeller-driven, twin-engined airliner. A plainclothes man shouted (someone translated for me), 'Stop making fools of yourselves. Today one should behave correctly.' A Polish journalist told me he thought one reason for the enthusiastic welcome was that VIPs rarely come to Rzeszow, which is in the Polish outback.

Khrushchev bantered with Gomulka, who was not supposed to speak at the airport, and persuaded him to do so. Gomulka denied that there was any dictation by the Soviet Union to Poland. He said the Polish Communists decided all their own affairs. Khrushchev made no mention of the Soviet Union's acquisition of former Polish territory just to the east of Rzeszow. Instead he spoke in very warm terms of the present relations between Poland and the Soviet Union.

We were refused admission to Khrushchev's next call, a factory, and to the onion-domed castle – sixteenth-century, I was told – which formerly belonged to the noble Potocki family, who used to be one of the richest Polish landowners. The last Potocki to live there, Count Alfred, left with the Germans in the Second World War, when the Russians came.

In a café outside the castle, two leathery-faced labourers, who goggled when I told them that I was English, made no bones about their distaste for the Russians. One of them grasped the red ribbon which his companion had donned for the day, tore it off and stuffed it into the man's pocket.

'I am a Pole,' he growled at me.

During our drive up to the castle, and again on the way down, in the tail of Khrushchev's procession, we were the recipients, mainly through the sun roof, of about half a dozen bouquets, which we duly presented later to the two women teleprinter operators in the Rzeszow office of the Polish Press Agency, from where I sent my story. We also got lots of waves and claps, and one or two shouts of 'Volkswagen' – recognized here even though the cars are more than rare in Poland.

We had a pleasant chat with Mr Krucrek, the Rzeszow party secretary, who had been with Khrushchev and Gomulka in yesterday's motorcade. We found him likeable, which may explain how he has managed to retain his post, even though he was once a Stalinist. He told us that on several occasions when Khrushchev's car had been stopped by the crowd, people had shouted, 'Keep peace, Khrushchev.' He seemed surprised at the warmth of the welcome given to the Soviet leader, which was indeed quite impressive.

We sped up to Warsaw – about 200 miles – in around four hours. Khrushchev addressed a formal meeting held in the towering Stalinist 'palace of science and culture', which most Poles find out of character with the city which it dominates. I found the large amphitheatre where the meeting was held not unattractive in a somewhat Victorian way. Much of Warsaw has been rebuilt after terrible wartime damage, and a lot has been recreated in the old style. Some areas reminded me of Paris, with tree-lined boulevards and stylish buildings. One street has been renamed after Winnie the Pooh since the war.

It was my turn tonight to attend a reception in the Prime Minister's official residence, but Khrushchev was not saying anything. The place was swarming with plainclothes men and military security officers in uniform, keeping us away from the big nobs. As Khrushchev and Gomulka watched Polish folk dancers perform on an outdoor stage, fireworks shot up from near the

Vistula. Shortly before Khrushchev left, a band played the old American jazz favourite, *In the Mood*. That would not have happened in most Communist countries.

19 To Elfi's home village

23 July 1959 : Khrushchev flew off home today, kissing Gomulka heartily and, according to David, looking truly moved at the reception he has had here. I took time off to pay my first visit to the Polish (southern) half of what was once Elfi's home village, Schönbruch, in former East Prussia, about 190 miles north of Warsaw. The northern half of what was a large village, with about 2,000 inhabitants, is in the Russian region of Kaliningrad, closed to Westerners and reliably thought to include some Soviet missile bases. Its main city, also called Kaliningrad, was formerly Königsberg, the capital of East Prussia, then Germany's most easterly province.

[The territory which came to be called East Prussia was invaded in the thirteenth century by the Order of Teutonic Knights, a partly religious and partly chivalrous organization, which was founded in 1190 in Palestine by crusaders. After the Christian forces had been defeated in Palestine, the Order, composed mainly of Germans, moved its headquarters to Venice in 1291. With the approval of the Pope and the Holy Roman Emperor, the Teutonic Knights started a new crusade along the Baltic Sea, to the east of Germany, and in 1309 moved their headquarters to the castle of Marienburg, which is now in Poland near Gdansk. They defeated and Christianized the pagan Baltic tribes – the Prussen (who gave their name to the later state of Prussia), the Lithuanians, the Latvians and the Estonians – and set up their own state ruled by the Order.

In the early sixteenth century the Order suffered military defeats, and lost most of present-day Lithuania, Latvia and Estonia. By 1526

the earlier idealism of the Order had paled, and the state was secular-
ized and made Protestant by a German duke. It became one of the
constituent parts of what developed into the state of Prussia, the most
powerful German state, which brought about the unification of
Germany in 1871. The history of East Prussia and neighbouring West
Prussia was closely linked with that of Poland. For nearly 200 years
from 1466 they were vassals of the Polish crown.]

I left Warsaw early in the afternoon. About 12 miles south of
the onetime Polish–German frontier, now just an administrative
border, a woman ran out on to the road waving. An old woman
had been taken ill and needed to see a doctor some ten miles further north. As she got into my car, I took a snap of a crowd of
Poles – adults and children. Their clothing was somewhat ragged
and some of the men were unshaven. In the car the old woman
told me in German where the frontier used to be. After dropping
her and travelling past what had been the frontier – a barefooted
peasant woman confirmed this – I took my long-awaited first look
at former East Prussia, my wife's homeland.

Here it was slightly rolling countryside, with a sprinkling of
trees. Most of the land was under cultivation. I saw some farmhouse shells, relics of the war, and those occupied looked rather
down at heel. I gave lifts to, first, a soldier and another man, the
latter smelling, I suppose, of vodka, and then to two pleasant students, a youth and a girl, who waved their book of *Autostop*
coupons. I ran over my fourth hen since entering Poland; I had
already dispatched one hare, two birds and a cat, after running
over nothing during four years in Germany, so far as I can
remember.

On northwards, through the Polish towns of Szczytno and
Biskupiec, which the Germans called Ortelsburg and
Bischofsburg. Here and there considerable war damage, but the
general impression was better than I'd expected after reading the
accounts of travellers who went there three or four years ago. It
was a great thrill to see the black-on-yellow road sign saying
'Bartoszyce', telling me I had arrived at what had been Elfi's
county town, Bartenstein, where she went to grammar school.

I went into the police station to tell them I wanted to see my wife's birthplace in a village that used to be called Schönbruch, the present name of which I did not know. After a little humming and hawing, I was introduced to a smallish chap in civvies, who spoke some German and Russian and was very helpful. He told me he knew where Schönbruch was, divided by the frontier. He agreed to drive out there with me.

We drove into the centre of Bartoszyce through the typically German redbrick arch, once no doubt part of a city wall, and onto the main square, with its gaily-painted house fronts, as in other Polish towns – unlike Germany where the brickwork is not normally painted. There are a few gaps in the square, but it is generally in good shape. After checking in at Bartoszyce's only hotel, I drove the ten miles or so along the increasingly bad road leading to Elfi's home village, the Polish half of which is now called Szczurkowo (Shchurkovo in English imitated pronunciation). *[Years later I learned that* Szczur *means 'rat'. The German name, Schönbruch, meant 'beautiful marsh'.]*

As we topped a small rise, my companion told me we had arrived. Through trees I could see a large white building, the former manor house which had been the home of the local bigwigs, the von Bolschwings, who as refugees are now running a chicken farm in the Rhineland. The Polish half of the village is, as far as I could see, mainly a one-street affair. We stopped at the first houses and a crowd of about 30, mainly children in a scruffy state, gathered around. Some of them, a little timid at first, agreed to stand by my car while I snapped them. We were told no Germans now lived in the village. My companion said that about 200 Germans lived in Bartoszyce county now, together with about 50,000 Poles.

An unshaven Polish farmer, wearing a peaked cap, showed us the way to the ruin of the large dairy which Elfi's father managed and where she was born. The ruin is on a slight rise just off the main street. The dairy appears to have been used as a strongpoint in the last days of the war, for other nearby buildings are undamaged or only slightly damaged. I clambered down into a tiled basement and had my companion take my picture, and took several myself. At first he had not wanted me to take pictures, saying it was too near the frontier, but I mollified him by pointing out that I was merely taking pictures of stones.

Near the dairy ruin is a field full of beehives. I asked the Pole who kept them if he would sell me some honey. He said he had none today as it had been raining. *[Later we used to joke about honey from 'Polish-administered German bees'.]* The hives looked badly kept, and the whole village had a decrepit air. Saddening. It made me think of how I know it had been once, trim and neat and not split in two by a frontier. An untidy looking frontier guard came along, saw me taking pictures, and ordered us to go along to the guardhouse at the village school.

A metal sign above the entrance said: 193 /1937 (one number had dropped out). The school is close to the frontier. Near it is a short pole, striped in white and red, with a sign on it saying in Polish: 'Polish Republic, State Frontier'. At that point there is a barbed-wire fence crossing the road. A few yards behind that is a Russian fence, not very high, among trees, and a Russian frontier pole. I could not see that pole very well but another one, along to the left, was painted green and red and had a metal plate – it looked like brass – bearing the Soviet coat of arms – hammer-and-sickle surrounded by ears of wheat.

Beyond the school, a hundred yards or so inside Russia, is the village's redbrick Gothic church. Elfi was christened there. *[Originally a Roman Catholic church, built by the Teutonic Knights in the fourteenth century, it became Protestant in the sixteenth century during the Reformation.]* The church looks largely intact, except that the roof of its tower has been removed and replaced by a balcony and watchtower for the Soviet guards. I saw one walk round the balcony. *[I was told years later that the Polish authorities had asked the Russians to agree to a slight change in the frontier, so that the historic church could be used by the Poles, but the Russians rejected this. Later the Russians destroyed the church, along with the other buildings in their half of the village, which they named 'Shirokoye' (wide).]*

196

As we waited for about 20 minutes in the school for an officer to appear, I noted on the wall a red-and-white Polish flag, a picture of Prime Minister Cyrankiewicz, a noticeboard showing examples of valid passports, a map of Europe and a poster calling the Polish United Workers' (Communist) Party the 'leading force of the people'. For a few minutes I played table tennis with one of the young guards. In front of the school building, in the garden, are two depictions of Polish eagles shaped from stones.

A khaki-uniformed officer, who drove up in a jeep, was most polite and friendly. I told him in Russian why I had come to Schönbruch. He took my name, looked at my East German press card, and said everything was all right. With my plainclothes companion, I drove back to the Bartoszyce hotel, where the quite trim and clean restaurant was closing at about ten. I was able to get a couple of cheese sandwiches and a glass of not very good, but definitely alcoholic beer. My companion declined both refreshment and the 50 zlotys I wanted to give him for showing me around. (Of course, it might have been his job to keep an eye on me.) As I started to type this in my hotel room it was strange to hear youths outside, singing in Polish.

24 July 1959 : For breakfast in the hotel restaurant I ordered a boiled egg – my first 'former East Prussian egg' – some bread and butter and a glass of tea. There were at least two uniformed waitresses. One of three men to whom I spoke said he was a waiter earning 800 zlotys a month. One of his companions, a motor mechanic, said that to live one needed 1,500 zlotys, which was what he and the third man, a lorry driver, earned. How did the waiter manage then, I asked. The mechanic made a gesture, indicating some kind of double-dealing, and grinned.

Two of the men were unshaven or half-shaven, like many men in Poland. I invited them to have a drink with me and they chose a small glass of vodka, small for them, that is, about an eighth of a pint. They downed theirs in one. I sipped.

The motor mechanic said, 'I can drink one-and-a-half litres of it and still drive.' I asked why they drank so much if they earned so little. He said they had to work so hard and were paid so little that they got into the habit of having a vodka to make the world seem a more hopeful place.

One of the men, or our waitress, said they would have to work all their lives to afford a car like my Beetle. I said I hoped that in ten years things would have improved, and paid for the men's second vodka. The waitress declined everything. (Gomulka's regime has introduced strict anti-vodka rules, such as no vodka sales on paydays or certain holidays. Foreign journalists, I'm told, usually get round this by persuading the waiter to bring vodka in a soda water bottle.)

I chatted later with Frau Erna Becker, one of the few Germans still living in Bartoszyce, born in the area, the wife of a joiner. She said they both had to work to make some kind of a living and wanted to leave for Germany, but had not been given permission, perhaps because her husband was a useful craftsman. On the other hand, she added, they were still attached to their homeland, even in its present state. She said things had improved in the past year or two – a statement I heard from others. Of course, the improvement is only comparative.

At the police station I again picked up my companion of yesterday whose name, I learned, was Baranowski. When I asked him if he were a detective, he expressed surprise and said, 'No.' In the police station I was told that, according to the law, I should not have taken pictures of the village, as it was so near the frontier. After I explained that they were purely for private purposes and did not show the frontier itself, I was allowed to retain the films.

Then Baranowski and I set off again, but not for Schönbruch, as he said I should not go there again as it is right on the frontier. (I'd been told earlier that the Poles did not guard the frontier, but left it to the Russians.) We drove instead to Trosiny (in German, Trosienen), a former estate about half a mile south of Schönbruch. It comprises a large farmhouse or manor house and surrounding buildings, formerly owned by a family called Rohde, now living in West Germany. Elfi went to school with their daughter.

Baranowski said I must not take pictures there; this was forbidden without special permission within 50 km (30 miles) of the frontier. But he was most helpful in interpreting what I said to some of the local Polish inhabitants. As in Schönbruch, the buildings looked neglected. A dozen or so children played around the buildings. Lots of ducks and poultry about. Men harvesting in the fields. I noticed grain, clover and potatoes. A little girl let me into what was once the Rohdes' handsome house, now occupied by several private farmers who have been given land, once part of the big farm. Most of the locals are expellees from former Eastern Poland, which became part of Soviet Ukraine in 1945.

The little girl's family evidently lived upstairs, for she let me into the attic, where I scuffled about looking for a bit of paper with German on it – 14 years since this territory became Polish. At last I found a little card, the sort one gets with crackers or a box of sweets, with a German motto on it. One of the adjoining buildings still bore the 'R' (in concrete) of the Rohde family, and the date 1836 or 1856. A dirty half-shaven old man produced a Nazi medal for Labour Day (1 May) 1934, and another medal, with the word Schönbruch on it, awarded for a shooting competition in, I think, 1935. I bought the medals for about 150 zloty, had some of the children and a woman fetch me some apples and bought ten eggs. I delighted each of the children by giving them either a West German or East German 10-pfennig piece. One or two of them started chewing them; I used to do that too.

As we left Trosiny, men working in a field waved and one took off his cap as though I were a feudal lord, though I imagine it was merely Polish courtesy. Poles spatter their conversation with 'prosze pana' ('please sir' or 'please mister'). Polish is easier to pronounce than it looks when written. Take Szczecin, for instance, which looks unpronounceable if you give the letters their English values. But in fact 'sz' is English 'sh' and 'cz' is English 'ch', so that Khrushchev in Polish would, I suppose, be Kruszczew.

Elfi did not exaggerate when she told me of the beautiful countryside around Schönbruch. It is mainly flat, but with one or two small rises making it more interesting. Today, at harvest time, with the grain partly standing and partly in haycocks and the trees in full leaf, it looked really lovely. In Bartenstein I bought a large bottle of perfume each for Elfi and Mutti (my mother-in-law) as a memento of their home area.

As I drove back towards Warsaw, I picked up an elderly motor mechanic who, when I asked him what he thought of Gomulka, replied with typical Polish frankness, 'Oh, he's just a Red, same as Khrushchev.' He had visited Russia a year or two ago and did not think it had improved since the 1917 revolution. But he agreed that things seemed to be going ahead now and that the last war had thrown them back a lot. Had a good lunch in the regional capital, Olsztyn (formerly Allenstein), served by a young German who had not been allowed to move to Germany. The city of about 65,000 looked in good shape, with much new building evident. *[Nearly 40 years later, thanks to a coincidence, the first volume of my memoirs, was printed – cheaply and well – in Olsztyn.]*

Back in Central Poland again, I picked up a couple of hitch-hiking scouts. One of them said Poland had a low cultural standard and needed to emulate certain Western nations, including Britain and France. Did they drink vodka? Horrified cries of: 'No, we are scouts.' It was dark when I reached Poznan, about 120 miles from the German frontier. I was so tired that I kept having to stop the car, get out, walk round it a few times, swinging my arms until I woke up sufficiently to drive a few more miles. At a level crossing where I had been stopped, I dozed and then woke up to find it open again. Reached my East Berlin hotel around 05.00 and fell into a deep sleep.

26 July 1959 : Attended a Quaker Meeting for Worship in East Berlin. Two old women spoke, basically on the theme that for the person who loves God everything turns out right. During the meeting, the thought came to me that I ought to try to help someone in poor Poland. It's not right that we live so well and other countries do not. In fact it is a sin on our part but, of course, we keep on sinning.

30 July 1959 : A delightful couple of hours at the big house in Charlottenburg, West Berlin, owned by prominent West German banker, Hermann Abs, but commandeered by the British occupation authorities. It is the home of George Turner, chief British information officer in Berlin – a Yorkshireman – and his wife Marjorie. George's personal view was that the Berlin problem should first be tackled by offering a deal to the Russians under which propaganda and espionage would be cut down on both sides. Judging by the latest news from the foreign ministers' conference in Geneva, it is getting nowhere.

George and I agreed it was vital that West Berlin be allowed to choose its own destiny and not to be swallowed up by the Communists by force. If it wants to go Communist in 20 years, should the Communist system have proved so attractive by then, good luck to it, I say. I expressed my view – which goes against the official British and West German view – that East Germany ought to be recognized by the Western powers as a way of getting something in return for that recognition. In my view, recognition will come sooner or later.

[The centre–left government of West Germany, led by the Social Democrat Willy Brandt, recognized East Germany as a separate, though not foreign state in 1972. The three Western Powers, and other non-Communist countries, accorded diplomatic recognition to East Germany later in the seventies.]

20 Nixon in Warsaw

1 August 1959 : After a little holiday with my family in Berlin, they left for Bonn and I drove off again towards Warsaw, to cover a visit by the United States Vice-President, Richard Nixon. Overnighted in Poznan, in a good hotel, the Bazar, where two men from Krupps of Essen told me they did not think it right that one man should own such a firm. However, they admired the present Krupp, Alfried, personally for his declared intention, largely fulfilled, to keep out of arms production. (The firm is, however, making some military aircraft.)

In the hotel the barber is named in French (*coiffeur*), Polish (*fryzjer*) and Russian (*parikmakher* – the old German word for wigmaker). An old Polish man told me over coffee that he had been expelled from Poznan, his hometown, by the Germans when they annexed the area to the Reich during the Second World War.

2 August 1959 : A good drive down that excellent road to Warsaw, but sadly I bagged one hen and three birds – Polish poultry and birds have not learned about motorcars yet. Asked a boy and girl student, whom I picked up, what they thought of Poland's present frontiers. The girl, who had taken me for a German because of my Volkswagen, said, 'We want that land and you want that land.' Later picked up two perfumed young men who turned out to be apprentice barbers. A haircut costs five zloty – about 1s 6d *[7¹/₂p]* at the official rate.

Around five pm, Nixon arrived in his long-range Boeing 707 jet at Babice military airport. On the way out to the airport with

David and his two local Polish assistants, Anna and George, there were not many people waiting on the streets because the authorities had not, as in Khrushchev's case, announced the route or the exact time of arrival, nor had they flagged the streets. But by the time Nixon entered the city, the crowds had grown a lot, and David, who saw the reception for Khrushchev, said they were nearly as large as the 100,000 which was estimated then by Polish newspapers.

I stood at one point where the crowd surged round the American Vice-President's car, clapped and cheered. Nixon called to them. At another place, George told me, Nixon shouted in Polish, 'Long live Poland.' It is pleasing that Nixon can come to Warsaw and be received warmly both by the people and the Communist authorities.

3 August 1959 : The main thing about the Nixon story is how the people are reacting. David had a good story on enthusiastic scenes when Nixon laid a wreath at a war memorial, and I did one on Mrs Nixon being warmly welcomed by a small crowd when she visited a trim nursery school. A few old men in overalls and open-necked shirts pushed forward in the crowd so they could kiss her hand. Mrs Nixon has a pleasant face and – like her husband – knows how to give the photographers a good picture. David and I keep swapping remarks about Nixon doing presidential election campaigning in Poland. *[Nixon stood as the Republican candidate in the 1960 US presidential election, but lost to John F. Kennedy. He was elected President in 1968, when he narrowly defeated Vice-President Hubert Humphrey.]*

Tonight the Poles gave a reception for Nixon in that same baroque palace – the Prime Minister's residence – where Khrushchev was entertained on 22 July. Fewer secret policemen around this time. Nixon spoke without notes, quite an appealing voice, about the overriding need for peace in spite of different political and social systems.

Today's most important event was the announcement in Washington and Moscow that Khrushchev is to visit the United

States and President Eisenhower the Soviet Union. As Nixon helped to lay the basis for this by paying a visit to Moscow, his reaction to the announcement, after he had been in conference with the Polish leaders, was a good story. The gist was that he favoured the visit, not only because it gave the opportunity for talks on world issues, but also because it would enable Khrushchev to learn more about what the United States really was like.

4 August 1959 : Trailed Nixon, first to the site of the former ghetto, where he posed sombrely in the ruins of a prison where the Nazis carried out poison-gas experiments. David and I both thought he overdid the posing for photographers, and we made snide remarks about his bid to win the Jewish and Polish vote in the States. On to Palmiry cemetery, in a wood outside Warsaw, in an area where the Nazis shot about 20,000 Poles. The bodies of about 2,200 were found and buried in that cemetery. No wonder, after their past, that the Poles are strongly nationalist.

A little boy wandered into the cemetery and gave Nixon flowers he had plucked in the fields. The Vice-President gave him a propelling pencil, with Nixon's name on it, and told him he could do his schoolwork with it. Back to Warsaw's Old City, where gabled houses and a picturesque square reminiscent of Brussels or Ghent have been lovingly rebuilt. Several thousand people waited to see Nixon, though many were kept away from him by police. Outside the redbrick cathedral of St John, the crowd clapped and cheered and threw flowers, often white and red ones, the Polish national colours. There were more claps when Nixon said one of his Polish phrases, 'Long live Polish–American friendship.'

There was an even more enthusiastic scene when Nixon visited the university. As well as cheers and claps, there was the singing of *Sto Lat (Let him live a Hundred Years)*, a signal honour to a visitor, a sort of Polish *For he's a Jolly Good Fellow*. True, Poles sang this for Khrushchev, too, here and there. No doubt they were different Poles, though perhaps just as sincere about it.

With horns blaring, the Nixon motorcade had to nose its way through the crowd to get out of the university yard.

Tonight it was the turn of the Americans to give a reception, in their embassy or, mainly, in the leafy garden dotted with lights. Nixon kept to his basic theme: let us maintain peace in spite of differences in the social order, and let us strengthen traditional Polish–American friendship. Cyrankiewicz, who spoke for the Poles, also stressed the need for the peaceful settlement of disputes and the absurdity of war, but once again attacked 'West German militarism'.

By chance, David found out that the Poles had got nowhere in their attempts, during their talks with Nixon, to bring about some change in the United States' positive attitude towards West German rearmament. The Poles had also failed to obtain the prospect of some kind of final US assent to Poland's postwar Western frontiers, which were demarcated at the Yalta and Potsdam conferences in 1945, but are still officially regarded by the Western allies as provisional, pending a peace treaty with Germany, even though few people regard any change as possible or desirable.

Incidentally the American Associated Press correspondent, another Johnson, Stanley, was expelled during the Khrushchev visit after he had mistakenly reported that Gomulka had referred to General de Gaulle as a dog. In fact, Gomulka had referred to West German irredentists calling de Gaulle a dog, because the French leader had spoken out in support of Poland's present frontiers. Bearing the same name as a correspondent who had just been expelled made me a little worried.

5 August 1959 : David takes the view that the Nixon visit is one up for the Polish Communists under Gomulka, in that it gave some backing for the *status quo* in Poland. I think that's true and I also think that it is right to back the *status quo* in Poland, which is a far more acceptable state of affairs than if Gomulka – and Khrushchev – had not come to power. Nixon received a warm send-off.

Lunch with George, who told me he was from the former upper middle-class and was a member of a hunting club of about 25 persons, including several former noblemen and no workers. George looks like a minor English country gentleman. With his appealing smile, just visible under his gingery moustache, he said, 'I love to kill animals and eat them afterwards.' He told me that, while in the Stalin era he was not allowed to have a hunting licence, as he worked for the British embassy – which he still does now, as well as for Reuters – anyone could have one now. Hunting licences used to be issued by the secret police. Now the ordinary police do that.

Took a few farewell carnations to Leszek's mother. In a toast, his father said, 'To our freedom.' When I said it all depended on what you meant by freedom, he retorted, 'Well, we haven't got freedom anyway.' That is indisputable. The question is, who has? Or to what degree? Britain has a good portion, so much so that people don't appreciate it.

6 August 1959 : As I drove back to Berlin today, one of my hitch-hikers in Poland was a 45-ish man who had lived in France for about 20 years and greatly regretted his decision to return to Poland in 1947. Since then, he said, he had not been allowed to leave. He added that, with his good job in France, he had been able to earn as much in 14 days as in 6 months in Poland. He'd been a factory economist in France and is a clerk in Poland. He also spoke highly of German organization compared to Polish.

Another Pole told me today that some Poles he'd met in former East Prussia said they had been better off under German rule there, because their work was better paid and things were better organized.

8 August 1959 : In East Berlin saw a full-length Czech cartoon film, based on drawings by Jean Effel, called *The Creation of the World*. Though avowedly atheist, it had some heart-warming touches. It showed, for instance, how a white-bearded God created a rose by drawing it in mid-air; then the Devil got to work and put some thorns on it. The Devil and his aides were also shown as responsible for creating opium, coffee and alcohol; and they had something to do with woman.

There were some political cracks in the film, some of which could be seen as anti-Communist as, for instance, when God plants a forest of trees and tells them that if they don't behave they will be on half rations, but that if they follow orders they will be all right.

11 August 1959 : Am spending much of my time scouring East Berlin for office furniture, which is scarce. Why? I suppose partly because production has not increased quickly enough to satisfy the increased demand caused by the economic upsurge. Add to this bad organization, causing the production of some things not so necessary instead of ensuring basic needs. It's hard, for instance, to get a simple kitchen chair, but you can buy a home bar with a built-in refrigerator.

12 August 1959 : Still chasing furniture. Had to appeal to the Foreign Ministry to get me priority for a desk, which will be ready in early September.

13 August 1959 : Managed to buy a handsome oak bedroom suite for 1,800 East marks (£158), including bedding – about twice the West German price. (The official exchange rate is one East mark for one West mark.)

Rang up one of our closest West German friends, Fritz Söhner, who lives in Bonn, to tell him I had been able to get news of his 60-ish East German mother who, I learned yesterday, had been arrested by the East Germans for illegally – under East German law – changing East German money into West German money in West Berlin and sending the proceeds to Fritz.

I'd spoken to the prosecutor in Delitzsch, near Leipzig, where Frau Söhner lives. He said, in answer to my question, that it would certainly do no harm if Fritz sent the money back, and this I advised him to do. The prosecutor said he expected Frau Söhner would be tried in about three weeks. This is one of the countless sadnesses that arise from the division of Germany.

14 August 1959 : Moved into my office/flat, Reuters first office in East Germany. Am typing this late tonight in the office of the three-and-a-half room (plus kitchen and bathroom) accommodation at 27 Schönhauser Allee, first floor. At this point the wide road is a pleasant boulevard with trees on the pavements and also on a centre strip where one can sit. It is planned to make the road into a kind of East Berlin Kurfürstendamm, that is, a high-class shopping and entertainment area. The road has already had its face lifted here and there. *[After the Communist regime collapsed in 1989 I learned that, at some stage, the Stasi had rented a room next to the Reuter office to ease its surveillance of the agency.]*

By lunchtime all the teleprinters needed to start work were operating. I get Reuters service from London via ADN, the East German news agency, and Bonn sends me service messages along the same line. I receive ADN's news service direct from them. I am sending my stories for the time being by telex to Bonn. Later I shall send them on a leased line to ADN, which will pass them on to Bonn, with which they are already connected by a Reuter wire.

Still have not obtained the office chairs I want. Am sitting on an easy chair at a desk, having raised myself on a pile of newspapers. My West Berlin colleagues, Alfred Klühs, a German, and Fred Ungeheuer, an American, together with Alfred's doctor wife, Gaby, came over this evening. We toasted the new office, which looks smart after redecoration, in Romanian champagne and East German vodka. Have failed to buy a bucket, of all things. One shopkeeper told me he had had none for four months. He had been able to get them regularly until two years ago. Begged him to save me one when, as he hopes, a few come in next month.

16 August 1959 : After the East Berlin Quaker Meeting for Worship, chatted with a Jordanian medical student who was of the view, as am I, that the majority of people in East Germany do not want the kind of state they have got – however good it may be in some respects. He said that even if a people wanted to do something silly, they should be allowed to do so.

Also talked to a West Berlin Quaker lady who had been working at a hostel in West Berlin, financed mainly by the West German government, where people from West Germany can meet relatives from East Germany who are not allowed to travel to West Germany but can come to West Berlin. (Clearly the East German travel restrictions turn many people against the regime; one can imagine the conversations that go on at this hostel.) The Quaker lady told me she had given up the job when she found out that the West German authorities were using the hostel to make propaganda instead of solely for humanitarian purposes and to serve peace, as she said she had wanted to do. That's the Cold War – on both sides.

Sunday is also the day when, whenever I can, I nip over to West Berlin to have *Kaffee und Kuchen* with three of Elfi's old aunts, who share a comfortable nineteenth-century flat in the suburb of Friedenau. The flat survived the war thanks to the fact that a British landmine which came down in its back garden was a dud or, in that expressive German word, a *Blindgänger* or 'blind goer'.

Today, as well as the cake, with cherries and whipped cream, there was much talk about East Germany. They objected most of all to the pressure put on people to do what they don't want to do – for instance, to join a collective farm. They also condemned the travel restrictions. One of the aunts' lady friends argued that the East German leaders were bad people who were exploiting the workers and so on, but I contested this, saying they were trying to improve things for the workers but were sometimes using bad methods.

17 August 1959 : An East German man I know said one could accept most of what is being done by the regime if only one had the freedom to travel where and when one wanted. (The Poles do have this freedom to a large extent.) He also thought that the regime was often motivated by sheer dogmatism: for instance, using various means of pressure to force small craftsmen into cooperatives and shopkeepers into state sales trusts. I don't think Marx would have wanted that. He wanted to get rid of evils, not to make people unhappy and harm the economy.

18 August 1959 : All my teleprinters went out for a couple of hours thanks to an electrical fault. Our German odd-job man and cleaner traced the fault to an old piece of wire.

In a West Berlin restaurant, the waiter told me he'd been a British citizen, though German-born, but had returned to Germany before the Second World War and had joined, of all things, the *Waffen SS*, an elite Nazi military formation. He said he had been very keen about the *Waffen SS* in those days. He did not seem much less keen today, though he deprecated what was done to the Jews; not by the *Waffen SS*, he said, but by the *General* SS (which included concentration camp guards). He said, former *Waffen SS* soldiers dissociated themselves from the *General SS*.

[Although the Waffen SS *were mainly elite troops, some* Waffen SS *units did take part in mass murders of Jews on the eastern front.]*

19 August 1959 : More teleprinter trouble. This time paper jammed because the machines were on the floor. Put them on a trestle and it shouldn't happen again. Soon afterwards my telephone dial stuck, so I have to push it backwards by hand until it is mended. A silver lining: have found lots of buckets, zinc and enamel, in a shop near my office. Summing up my shopping experiences so far: there is a great variety of stuff for sale, including consumer goods of all kinds, perhaps too great a variety, which sometimes causes simpler things to become scarce. Food shops are well stocked, prices in general bearable by comparison with West Germany.

A visiting correspondent of the Soviet Communist Party newspaper *Pravda*, Naumov, told me he thought the atmosphere in factories had improved a lot since he was last here about two years ago. Although I agreed with him, I added that I thought the majority of the population was still anti-government. He accused me of saying that to be nice to the Bonn government, as if I'd do a thing like that! I think the anti-government feeling is partly a backlog from the Stalinist period. In addition, while most people probably agree with many of the recent reforms, they do not agree with the way they were imposed nor do they like the travel restrictions, the instilling of Communist dogma and the use of pressures against church members.

There is something about running the office on my own that occasionally gives me the exhilaration I knew when, aged about 14, a boyhood friend and I brought out a 'magazine' on a typewriter which was so antiquated that you had to go round the back of it to read what you had typed.

20 August 1959 : The new East Berlin correspondent of *Izvestia*, the Soviet government newspaper, Yenakiev, is an appealing youngish chap. *Izvestia*, he said, is more interesting than *Pravda*; it even carries children's funny sayings. One he retailed to me: about a bald-headed father who suggested to his offspring that he or she should draw Daddy. Reply: 'I'm sorry but I haven't got a bald-headed pencil.'

Over dinner I tried to convince Yenakiev that in Britain, if a wrong is done, there is far more chance of righting it than in a Communist country. He disagreed, saying that, in the post-Stalin era, the Communist parties were very active in preventing wrongs. However, he did concede I had a point when I said that in the Stalin era, if he had known about atrocities such as those committed by British prison authorities in Kenya some months ago, he could not have done anything about it for fear of losing his head, whereas in the British case the opposition and the press took the matter up. Yenakiev appeared to me to be so sure of the basic rightness of communism that he accepted all its twists and turns, and its propaganda, as gospel.

21 August 1959 : Sutulov, one of the Soviet embassy officials who deals with the press, told me today that capitalism was doomed by history and would, one could not say when, vanish because it was ill. I retorted that Communists were ill in thinking that capitalism was bound to vanish, rather than modifying itself, which communism was doing. I maintained it would be possible to keep some elements of capitalism within a planned economy, and said that the free enterprise system sometimes gave better results for the consumer than socialist planning did; it put more desirable goods in the shops. I was thinking of my efforts, recently crowned with success, to buy a bucket in East Germany.

21 Frontier trouble

22 August 1959 : ADN tipped me off that a good story was shortly to come on their printer. This enabled me quickly to send my version of an East German Interior Ministry announcement that about 30 people from West Germany had destroyed frontier defences near Erfurt, Thuringia, early yesterday. The statement called this 'a serious provocation'. (The sort of thing, I suppose, which could be a pretext for war if someone on one side, or both, wanted this.)

West German police said they suspected that young people were responsible for the incident, in which 12 concrete frontier posts were uprooted and wire was removed. The East German statement said West German border guards and customs officials were present and did nothing to stop the incident. ADN interpreted it as another effort by West German leaders to harm the international atmosphere on the eve of talks between Eisenhower and Khrushchev. Not impossible, of course, but I wouldn't know – and neither would ADN.

23 August 1959 : Drove out to the village of Altenhof on Lake Werbellin, about 50 miles northeast of Berlin, passing a few miles from the ruins of Hermann Göring's country home, Karinhall. My destination was the 'Wilhelm Pieck Pioneer Republic', named after the 83-year-old East German President, a veteran Communist. *[Pieck died on 7 September 1960.]* This is a permanent camp for active members of the Communist children's organization, the Thälmann Pioneers, named after the pre-war leader

213

of the German Communist Party, Ernst Thälmann, who was murdered in the concentration camp of Buchenwald, near Weimar, in 1944. The Thälmann Pioneers, children aged between 6 and 14, are the junior section of the Free German Youth. They wear white shirts and red neckerchiefs.

The camp houses about 1,000 in handsome stone buildings set in woods, plus a further 500 in tents in summer. I went there to meet 19 British boys and girls, led by two adults, members of the Woodcraft Folk, a youth organization founded in 1921. It is linked with the cooperative movement. One of their leaders, a pleasant 30-ish man from Harrow, northwest London, said their organization aimed at international friendship. He told me he did not believe in trying to force politics down kids' throats. He did not realize his words could have been taken as a criticism of the Thälmann Pioneers who, like Catholic clerics, do force ideology down children's throats. However, perhaps 'force' is unfair, as I'm sure the Communist instructors think they are acting for the best – like the Catholics, even though they may both be wrong.

24 August 1959 : The main Communist newspaper, *Neues Deutschland*, published a policy statement to prepare for the tenth anniversary of the East German state, which falls on 7 October. This statement annoyed me for suggesting that, years ago, the majority of East Germans were behind the SED, when it was obvious – even to SED members – they were not, whatever may be the case now. It also referred to the June 1953 uprising as having been defeated, but did not mention that the defeating was done by Soviet troops.

It claimed that the rising was fomented because of bourgeois fears about the attractiveness of socialism in East Germany. In fact, life in East Germany then was not attractive, but highly unattractive, so that discontent was genuine and did not need to be fomented. While mentioning, rightly, production achievements of recent years, the policy statement omitted any mention of the numbers who have left East Germany for the West – between one and two million since the state was founded.

214

25 August 1959 : I finally got my longed-for office chair, so I can stop sitting on a low armchair, raising myself on an extra cushion or a typewriter lid. A real joy.

26 August 1959 : As the only Western non-Communist reporter accredited in East Germany, was invited into the trial of four East Germans accused of espionage either for the American or West German secret service. About 300 'factory delegates', many in shirtsleeves because of the heat, made up most of the audience in the wood-panelled East Berlin courtroom. The East German hammer-and-dividers symbol was on the wall behind the bench of three judges in dark business suits. The four accused were in a wooden dock at one side of the bench, with a soldier sitting behind each of them. Two more soldiers were outside the dock. Below the dock were the four defence lawyers.

Three of the accused gave evidence today. They were two middle-aged men a Leipzig mechanic and a Rostock docker – and a young woman. Questioned by the presiding judge, all three told in detail how they had been hired by a secret service in West Berlin, had been trained there and had transmitted information from East Germany to West Berlin or had taken it there while on visits. The mechanic said he had sent 150 letters in invisible ink to West German cover addresses. Later all three had been trained as radio operators and equipped with small radio sets, with tape recorders, used for recording coded messages received on their home radios. Using the tape recorders, they could play back the messages slowly and decode them. Two of the accused said they had been told to be ready by 28 May: the start of the period in which the Soviet Union had originally been threatening to hand over its Berlin control powers to East Germany.

The young woman, who lived in East Berlin, close to the sector border with West Berlin, said she had been equipped additionally with an infra-red walkie-talkie which, I understand, cannot be tapped. Its signal is transmitted only in a straight line. She had used it by a window in her flat to send a message to an American car standing in a nearby West Berlin street. This method would have enabled her to communicate with the Americans if the sector borders had been closed, as was thought possible before the East–West negotiations began. The docker said he had provided information on shipping and on East German and Soviet military units. I have no doubt that the confessions of these three people were materially true. They had been betrayed by a Western agent who defected to East Germany a few months ago.

The prosecutor and the presiding judge, by loaded questions or mere allegations, sought to make it appear that these spying efforts were part of an American and West German plan to launch an attack on East Germany, in which nuclear weapons would be used. There was, however, no evidence of plans to launch such an attack. The evidence was that the two secret services were making preparations for a possible crisis or war. (It was stated that the agents were issued with special abbreviated coded radio signals about military movements which were to be used in case of war.) In my view, with the situation as it was after Khrushchev started the moves intended to change the status of Berlin, it was the duty of any intelligence service to make such preparations.

I found it interesting how the presiding judge sought to explain to the audience of factory workers the political background of the case, according to Marxist ideology. For instance, he said that the docker, as a young man before the war, had been a member of the right-wing *Stahlhelm* organization (later incorporated into the Nazi party), and that after the East German land reform of 1945, when he was the owner of a medium-sized farm, he had been angry because farm labourers who had worked for him had quit because they had been given land of their own by the state. The judge said that these two factors, and the man's readiness to become a spy, were in a direct line. The judge reproved the fourth accused, a physicist, who gave his evidence later, for having 'betrayed the state' which had enabled him to study at no cost for several years.

27 August 1959 : After many talks with East Germans, I have come to the conclusion that the worst thing about this system is that it denies a people the right to develop in the way it wants, by putting them in an ideological straitjacket called Marxism–Leninism. That does not mean that the things the regime wants to do are necessarily bad – i.e. to cut out exploitation of man by man and continuously increase production for everyone's benefit, and gradually replace the profit motive by, at least partly, the motive of socialist cooperation. What is wrong is to force people to do such things, instead of gradually persuading them to accept socialist reforms, as was the case in Britain.

I can understand that Russian and Chinese Communists, faced with dictatorial and corrupt opponents, decided that the only way of achieving their aims was by taking totalitarian power themselves. But by doing this in East Germany, the Communists have made themselves once again the 'red bogey' for the rest of Germany and have made it even harder for the Social Democrats in West Germany to win a parliamentary majority to carry out, democratically, some of the things the Communists are carrying out undemocratically. All I can hope for is that communism as a whole will liberalize itself further – there's been definite progress in that respect since the Stalin era – and adopt at least some of what Communists dismiss as the 'so-called bourgeois freedoms', such as the freedom to read what one wants (even if one can't do as one wants) and to travel where one pleases.

28 August 1959 : Have been preparing a background report on the coming tenth anniversary of the East German state. My main conclusion is that a terrific amount has been achieved in the past few years and that there is no question of West Germany absorbing East Germany, as some dreamers in Bonn appear to think. That means that one has to consider, at least in the long run, recognizing East Germany and making some practical arrangement regarding Berlin.

Alfred Klühs presented me with an old kitchen chair from his palatial West Berlin home for the East Berlin flat, as I had not chased one up yet. I learned that the last occupant of the flat had fled West after serving a prison sentence for black-marketeering.

29 August 1959 : Covered the closing stage of the spy trial. The mechanic and the docker each got life, the physicist 15 years and the woman 12 years. It is difficult to decide whether one regards such sentences as just, but I suppose similar sentences would be imposed in similar circumstances in Britain or the United States. The judgement included much political polemic, which was not justified by the evidence, but fitted the official line. Perhaps the trial was put on this week because of the presence of Eisenhower in Bonn – to show him that West Berlin really is an important espionage centre (as if he didn't know), or to gain more publicity for this in the West.

30 August 1959 : In Leipzig for the autumn fair. This is always smaller than the spring one, as it lacks the large industrial exhibits. I missed Khrushchev too. However, this year's autumn fair is the biggest ever, as its area has been slightly increased to about 112,000 square metres (around 1,200,000 sq ft) and 45 countries are represented, compared with 38 last year and fewer than 10 when the fair restarted in 1949. An important feature is the entry of the Soviet Union and China into the autumn fair as large exporters of consumer goods and foods. (Most of the fair is occupied by the two Germanys.)

I was allowed to have a preview of the Soviet and Chinese exhibits, before the fair officially opened at midday. I followed Heinrich Rau, the Foreign Trade Minister, and his official party. The Soviet Union showed about 6,000 articles which, as well as traditional items such as furs, vodka and handicrafts, included the Moskvich small family car, motor scooters, mopeds, three or four types of refrigerators, two or three kinds of washing machines and 33 different radio and television sets and tape-recorders.

The radios and televisions looked old-fashioned and most of the TVs had smaller screens than in the West. Picture quality did not seem as good either. A spokesman talking about the watches being exhibited amused me by his strong insistence that they were reliable. Another spokesman told Rau that the watches did not lose more than five seconds a day. There were also some attractive-looking clothes and textiles, and a variety of cameras. An East German official, inspecting some of the washing machines, was critical, saying he thought they would take too long to heat up and were made of metal that was too thin.

China's exhibit, though more tastefully set out than that of the Soviet Union, had a much smaller range, though it included three or four radios, made partly from East German parts. The accent was on textiles, including some lovely brocades and finished kimonos, if that's the right word for China too. There were also American-type mechanical toys, and toothpaste with the label 'spearmint chlorophyll'. As for the prices, a Chinese spokesman said they would differ according to the buyer. Later I saw some of the British exhibitors — only 13 altogether — who did not seem enthusiastic about increasing sales.

At a reception given by the Chamber of Foreign Trade tonight, chatted with Arthur Lewis, a Labour MP, and G.B. Drayson, Tory MP for Skipton, Yorkshire. Both have some commercial interest in the fair, which they have been visiting for years. They were impressed by the improvement in East German goods.

I also spoke to a West German 'defector', Karlfranz Schmidt-Wittmack, a former Christian Democratic member of the *Bundestag*, who moved to East Germany in 1954 and was made a vice-president of the Chamber of Foreign Trade. Lewis and I quizzed him about the East German travel restrictions and I gained the impression that he did not approve of them and thought they were likely to be lifted if more confidence was achieved between East and West Germany.

[According to the West German Ministry for All-German Affairs, Schmidt-Wittmack, born in 1914, joined the Nazi party in 1938, was a junior officer in the German air force during the Second World War and after the war became an informant of the East German intelligence service.]

31 August 1959 : Spoke to more British exhibitors, mainly textile manufacturers, and found some optimism about improved trade, partly due to the new trade agreement signed earlier this year between the East German Chamber and the Federation of British Industries. *[That agreement sidestepped the question of the diplomatic recognition of East Germany.]* Have obtained a nice little story about a West Berlin agent for Scotch whisky and other capitalist drinks who has recently started selling this stuff to Communist countries, which keep coming for more. This is an illustration of how things are changing economically. Up to now, though, he told me, the Russians had held out.

After weeks of lobbying, was today presented with a short statement – exclusive to me and ADN – announcing that Klaus Fuchs had been given the same job in East Germany – deputy director of the central nuclear research institute – as he had in Britain before he was arrested. Managed to get a good interview with Fuchs' new boss, Professor Heinz Barwich, the head of the institute, which is in Rossendorf, near Dresden. Later got a few words from Fuchs expressing pleasure at his appointment. He is in a sanatorium in Thuringia and intends to start work in September.

[Fuchs remained in the Rossendorf post until his retirement. He died in 1988. Barwich, a former Siemens employee, was one of the German physicists who worked in the Soviet Union for several years after the Second World War. As well as his post in Rossendorf, he was deputy director of the Soviet bloc's nuclear research centre at Dubno, near Moscow, from 1960 until early in 1964. While attending an international conference on nuclear energy in Geneva in 1964, he defected to the West and was given political asylum in the United States. He moved to West Germany in 1965 and died in 1966.]

2 September 1959 : Hedda Zinner, a prize-winning East German playwright, has written a semi-comedy entitled *What would happen if . . .* In it, three photographers arrive at an East German village near the West German frontier and are thought to be Western officials who have come to restore the old regime.

The play, I was told, shows that there are some people who want the old regime back and that there are some who are hesitant, but ends with firm backing for the 'workers' and farmers' state'. I don't think the Communists have anything like the popularity which would enable them to make such an experiment in reality. Maybe they will have, some day, if they continue to improve their methods and the standard of living.

4 September 1959 : Took one of Elfi's West Berlin old aunts, Trudchen, to see a German translation of *Macbeth* done by an East Berlin theatre, the Volksbühne. We had a good laugh when she maintained it was not by Shakespeare, but Schiller. With the aid of the programme, I managed to put her right. The play was well done. It was fun to recognize bits like, 'Is this a dagger I see before my eyes?' coming over in German. Trudchen, who has not been to a show in East Berlin for some months at least, commented with amazement on how well-dressed the theatregoers were. There is indeed a great difference from the overall dowdiness of three or four years ago, when I first visited East Berlin.

22 Visit to a Stasi agent

7 September 1959 : On my way home to Bonn, called on an East German agricultural journalist and Communist, Wolfgang Warzok, in the regional capital of Erfurt, close to West Germany – had got to know him last year. He told me that collective farms were improving, but also said that, as a result of watching a programme on West German television, some farmers in his area had left a collective. I was surprised to learn they could do this at all, after once joining.

The young Communist headmaster of a secondary school, where Warzok is the chairman of the parent–teacher committee, visited the Warzoks this evening. He made a good impression on me, as did the Warzoks and their two teenage children, a girl and a boy. I felt that, if this were communism, we could live with it, without necessarily adopting it ourselves.

[After the reunification of Germany in 1990, I learned from formerly secret documents of the East German State Security Service, the Stasi, that Warzok had been informing on me to the Stasi, which suspected I might have been working for British intelligence. I was pleased to see that the reports Warzok wrote on me were truthful. I let him know that I had seen the documents, but he did not react to that. Parts of his reports were unintentionally amusing. For instance, he quoted Elfi as saying that had she known beforehand that, as a result of my career, she would have to move house 20 times, she would never have married me.]

8 September 1959 : After passing through four or five sets of

East German frontier checks – a terrible advertisement for communism – and one West German one, I drove about 40 miles further westwards to call on Henner Pflug, our Social Democratic (ex-Nazi) schoolteacher friend and his wife Hanna in Altenbauna, near Kassel. Henner, from the Kassel area, was a schoolteacher in Elfi's home village, Schönbruch, in East Prussia, where he married Hanna, an East Prussian widow.

We talked a lot about West German government claims for the restitution of former German territories that were placed under Polish and Soviet administration in 1945. These claims are taught in detail in schools. I criticised this as only keeping old wounds open, because no realist thinks there is any hope of Germany getting any of this territory back, and harping on it only tends to harm East–West relations. Henner at first defended the claims but, after thinking the matter over further, said he agreed with me. We all feel that it is sad for individuals to lose their homes, but I agreed with Henner that, until a peace treaty is signed with Germany, one cannot expect the West German government to drop claims in advance, but that same government seems to be doing all it can to prevent the conclusion of such a peace treaty. We agreed that there is only one solution to such questions in the long run: an end to frontiers and travel restrictions all round.

12 September 1959 : Played tennis as Fred Ungeheuer's guest at his Bonn tennis club. Club subscription about £18 a year, compared to 12 shillings *[60p]* at my East Berlin club. Very few public parks with tennis courts in West Germany, unlike Britain.

Walking in the hilly Bergisches Land, northeast of Bonn, Chris kept asking if there were wolves in the woods we saw.

13 September 1959 : The evening was enlivened by the news – what news! – that the Russians had landed an (unmanned) rocket on the moon, two days before Khrushchev arrives in the States. Listening to the radio news was like listening to a futuristic novel, except the future's here.

223

14 September 1959 : Elfi's 35th birthday. Inspired by the example of Klaus Fuchs' father, who in his biography mentions that he wrote poems for his wife on birthday cards, I did the same; a long time since I've done this. In this poem, after mulling it over a long time, I mentioned Jesus as being 'our guide'. I wondered if I wasn't being hypocritical, as I completely accept only very little of what is regarded as the Christian religion. But on thinking it over, I believe that I do regard Jesus as a guide in many important things and am thankful for him.

Left my folks again this afternoon to start my last three weeks in East Berlin. After about 200 miles – about halfway to Berlin – I overnighted in Vlotho, Westphalia, in the home of 60-ish Ursula Rohde, who used to be the lady of the manor at Trosienen, now Trosiny, the large estate that I visited recently, near Elfi's birthplace in former East Prussia, now in Poland. We talked for hours as she naturally wanted to know all I could remember of what I had seen, for I was the first person she knew who had been able to get there since the war.

She showed me photographs of the manor house and surrounding buildings in their smart pre-war and wartime state. Saddening to think of its present neglect. At the same time, I had to think of Hitler's attack on Poland and the fact that Herr Rohde, who died a couple of years ago, was a *Luftwaffe* officer recalled from the reserve to take part in the Polish campaign. No doubt he was right behind Hitler, at that stage anyway. I was glad that Frau Rohde, whom I like, expressed no hatred of the Poles or the poor farmers who now live in her former house. Frau Rohde's maiden name is Perkuhn, indicating that she is descended from that Baltic tribe, the Prussen, akin to the Lithuanians, who inhabited what became East Prussia when the Teutonic Knights conquered the region in the thirteenth century. Perkunos was the name of one of the old Prussen gods.

[The Rohde family later managed to establish friendly contacts with some of the Poles living on their former estate, visited them and sent them gifts.]

15 September 1959 : On my way to East Berlin, was given a drink of English tea by the captain in charge of the British checkpoint on the zonal frontier near Helmstedt, before I re-entered East Germany in growing darkness for the last 120 miles or so of my journey back.

16 September 1959 : In the East Berlin press club, bumped into owlish, appealing Richter, editor of *Das Volk*, the Communist regional organ published in Erfurt, whom I first met last year. As a refugee during the Second World War, he worked in Leeds and London, and joined the British engineering union. Richter accused me of being a member of the capitalist class, to which I retorted that I was, in working hours, a journalist who tried to be objective, and that he did not know what my off-duty politics were. He said I also seemed to be defending the capitalists or the Bonn 'fascists', to which I retorted that when I was talking to anti-Communists I always seemed to be defending the East German Communists. I think I must be too fair-minded!

17 September 1959 : Interviewed the first of four applicants for the post of office secretary, Erdmute Behrendt, a pleasant 22-year-old East Berliner with red-tinted hair, who is working as a translator for a state trading concern. She looks a likely choice. *[She got the job and stayed with Reuters in Berlin until she retired in 1998. I turned down the other three applicants for various reasons. One of them had excruciating English. She wrote, for instance: 'I shuold (sic) like to apply for the pointed out vacancy. I am sure my Englisch is in time not as god (sic) as necessary but I am as well sure that I got into it in a short time, since I lived in Great Britain up to 1939 till 1946.'*

My efforts to recruit a secretary taught me a little more about the East German dictatorship. I had innocently inserted a recruitment advert in an East Berlin newspaper. This produced several replies. When my action came to the notice of the authorities, a Foreign Ministry official reprimanded me and asked me, with annoyance, whether, if he were working in London, he would be allowed to insert an advert in a British newspaper. He seemed surprised when I told him he would.]

My West Berlin colleague, Alfred Klühs, is about to start a month's holiday; the Germans get more holiday than we do, thanks to their labour laws.

19 September 1959 : Read an interesting analysis in a French legal journal – not a Communist one – which came to the conclusion that West Germany's claim to be the only legal German state is untenable.

The *Izvestia* correspondent, Yenakiev, jokingly (I think) called me a 'Communist eater'. I told him I had a lot of respect for some Communists and that, if I'd been born a Russian or a Chinaman, I might well have been one myself, but that I didn't think they were necessary in my country. He said I was a patriot.

20 September 1959 : Attended the opening by Ulbricht of an exhibition marking the tenth anniversary of the Communist republic, which he described as the greatest revolution there had ever been in Germany. In my view it was not a revolution in the real sense, but the imposition of a new regime from outside – one of the reasons it has had so many difficulties. The exhibition itself shows that a lot has been achieved, though there is still a long way to go. However, the trend is continually upwards and there is no evident reason why this should not go on.

If one looks at the difference – displayed in a showcase – between what 500 East marks would buy in 1949, compared with today, and one thinks what the situation will be in another five or ten years, then the East Germans will have nothing to complain about materially. In 1949, 500 East marks (about £43), then about five weeks' wages for an average industrial worker, would buy: one bicycle tyre and tube, a pair of women's shoes, a pair of cotton socks and a 40-watt bulb. Today it would buy: a complete bicycle, a pair of men's corduroy trousers, a simple dress, a poplin shirt, a set of artificial silk underwear, a pair each of men's and women's shoes and stockings, and some cosmetics.

The exhibition also showed, in the form of treaties and trade agreements and pictures of delegation visits, East Germany's increasing international links. It represented West Germany, with former Nazis and Hitler generals again in leading positions, as a state of 'monopoly capitalists' who 'want war'; while it claimed that East Germany was devoted to the peaceful building of socialism and the ending of exploitation. There is no doubt that some former Nazis and generals are in positions of power in West Germany, but I don't think that any appreciable number want war.

I asked a Polish Communist journalist over lunch why he liked living. He said that, being an atheist, he could not advance the reasons of a Catholic. However, he added that he found life beautiful, though not some of the people in this world; he immediately excepted me. I told him I thought that Poles were some of the people who made life particularly interesting. As for why I like living I told him one reason was my family, another that life was interesting, and a third, to which he assented, that I wanted to do something to improve the world.

21 September 1959 : After trying without success for about six weeks to get an office desk, I decided today to buy one actually made for a living-room, which I tracked down some time ago at a joiners' cooperative. I would have to wait at least another month or two to get a normal office desk, I'm told, as the demand is so great. No shortage of work for anyone here at least, whatever else may be wrong. Have been perturbed that Khrushchev, during his visit to the United States, has several times lost his temper under questioning by admittedly not always very polite Americans, and has even threatened a couple of times to break off his trip. This is a bad sign in a man with so much power, even though he has in my view many good qualities.

My successor, lanky bespectacled Brian Horton, scion of a New Zealand newspaper-owning family, arrived today. *[I was disappointed that Gerry Long had stood by his decision to have the East Berlin post filled by a single man in the long term.]* In the Johannishof we celebrated his arrival with vodka and caviare.

Brian, who is a gourmet, complained that the caviare had been slightly salted.

A grand story fell into my lap today. Was told casually that Klaus Fuchs had married and followed up the story. Gleaned some details about his bride, Greta Keilson, 53, an associate of his Communist past, whom he first met after fleeing Germany in 1933, when he lived in Paris. *[She was the widow of Max Keilson, a former head of the East German Foreign Ministry press department, who died in 1953. She had held a number of posts in the SED party apparatus and in 1959 was an official of the Foreign Ministry press department.]*

When I phoned Fuchs, he declined to give me more than minimal additional information, but did tell me that he's started work today in his new post as deputy director of the central East German nuclear research station. Correspondents of British national newspapers kept ringing us up to help them on this lucky scoop, but we kept mum. That meant their papers had either to use our story or pretend it was their own man's and omit our credit. (The story was Reuters best European story of the day, according to the head office log.)

In a chat with Anatoli Gubanov, *Pravda* correspondent – a man with a face of character and humanity – he said I should have sent the boys to school in East Berlin. I would like it to be possible for the boys to go to a school where they were taught as objectively as possible, so they could make up their minds for themselves later. But I prefer them in a West German school to an East German school in the present situation, because they are not forced as much into one mould – however good – as is also the case in a Catholic seminary.

I see that Khrushchev has calmed down again, charmed by his reception on the way to and in San Francisco.

25 September 1959 : Took my leave from a number of East German and Soviet officials, and introduced them to Brian.

23 A model collective farm

29 September 1959 : Visited a 320-hectare (about 800-acre) collective farm, called 'The First of May', in the outer East Berlin suburb of Wartenberg. Was told this was one of the most successful collective farms. Its members receive 13.50 marks, roughly 23 shillings *[£1.18]* at the official rate, for a unit of work, a job taking between four and seven hours. The unsuccessful neighbouring collective pays only seven marks per work unit, the minimum allowed. It actually earns only 3.80 marks of this. The rest is made up by subsidy or state credit.

The Wartenberg collective started with four or five farms totalling about 100 hectares (250 acres) in 1953, one year after collectivization began in East Germany. At first the members merely tilled and harvested together, but retained individual ownership of cattle, horses and equipment. They were collectivized later. Each member who brought land into the collective retains title to it. If a member leaves, his or her land can either be sold to the collective or it can be exchanged for land of equal value on the edge of the collective's fields, which have been joined together to enable large-scale cultivation.

Almost one-tenth of the collective's land used to belong to private farmers who fled to the West, partly because they did not want to collectivize. Several members to whom I talked denied that they had been forced to collectivize, but admitted that as private farmers they had to pay more taxes, were not allowed to buy farm machines and were not as well served by the state-owned machine and tractor station as the collective was. I'm not against

229

collectives – I think they are a better idea than large capitalist farms – but too much pressure has been exerted to create them in East Germany, and not enough persuasion. The result has been that many farmers have fled, with consequent production losses.

Several members I spoke to were enthusiastic. Monthly wages worked out to between 400 and 600 marks (between £35 and £53 at the official rate) for farm workers, 800 (£70) for foremen and something over 1,000 (£88) for the chairman. All these pay rates are good by East German standards which, I suppose, partly explains the large wad of applications to join the collective which the chairman, Dietrich Besler, a 41-year-old Communist, showed me. Besler, who was a farm worker in his youth, was Minister of Agriculture in the state of Brandenburg from 1950 until 1952, when the East German states were abolished and replaced by smaller administrative regions.

[Clearly I had been directed to a model collective. I learned later that Besler, who had become chairman of the collective in 1956, had held some political positions after his ministerial post in Brandenburg was abolished. When we met he was, among other things, a member of the Volkskammer, *the rubber-stamp parliament, though he didn't tell me that.]*

One factor praised by some of the members I spoke to was the shorter working hours in the collective, where shift work is possible, compared to the hours worked by private farmers. The greater cultural and educational opportunities were also mentioned. Members achieving the best results, say in pig production, are given a free holiday. Some have been sent to Russia on holiday, some to Bulgaria. Planned and actual production figures are posted up everywhere and there are signs of major building extensions. The atmosphere is confident. The farming is intensive, with much Berlin kitchen waste being used for pigs.

The Wartenberg collective farmers, feeling well off, are trying to help their poorer neighbours to improve their methods and increase their income. Each collective farmer is allowed to retain up to ½ hectare (1¼ acres) of land for individual use and can keep some 'private' cows, pigs and poultry. The result of this, in poor collectives like the one next to Wartenberg's, is that the members, because they are not earning enough from the collective, tend to spend too much time on their own plots, which makes it still harder to improve the collective: a vicious circle.

Besler told me his roughly 180 members would probably be willing, after discussion, to amalgamate with their neighbours, if calculations showed this would not reduce their income too much; he did not think it would. He said their neighbours' land would complement their own. The production figures at Wartenberg looked good, even though Besler said they still had a lot to do.

I spoke to a middle-aged widow who had worked for years for the former owner of a nursery, now part of the collective. She said she was earning much more now, and did not appear to regret the departure for West Berlin of her former boss, after he had served a sentence for alleged black-marketeering.

[Threats of prosecution for alleged black-marketeering, with or without foundation, were sometimes used to pressurize private farmers into joining collectives.]

An elderly foreman cowhand told me that he and his working wife had been able to save enough in two years to buy the small house he had yearned for all his life. Several members spoke of the rights they have through their votes in the farm's monthly meeting or in the meetings of their sections or 'brigades' as they are called in Communist terminology.

I think the idea of collectives is good, but in East Germany they have been introduced through undue pressure. The result has been that many farmers have fled to the West and that many uneconomic collectives have been founded. One should let the hard facts of modern economics – which apply everywhere – work on the private farmers, so they realize that collectives are the only alternative to big capitalist farming, with most farmers reduced to farm labourers or, at any rate, employees instead of members with equal rights. *[I realized rather later that there was another alternative: highly mechanized family farms requiring no or few outside employees.]*

Collective farm members, too, also have the advantage of normal working hours – and, being in Reuters, I know what that means!

30 September 1959 : Klaus Fuchs is proving a gold mine for news. Today Reuters was granted an interview with him in the government press office opposite the mangled ruin of Hitler's bunker on the Wilhelmstrasse, in which – the interview, not the bunker – Fuchs told Brian and me something of his new work as head of a theoretical physics division of the central nuclear research institute in Rossendorf, near Dresden. He has applied to 'rejoin' the SED as a former member of, first, the Social Democrats and later, the Communist Party, which were merged in East Germany in 1946 to form the SED.

Fuchs also gave us some of his impressions of the British murderer, Brian Donald Hume, with whom he was in Wakefield Prison, and who was sentenced to life in Switzerland yesterday. He denied a statement made by Hume during his trial that he had taken a message for Dr Fuchs to his father in East Germany. Fuchs added that he thought Hume had some good in him and, according to his account, had had a tough childhood in an orphanage.

Had to leave Brian to finish off our report of the interview, so I could dash off to see Wolverhampton Wanderers, British league champions, suffer a surprising 2–1 defeat by the East German champions, the army club Vorwärts, in a European cup match. I dislike sports reporting, partly because it bores me and partly because I'm not an expert at it. One thing nice about it though: the fresh air.

We had started the day by listening to part of a long Ulbricht speech introducing the seven-year plan, which is intended to increase real wages by 60–65 per cent between this year and 1965. This, I reckon, should bring the East and West Germans to more or less the same standard of living.

[That forecast proved to be way out, thanks partly to a continuing good growth rate in West Germany.]

1 October 1959 : Klaus Fuchs has been really nice to me. When we met today, to go over our version of yesterday's interview with him before we transmitted it to London, he said smilingly, knowing that I'm leaving, that he supposed we should not meet again. I jokingly suggested I might become press officer at his institute, and he replied that they had not got one yet. I thanked him for his courtesy and help, and told him it had been very useful to me.

Introduced Brian to the office's 'local' restaurant, a rather dingy place called 'U-Bahn' ('underground railway', which adjoins it). It has, however, a pretty good menu at prices often cheaper, mark for mark, than in a comparable West Berlin restaurant, something which would have been incredible a few years ago. Brian's initiation there was not too happy, as his tum, not too strong, revolted at something in his Holstein Schnitzel dish and he had a bad night.

Brian and I are having fun pretending – and believing – that our wires in the office are being tapped. We say mock provocative things into the phone where, maybe, the secret police microphone is located. We know that this sort of thing is done here – as in some other countries, including West Germany. There was the recent glaring case of a Catholic suffragan bishop in East Berlin who, suspecting something of the sort, called in a West Berlin technician, who discovered the hidden microphone. Somehow the East Berlin police got to know. The two were stopped in the street, interviewed by the police for some hours in a correct manner and released. Later some East Berlin papers said that an investigation had shown that the wire-tapping apparatus had been installed by the Americans.

2 October 1959 : We held a cocktail party in the office flat to introduce Brian, and for me to say goodbye. I borrowed a large photo of the Queen from West Berlin to decorate the wall of the bare dining-room of the flat, where we had decided to hold the do, as East Berlin's main hotels had been commandeered for guests attending the celebrations of East Germany's tenth anniversary.

Was pleasantly surprised by the turnout. We invited around 40 people and about 30 came, so many in fact that the drinks we had bought in both East and West Berlin just lasted out. All the guests were from East Berlin, as we thought it impolitic to invite Westerners at this stage.

The guests included Ambassador Heymann, head of the Foreign Ministry press department, Frau Wieland, the ADN chief – who drank a little whisky in training for a visit she is shortly to pay to Britain – and, probably the most important person, Horst Sindermann, head of the press section in the SED Central Committee.

Sindermann who, like several others, said very warm goodbyes to me, told us that when Klaus Fuchs arrived in East Germany last June, his present wife, then just an old acquaintance, who was to be among the airport welcome party, had asked Sindermann in Ulbricht's presence what she should say if questioned by reporters. Sindermann had jokingly told her, 'Tell them you are his bride and have been waiting for this day for ten years.'

I was touched by little presents brought along by three Communist journalists – a Polish man, a Finnish woman and a Bulgarian woman. The Pole brought two little traditional Polish dolls on a stand, the Finn a tiny dagger in a sheath – don't know whether this is Finnish – and the Bulgarian a little bottle of Bulgarian rose oil in an ornamented wooden tube. *[After writing this, on 15 September 1999, I found the bottle of rose oil and gave it to Elfi to mark her 75th birthday, which fell on the previous day.]*

During our party the news came out in Moscow that Khrushchev was not coming to the anniversary celebrations here. Instead his 'crown prince', Frol Kozlov, First Deputy Premier, would head the Soviet delegation.

3 October 1959 : Brian and I were the hosts at lunch in one of East Berlin's best restaurants, the Budapest in the Stalinallee, which not surprisingly does Hungarian specialities. Our guests were George Turner, information chief of British Military Government in West Berlin, and his wife Marjorie. George sympathizes to some extent with my views on East Germany – namely, that life is likely to improve economically and, as a result, politically – but does not think we should move towards diplomatic recognition. I cannot understand why not.

4 October 1959 : Called on Elfi's East German uncle and aunt, Fritz and Friedel Engler, in Schönow, just outside East Berlin, to say *Auf Wiedersehen. [See 30 May 1959.]* We watched East and West TV alternately. They are just about to buy a fridge from savings, at about three times the West German price in marks *[which in real terms was an even greater expense for them, as their income was smaller than that of a comparable West German family].*

Fritz gives the impression of being basically in favour of the Communist system, but criticizes it on the ground that things have moved too fast. For instance, he does not think the old system of land ownership was right, with large landowners lording it around, and he finds the principle of collective farms good, but not when private farmers are put under pressure.

Glanced at a torchlight official 'demonstration' of blue-uniformed members of the Communist Free German Youth in East Berlin, calling for West Berlin to be made into a 'free city' [the Soviet demand]. Then to the première of a comedy drama by East German national prizewinner, Hedda Zinner, 52, depicting what happened in an East German border village when, thanks to a misunderstanding, inhabitants thought it was going to become West German. *[See 2 September 1959.]*

The early parts of this piece are very well done, with private farmers bluntly putting forward arguments for not joining collectives: for instance, that the collective farmers do not work as hard as they do and that if they joined a collective it would mean that they, the most efficient individual farmers, would be working for others. The chairman of the local collective farm in the play has to admit the force of some of the private farmers' arguments. One private farmer bitterly complains that he is not allowed to buy machinery – in my opinion an arbitrary way of forcing farmers into collectives.

In fact the play puts over no convincing argument for collectives as they are at present in East Germany. It shows that the main force keeping some of the farmers loyal to the present regime is the fear that, if the old big landowners returned, they would lose the land they were given in the Communist-run postwar land reform.

[Hedda Zinner, a Viennese-born former actress, became a Communist journalist, poet, novelist and dramatist. She lived in exile in the Soviet Union from 1935 to 1945. She was awarded several East German prizes and decorations. She died in 1994.]

5 October 1959 : Had my first glimpse of wavy-haired greying Frol Kozlov, the 51-year-old Soviet First Deputy Premier, generally regarded as Khrushchev's crown prince. He flew in for the anniversary celebrations in a gleaming turbo-prop Ilyushin-18, the first turbo-prop to land at East Berlin airport. Much of his airport speech was praise for the results of the Khrushchev–Eisenhower talks in the USA and the hopeful atmosphere arising from them.

Brian and I enjoyed Prokofiev's opera, *The Betrothal in the Monastery*, at the East German State Opera. I preferred the music to the singing, which somehow seemed to conflict with Prokofiev's surprising melodies. *[Forty years later, I seem to recall that the opera included some anti-religious spin – perhaps drunken or corrupt priests.]*

6 October 1959 : Brian, having evidently been brought up to boss other people around, has been trying it with me a little. I am happy that I have been able to bring him to heel without losing my temper and to keep relations otherwise very good. *[Horton, a protégé of Gerry Long, had an impressive career in Reuters, culminating in his appointment as editor-in-chief and an assistant general manager in September 1968, when Long was general manager. Horton resigned from Reuters in December 1973.]*

Nothing new politically emerged from a ceremonial official meeting held this afternoon to mark East Germany's tenth anniversary, which falls tomorrow. In speeches lasting some five hours, Kozlov again emphasized the 'we must talk reasonably with each other' angle, and Grotewohl warned that it was no use West Germany thinking it was going to swallow up East Germany.

24 The tenth anniversary of East Germany

7 October 1959 : Today's tenth anniversary of the East German state was not a happy day for most of its inhabitants, in my opinion, but at least happier than it might have been. While East Germans have no prospect that their state will become a Western democracy, they have the definite prospect of considerable economic improvements and, with that, some political relaxation.

I started the day by watching more than 200 East German soldiers, in *Wehrmacht*-style uniforms, but with Soviet-style steel helmets, lay more than 50 wreaths at the massive Soviet war memorial in the East Berlin suburb of Treptow. They were followed by East German leaders, Kozlov and other foreign delegates to the anniversary celebrations and by thousands of workers, in groups, carrying banners and hundreds more wreaths. This afternoon, using the television in West Berlin, I reported speeches at an anniversary rally. Ulbricht said that the status of Vatican City showed that the West Berlin problem could be solved. I don't think it shows that, as Italian–Vatican relations are based on mutual trust, which does not, and cannot, exist between the West Berliners and the East German dictatorship.

8 October 1959 : I wrote about the 'flag dispute'. Until 1 October the two Germanys had the same flag, the black–red–gold tricolour used in the Weimar Republic era. But on 1 October, East Germany superimposed its state coat-of-arms on its flag: a hammer, symbolizing the workers; a pair of dividers, for the intellectuals; surrounded by a wreath of corn, for the farmers.

On previous anniversaries of the East German state, the East German flag was demonstratively displayed on West Berlin overhead railway stations and railway buildings administered by the East German railway authorities under four-power agreement – another Berlin anomaly. As the two state flags used to be the same, the East German action, intended to indicate East German sovereignty over West Berlin's overhead railway system, used to be ignored by the West Berlin authorities. But this year West Berlin police pulled down most of the new East German flags and half a dozen West Berlin policemen were injured in a fracas with Communist workers at one railway depot. The West Berlin authorities then called off their action.

It was silly and provocative of the East Germans to put up the flags, and silly of the West Berlin police to try to take them down. It would have been sufficient to state that flying the flags did not make the railway property extra-territorial.

9 October 1959 : Kozlov visited the Leuna chemical works, near Halle, about 100 miles southwest of Berlin. It is East Germany's biggest industrial plant, with about 30,000 employees. I was present as Kozlov and his party were given a very warm welcome by the workers at this former I.G. Farben plant, now called after Walter Ulbricht.

At an open-air meeting Kozlov made a 'let's live together' appeal to the 'capitalists' and poked fun at US scientific and sputnik efforts. Later, enjoying a lunch of pheasant in the works' club, he accused the Americans of using West Germany as a tool to carry out their 'dirty imperialist aims' and interpreted the American invitation which led to Khrushchev's visit to the USA last month as being dictated by American awe at Soviet scientific successes.

Kozlov then passed a message to me through his interpreter – the chief East German government interpreter, Werner Eberlein, 39. *[Eberlein, I learned later, was the son of Hugo Eberlein, one of the founders of the German Communist Party, who fled to the Soviet Union in 1934 with his family and died in a Stalinist purge. Werner grew up in the Soviet Union. After his return to Germany in 1948, he rose in the ranks of the SED.]*

In his message, Kozlov asked me to leave out his attacks on the USA, as they would not contribute to the present atmosphere of East–West cooperation if they were published. I naturally acceded to his request, just as I would have done had a Western statesman done the same sort of thing. *[Today I doubt whether I was right to have censored the bits which Kozlov didn't want publishing; if he thought they were bad for East–West cooperation, he shouldn't have said them. However, he perhaps realized only after he had spoken that a Western reporter was present and genuinely did not want to cause East–West friction. Neither did I.]*

I am not so keen on Kozlov – not only because of this incident. He looks rather brutal and has not the appeal of Khrushchev; nor the brains, I'd say. To be fair, he does smile quite a bit and his manners are pleasant enough. *[In 1958 Khrushchev had indicated privately that Kozlov was his personal choice as his successor. In May 1960 Kozlov gave up his governmental post to become a member of the Communist Party secretariat, where he shared power with four others under Khrushchev. By autumn 1962 his role as heir apparent seemed to have become less secure and there were indications of political disagreement with Khrushchev. Kozlov, who had suffered a heart attack in the spring of 1961, died on 30 January 1965.]*

At supper with several Soviet and East German Communists, we discussed the results of yesterday's British general election. I maintained that the main reason for the victory of the Tories – increasing their majority from 58 to about 110 – was the general economic well-being, plus an extra lift from Prime Minister Harold Macmillan's efforts to relax East–West tension. The Communists argued that Labour had done badly because it had no striking alternative to the Tories. I retorted that, if this were the case, why had the Communists, who certainly had a striking alternative, lost their deposits in 17 out of 18 constituencies where they stood.

Overnighted in a pleasant privately owned hotel in the small picturesque mining town of Eisleben, where Martin Luther was born in 1483 and died in 1546.

10 October 1959 : Kozlov rolled in to Eisleben this morning – not on account of Luther. He drove past the house where Luther was born, now a museum devoted to the Protestant reformer, displaying the new East German flag. Kozlov came to lay a wreath on a metal statue of Lenin, which the Germans shipped from occupied Russia during the Second World War and which, I was told, was hidden by pro-Communist workers under scrap at the yard where it had been sent to be melted down. It was given to Eisleben in 1945.

On to the nearby Hettstedt steel rolling mill, where Kozlov got what seemed to be a genuinely warm reception. All over the works were charts showing how the sections were meeting the economic plan. In some departments there were machines up to 50 years old; in others there were new ones, some West German. Bad ventilation in some areas. Flags everywhere marking the anniversary.

Had a free evening in Quedlinburg, ancient small town at the foot of the Harz Mountains. Reminiscent of York, with its old half-timbered buildings. Hotel room, quite decent, five marks, which normally have about five shillings *[25p]* purchasing power. Hotel staff complained about the regime's restrictions on visiting West Germany, some 30 miles from here.

11 October 1959 : Before breakfast this Sunday morning, walked up the hill to Quedlinburg castle, once a monastery, where lie the remains of Heinrich I and his queen, Mathilde. My encyclopedia says he was known as Heinrich the Fowler. He was a Saxon duke, who was made German king in AD 919 and died in 936. He is buried in a Romanesque church, Protestant, where half a dozen people had arrived for morning service.

I had to leave to watch Kozlov visit a new dam in the Harz, at Rappbode, said to be Germany's highest, at 106 metres (350 ft) –

certainly an impressive piece of work. While waiting for Kozlov, chatted with three chaps, two industrial workers and a people's policeman, all homespun types who sounded very enthusiastic about their proletarian dictatorship, but were unable to deny that they have not the same chances of expression as people in Britain, though they contended that one could bring up grievances, or new ideas, in the party. (Of course, don't bring up capitalist ideas – that amounts to sin.)

For a time I managed to insert myself into Kozlov's motorcade, which drove at about 60 mph, which is a bit too much for my Beetle or, at least, for me. After a while, some over-clever police-man noticed that my Beetle was not a large Russian ZIM limou-sine, and I was stopped to have my papers checked. That done, the motorcade had vanished. But I managed, by driving cross country, to beat the motorcade by about five minutes to the next place on Kozlov's programme, the state farm of Barby, south of Magdeburg, once part of a large private farm which was broken up in the 1946 land reform.

The Russians were warmly welcomed, with lots of hugs. Eminently huggable is a cheerful pudgy woman member of the Soviet delegation, Frau Yefremova, a local party secretary. Welcoming Germans seemed to pick on her. Sergei Pavlov, the 35-ish handsome blonde head of the Soviet Communist youth organisation, was picked on by a pretty young Free German Youth girl, who put her arms round his neck and kept at least one of them there for quite a time. I heard an East German journalist say to a colleague, 'Pavlov ought to stay here.'

Some of the Russians took notes and made suggestions, as the delegation toured the farm. Later there was a meeting in the for-mer manor house, now used as a meeting place and state farm offices. Kozlov sat beneath two stucco angels and a red flag, while waiters in evening dress served soda water and cigarettes. A farm-ing expert from the Soviet delegation answered farm workers' questions and made some criticisms: for instance, that their new buildings were too expensive, which would burden their milk price. *[As a correspondent in the Soviet Union in the sixties, I soon realized that most Soviet state farms and collectives were in a far worse state than most of the East German ones. But in the fifties East Germans were being told they should learn from the Soviet Union.]*

An official of the state farm said that this year, for the first time, they were intending to make a profit, but drought was making this a tough task. When another official of the farm asked me for comments as we toured the farm, I said that the regime's agricultural policy had caused production to fall for a time by forcing collectivization when farmers were not ready for it. This had produced inefficient collectives and spurred many farmers to flee to the West, leaving their land fallow for a time. To my surprise this chap agreed with me.

12 October 1959 : Was landed with a three-mark fine last night, for turning round just inside a one-way street. At first I told them to take me to court, but dropped this line hastily when they started talking about taking away my licence until the case was heard. I thought they were being hard on a stranger, as I'd entered the street only by a few yards, just to ask my way. This happened in Magdeburg, a place-name I remember from schooldays, because of the 'Magdeburg hemispheres' invented by the seventeenth-century scientist and mayor of Magdeburg, Otto von Guericke. He placed two metal hemispheres together, producing a sphere, extracted the air from the sphere to create a vacuum and showed that two horses couldn't pull the hemispheres apart.

In Magdeburg there were signs of much rebuilding, but also many bomb-scarred sites. Stayed in a new hotel, not quite finished, with a ghastly stained-glass window showing the 'building of socialism' in East Germany during the past ten years and including, of course, a Soviet rocket. As a whole the hotel was smart and service good.

Must note a talk the other day with three lorry drivers in a café. They praised East German social services, but said they felt unfree, particularly because of the restrictions on travel to the West.

Back to Berlin today.

25 An angry farewell

13 October 1959 : My spell as the first non-Communist Western correspondent accredited in East Germany ended today. Had hoped to take with me to Bonn, Elfi's 16-year-old East German cousin, Hannelore Engler, a dairy apprentice, and her sister, nine-year-old Angelika. They have never been to West Germany. Their parents had been optimistic about getting permission, but Hannelore's application was turned down and Angelika's would have required more time to be dealt with. Tried to get the Foreign Ministry to help, but was told that apprentices were in general forbidden to go to West Germany. (Hannelore had been told there was no urgent reason for her to make the visit.)

This incident made me fume, made Hannelore cry and upset her parents, whom I called on last night in Schönow to say goodbye. This type of restriction on freedom is one of the worst things about the East German regime. It is even more of a disgrace when one remembers that quite a number of today's East German leaders themselves suffered restrictions on their freedom under the Nazis, whom they condemn.

Breakfasted with Elfi's West Berlin aunts, then took farewell flowers for Frau Wieland, head of ADN. A pleasant woman. Decided to go to the West by way of Schwerin, some 140 miles northwest of Berlin, near the Baltic and the West German border, to call on another of Elfi's uncles, Hermann Engler, aged over 70, the only one I haven't met.

At an East German checkpoint on the East Berlin border, I asked a people's policeman for the best route to Schwerin. He evidently mentioned my request to the occupants of a car behind me, because these people, including at least one SED man, told me they knew the rather intricate route and said I could follow them. Later I invited one of them into my car: Karl Artelt, a 45-ish director of the state-owned Elde jam factory at Parchim near Schwerin.

Because of what had happened about Hannelore and Angelika, I really set on him about travel restrictions, which he defended in the usual Communist way – i.e. that West Germany is a fascist state (he referred to former Nazi judges being in office again, the same ones who sent him to prison in the Nazi era) and it is thus wrong to send people there, especially young people, to get warped. I told him he was exaggerating the influence of Nazis or onetime Nazis in West Germany, though admitting there was some reason for disquiet.

Artelt told me his father had been called the 'Red Admiral of Kiel', being the first sailor to take part in the abortive left-wing revolution of 1918. Artelt himself had been in a Communist resistance group in the Second World War. He said that in the first months after the war, while living in West Germany, he had been happy at the cooperation with British occupation forces in rounding up former Nazis. But when the Western Allies and the Soviet Union fell out, he had been told there was no longer room for cooperation with Communists, and had been offered a good job if he would leave the party. Instead he had preferred to come to the Soviet zone – anything else would have been treachery to him. He was bitter about the change in attitude of the British, but I tried to show him that the breach with the Soviet Union had by no means been the fault of the Western allies alone, but was conditioned by what the West considered to be Russia's imposition of communism on Eastern Europe.

[In 1996 I received a large file from the German 'Federal Authority for the Records of the State Security Service of the former German Democratic Republic' in Berlin – my 'Stasi' file.

Under the codename 'Neumann', datelined Parchim on 14 October 1959, is Artelt's report on our conversation in my car, some 500 words.

It says in part:

'Johnson said to me: "I see you are an SED member, we could have a little talk." I then tried to get his impressions about the five months [he had worked in the GDR]. Johnson spoke very favourably of our build-up, particularly in the past three years. He said our efforts had been enormous. "You will certainly reach your target by 1961," he said, "although this target is very variable." He complained that there were still considerable shortages of consumer goods. I tried to explain that and made certain points which he took in. Whether he was in agreement with them I could not tell. In particular we discussed the situation in West Germany, and he began by saying: "Why are your citizens restricted from travelling? Everyone ought to be allowed to travel as much as they want. The British can't understand that." It was necessary to talk in detail about this question, and I gave as the main danger the abnormal situation that he knew about, from being in Berlin, and, as another reason, the radical fascist development in West Germany, with agents and other dirty elements trying to disturb and sabotage our work. I think he said things were not so bad, although he agreed that the Berlin situation was unhealthy.

From my own experience I depicted the situation in West Germany since 1945 and how the Bonn state had taken over former fascist war criminals and other officials and that this was a great danger, not only for Germany but also for the other part [sic – of Europe?], in particular for Britain too. After all fascism did not spare Britain in the last war and he conceded that. But he did not want to accept that the fascists might get the upper hand in West Germany. He said we saw things too darkly. I told him that we had to give some guarantee for the safety of the people in our republic and could not let random visits to West Germany be allowed.

He said that we should not use the word 'enemy' in regard to West Germany, and I responded that everything which is against us and, in particular, those who have so many people on their consciences, should not only be seen as enemies but as criminals. He said that there should be a renunciation of the use of force, and touched upon the Hungarian problem and the Berlin problem on 17 June [a reference to the abortive revolt of 1953]. To that I replied that the British had all *reason to give a good example in view of the Suez Canal* [a reference to British participation in the attack on Egypt in 1956]. *I said that the provocations in Hungary and here had been instigated.*

On agricultural developments he said that collective farming was good, but that our way was not right because many people had been forced to go along with it. I tried here too to explain our socialist transformation.

He said: "I know your republic and have already talked with many officials of your party, but we can't approve of that . . ."

I referred to the question of coexistence, the two social systems, and he agreed that, in particular after the talk between Khrushchev and Eisenhower, many things would change to the advantage of Germany. Above all he hopes there will be a good solution for Berlin, so that the Berlin problem is not a continuing subject of dispute.'

This conversation went on in a calm, decent way.]

Schwerin is a lovely spot, set amid lakes. I could see some of them glinting in the dark as I arrived at about eight pm. *[From 1815 until 1918 Schwerin was the capital of one of the many German principalities, the grand duchy of Mecklenburg-Schwerin. Under the Communist regime it became a regional capital, with a population of about 120,000.]*

I found Uncle Hermann Engler, a retired dairy manager, and his wife, Aunt Lieschen, in their two-and a half-room top-floor flat in the 1890-ish two-storey terrace house they own in a main road named after the Slav tribe, the Obotriten, who inhabited what is now the Schwerin region for several centuries. (They were conquered in 1160 by a German king, Heinrich the Lion, and christianized.)

I was joined at the Englers by their 35-ish daughter, Gerdi, and her husband, Jochen, who works in the loan department of the state bank's regional office. We chatted for several hours. None of them is a Communist. Uncle Hermann said he ought to be decorated for having listened to the BBC for ten years – more, actually, because he started doing that in the Nazi era. He was, in fact, doing it when I came in.

All said life had improved in past years, economically and

247

politically, but that the unfreedom remained. Aunt Lieschen told of being put under pressure by the Communist woman official who lives on the ground floor, to hoist a flag to mark the state's anniversary – not that she would actually have suffered anything had she not done so. Jochen was of the view that the country's leaders were *trying* to do good. Both he and Gerdi favoured the diplomatic recognition of the Communist government by West Germany. They thought it would improve the situation between the two Germanys, particularly regarding freedom of movement.

What better illustration of the difference between East and West Germany than the remark by one of them about how Gerdi's daughter, Angelika, when aged about four, came home from kindergarten and started telling the family what a lovely person Little Father Stalin was. And now, when the family talks about the time 'when the Russians came' (Schwerin was temporarily occupied by American and then British soldiers in 1945), Angelika, now about 12, says, 'You mean the Soviet soldiers.' At school she is taught the atheist view of life, and after school she goes to religious lessons. I said that, at least in such circumstances, the people who remain Christians would not be just nominal ones. If Christianity is mere superstition, it will die out. If it is worthwhile it will remain, or whatever part of it is worthwhile will remain.

14 October 1959 : Left for the West. About an hour's drive took me to the frontier near Hamburg. The usual three or four checks on the East German side and the perfunctory one on the West German side. Asked four or five customs and passport control officers what they thought of recognizing East Germany. Several were for, several against. One said the East German leaders were criminals. I disagreed, saying they sometimes did bad things, but for reasons they thought good. Of course, that does not prove they are not criminals, but I don't accept that they are. Capitalists allow a certain amount of unemployment – sometimes a large amount – for reasons they think good, but some people regard this as criminal.

248

Happy homecoming. Brought Elfi a bracelet – enamel on copper – which delighted her, and for the boys an electric torch each for the dark evenings.

22 November 1959 : I summed up my view of the East German regime in talking to our friends, Boris Yurinov, Bonn correspondent of the Soviet news agency, TASS, and his wife Inna, a former television journalist. I told them that in my view the East German system was a dictatorship that would collapse if the Russians got out, which is why they are not going to get out until it has got stronger. I made Yurinov grin by saying, and meaning, that if I were Khrushchev, I would not get out either. I also told him that I was for the diplomatic recognition of East Germany and for a gradual change in both communism and capitalism, making them not so much unlike one another.

[My view of East Germany did not basically change, though I considered that its leaders became criminals – murderers – when, after having the Berlin Wall built in 1961, they ordered the shooting of anyone trying to cross it without permission. I was able to express this view repeatedly in my broadcasts to the two Germanys as the BBC correspondent in Berlin from 1965 to 1970, and again for several months in 1981, when I returned to that post. I intend to write about that in a future volume – if I live long enough.]

Bibliography

Baker Eddy, Mary, *Science and Health* (Christian Science Publishing Society, Boston)

Connell, Brian, *Watcher on the Rhine* (Weidenfeld and Nicolson, London, 1957)

Fisher, H.A.L., *Our New Religion* (Watts & Co., London, 1933)

Mencken, H.L., *The American Language* (Alfred A. Knopf, New York, 1957)

Peter Brierley Johnson, born in 1925 in Bradford, Yorkshire, England, served in the Royal Navy from 1943 to 1946, latterly as a sub-lieutenant, Royal Naval Volunteer Reserve. His last naval appointment, in mid-1946, was to the Royal Naval Headquarters in Germany. At the headquarters, in Hamburg, he became engaged to his future wife, Elfi Kowitz, a refugee from former German East Prussia. They have two sons.

From 1947 to 1954 Johnson was a reporter on British provincial newspapers, mainly in Yorkshire. In 1954 he joined Reuters, one of the world's leading news agencies, as a sub-editor in its London headquarters. From 1955 to 1965 he was a Reuter correspondent, successively in Bonn and Communist East Berlin, and then chief correspondent in the Soviet Union and Germany.

In 1965 he was appointed BBC Berlin correspondent and, from 1971 until his retirement from the BBC in 1985, he was a London-based commentator for BBC External Services (now the World Service), specializing in German and Soviet-bloc issues. Since then he has become a freelance journalist, author and translator, living in London.

Reuter Reporter Among the Communists 1958-59 is the second volume of Peter Johnson's memoirs based on diaries that he began keeping in 1946. The first volume, published in 1998, entitled *Reuter Reporter in Divided Germany 1955-58,* won critical praise in both Britain and Germany. A planned third volume entitled *Roving Reuter Reporter* is to follow describing, among other things, the 1961 Jerusalem trial of Adolf Eichmann, an assignment in Tito's Yugoslavia and the early experiences of the author as a Reuter correspondent in Moscow.